Jewish Bible Translations

University of Nebraska Press | Lincoln

"Translating their Bible has been a major cultural activity of Jewish communities for well over two thousand years and on several continents, and yet few Jews today know about this history or why it matters. This massively learned but accessible volume admirably fills that glaring gap. I highly recommend it to Jewish and Gentile readers alike!"

—Jon D. Levenson, author of *Inheriting Abraham: The Legacy of the Patriarch in Judaism, Christianity, and Islam*

"This is an irresistible book. Greenspoon distills a lifetime of learning into a lively account of famous and not-so-famous versions of Hebrew scripture in diverse languages—even Chinese. Sages and eccentrics populate his pages."

—Ronald Hendel, Norma and Sam Dabby Professor of Hebrew Bible and Jewish Studies, University of California—Berkeley, and author of *The Book of Genesis: A Biography*

"No one has more information at their fingertips than Greenspoon, and this book will inevitably become a resource for anyone working in translation. The book should also appear on course syllabi in Bible studies as well as the history of Bible translation and inform scholarship in translation studies as well."

—Naomi Seidman, University of Toronto Department for the Study of Religion

"The only comprehensive guide on the subject, from earliest times to the present, *Jewish Bible Translations* is a masterful work from a master craftsman. By marrying profound erudition with lucid explanations, provocative questions and comments, and a light, sometimes whimsical touch, Greenspoon is sure to engage both scholars and laity alike."

—Alan Levenson, Schusterman/Josey Chair in Judaic History, University of Oklahoma

"Do all Jews understand the Bible in the same way? The answer can be found in this fascinating and comprehensive volume that explains how and why Jews translated the Bible—from the earliest translation into Greek to contemporary English translations and, along the way, to Aramaic, Arabic, Yiddish, and European languages. We encounter the translators, their interpretive traditions, and the agendas that inform their decisions. This book is a wonderful entrée into the Jewish engagement with the Bible."

—Adele Berlin, Robert H. Smith Professor of Biblical Studies (Emerita), University of Maryland, and coeditor of *The Jewish Study Bible*

"A masterfully broad survey—both chronologically and geographically—in a wonderfully engaging work by the dean of Jewish Bible translation."

—Marc Zvi Brettler, Bernice and Morton Lerner Professor in Judaic Studies, Duke University, and author of *How to Read the Bible*

Jewish Bible Translations

Personalities, Passions, Politics, Progress

LEONARD GREENSPOON

The Jewish Publication Society | Philadelphia

 Published by the University of Nebraska Press as a Jewish Publication Society book. Manufactured in the United States of America. ♾

Library of Congress Cataloging-in-Publication Data
Names: Greenspoon, Leonard J. (Leonard Jay), author.
Title: Jewish Bible translations: personalities, passions, politics, progress / Leonard Greenspoon.
Description: Philadelphia: The Jewish Publication Society; Lincoln: University of Nebraska Press, [2020] | Includes bibliographical references and index.
Identifiers: LCCN 2020007877
ISBN 9780827613126 (paperback)
ISBN 9780827618558 (epub)
ISBN 9780827618565 (mobi)
ISBN 9780827618572 (pdf)
Subjects: LCSH: Bible. Old Testament—Translating. | Judaism—History. | Jews—History.
Classification: LCC BS1132 .G74 2020 | DDC 221.4—dc23
LC record available at https://lccn.loc.gov/2020007877

Set in Merope by Mikala R. Kolander.

Contents

Acknowledgments

Doing research in the humanities—and that is the category into which this book fits—is necessarily a solitary activity in some respects. Sifting through masses of material, both primary and secondary, requires a singular dedication and focus. Ultimately, the researcher has sole responsibility for the thoroughness of documentation and the thoughtfulness of assigning a greater degree of credibility to some views over others. In this sense, the researcher is a scholar.

At the same time, doing research in the humanities ought not to be a lonely activity. Sharing insights, seeking out others' opinions, entering into the give-and-take of interactive discussion—these also are essential elements of what goes into the preparation and presentation of years, often many years, of combing through archives, grappling with difficult concepts, and trying to make sense out of accumulations of data. In this sense, the researcher is a member of one or more scholarly communities.

I have been, I think it is fair to say, blessed by the collegial friendships I have enjoyed over many years. For insights into Jewish Bible translations, the topic of this book, I especially want to recognize, acknowledge, and thank Harry M. Orlinsky, Fred Greenspahn, Ed Greenstein, Jonathan Sarna, and Naomi Seidman.

Every word, expression, sentence, and section of this book bears witness to the superb work of JPS's managing editor, Joy Weinberg.

From first draft to last, her insistence on excellence improved and enhanced my writing, even after I thought it was as good as I could get. JPS director Rabbi Barry Schwartz and the staff at the University of Nebraska Press, the publishing partner of this book, have also been unfailingly responsive and supportive.

More durable than even the closest professional connection are family relationships. I have been married more than fifty years (no, Ellie and I weren't quite child bride and groom!), with two daughters, Gallit and Talya, two sons-in-law, Elan and Andrew, and twin grandchildren, Gefi and Shoshi. And I hope the family continues to grow. Whether as dad or papa, my experiences with the family are more precious to me than any others.

And yes indeed, there is something especially meaningful and worthwhile now that I can share my love of teaching and learning with my immediate and extended family members, who don't ever seem bored with discussions of Septuagint translators or Saadiah Gaon or Max Margolis, among others. Who could ask for anything, or anyone, more!

Introduction

Anyone going into a large bookstore these days is confronted with, and perhaps perplexed by, an array of Bible translations. Most of these are produced by and marketed to Christians, primarily Protestants, but also Roman Catholics and adherents of the Orthodox churches. Either in the Bible section, or more often among books classified as Judaica or Jewish studies, one or more Jewish versions may be found. The relative paucity of modern-language translations by and for Jews obscures two related points of preeminent importance: (1) Bible translating began among Jews; and (2) all subsequent translations, whether under Jewish, Christian, or "inter-denominational" sponsorship, are profoundly Jewish.

Sadly, both Jews' and Judaism's substantial contributions to scriptural translation have gone largely unrecognized or underacknowledged, even among specialists who really should know better. In this connection, I call attention to non-Jewish scholars who, discussing the subject of English-language Bible translation, completely ignore the very existence of Jewish translators and translations. Such is the case with the well-known biblical scholar and translator Jack P. Lewis, who claims, with the title of his book, comprehensive coverage of *The English Bible from KJV to NIV* (1981)—and yet he mentions not even one Jewish version. And then there are the authors of three popular books, Benson Bobrick, Alister McGrath, and Adam Nicolson, who purport to provide full accounts of the *King James Bible*, but fail to make any reference to the profound influence Jewish exegetes and exegesis had on this translation.[1] I should also call attention to a scholarly work by Mary Wilson Carpenter, who never mentions English-language Jewish versions in her survey of British Bibles.[2] (See chapter 6 of this book for a corrective to such lapses.)

Even when Jewish versions are discussed, they are sometimes presented in what I would politely term an "odd" manner. Thus, the esteemed Bible scholar and translator Bruce M. Metzger devotes seven pages to modern "Jewish translations" in his wide-ranging study, *The Bible in Translation: Ancient and English Versions* (2001). But he gives considerably more space to two questionably Jewish versions—*God's New Covenant: A New Testament Translation* by the philosopher Heinz W. Cassirer, who was born Jewish but did not practice Judaism; and the *Complete Jewish Bible* by David H. Stern, who self-identifies as a Messianic Jew—than to the undeniably mainstream Jewish versions produced by The Jewish Publication Society. Many other examples could be cited as having failed to provide their readers with crucial information about these topics.

While I am far from the first researcher to consider significant aspects of this process (more on this to come), I am the first to do so in a full-length volume. It is my hope that this current volume—the first-ever book-length study solely devoted to Jewish Bible translators and translations—will help redress these and other imbalances.

Differing Jewish and Christian Understandings

Unlike the Jewish understanding of the Bible, translation of the sacred word is foundational to the Christian system of beliefs and practices. Jesus's very words, which he spoke for the most part in Aramaic, were presented in Greek in the New Testament—that is, in translation. Translation thus lies at the heart of Christianity. Whatever efforts, if any, Jesus's earliest followers made to preserve and transmit his words in Aramaic were quickly and completely overwhelmed by the urge to translate them.

Thus it is that for contemporary Christians, *the* Bible is a Bible in translation, not the Bible in Hebrew, Aramaic, and Greek. For this reason, very few Christian denominations or groups (outside of some Orthodox Christian churches) make a concerted effort to teach or preach the biblical languages among the laity. Additionally, large numbers of Christian clergy are, or appear to be, at best only superficially acquainted with the original languages of the Bible.

Not so for Jews and Judaism. Even the most nontraditional movements of contemporary Judaism continue to make use of Torah scrolls written in Hebrew, and expect the children in their congregations to be able to read, if not fully comprehend, portions of the Bible as part of becoming a bar or bat mitzvah.

And so it is that no Jewish Bible translation is intended as a practical or implicit replacement of the original. Jewish Bibles point to the original rather than attempt to replace it; in other words, they supplement but never supplant the original Hebrew (for more on this, see the conclusion).

Predominant Themes in Bible Translations

Throughout this book, other larger themes also emerge. One such motif is the contention that it is most productive to view translators in terms of the many contexts—both within and beyond the Jewish community—in which they worked. Appropriately generous room is given to the social, cultural, historical, political, and theological environments of these translators and to the influence of their often groundbreaking translations and commentaries on their environs. In this way, the word—especially, the word in translation—may come alive for today's readers in much the same way it did for the original audiences of each version. This, I hope, should in turn go a long way toward validating the observation that translations of the Bible have the power to transform society in addition to reflecting it.

Along with the recognition of historical and cultural realities goes an attendant realization that complex phenomena—which is what major Bible translations are—cannot be subjected to simplistic "either/or" analysis. Such an approach seeks to locate the development of a given project in a single origin, to the exclusion of any other causes. A prime example of this tendency relates to the origins of the Septuagint. According to one ancient narrative, Ptolemy II, the reigning monarch of Egypt, was the primary force initiating this monumental translation, motivated as he was by the desire to have a Greek copy of the Jewish Law in his prestigious library. These days, many Septuagint specialists reject this explanation in favor of the rationale that the Jewish community of Alexandria, Egypt, needed a Greek translation of the Bible, since Greek was then rapidly replacing Hebrew as the language of everyday life. Given what we know of that period, it seems more likely that both of these factors were at work, rather than one or the other. Life as actually lived is, I fear, messier and less susceptible to compartmentalization than many scholars would like to admit.

This is also true when scholars attempt to simplistically designate the overall relationship between a translation and the text it is rendering. Up until the middle of the twentieth century or so, the most frequently used descriptive terms were "literal" and "free," often presented as if they were polar opposites (that is, "either/or"). "Literal" meant word-for-word, and "free" referred to renderings that strayed from this approach. Most translations up until that time were perceived as literal, and they tended to be more highly valued than freer versions.

But when properly understood, neither "literal" nor "free" is absolute or monolithic. So, for example, most "literal" translators allow themselves to be flexible when handling metaphors and other figurative language, and almost all "free" translators strive for consistency when representing significant theological or historical terminology. So it is that any graphic representation of, say, twentieth-century English-language Bibles should be seen as a continuum from interlinear (hyper-literal) to paraphrase (showing little, if any, linguistic or stylistic connections with the source language). These then constitute further support for a nuanced approach to reading and evaluating Bible versions.

In the 1960s the linguist and translator Eugene Nida, a Protestant, introduced such a perspective to help not only in characterizing the work of Bible translators but also in explicating their motives.[3] For "literal," Nida substituted the term "formal equivalence"; "free" became "functional equivalence." Here, Nida intended more than a change in terminology. He correctly discerned that the more literal translator sought to maintain as much of the original's form (grammar, syntax, etc.) as possible, believing that the meaning of a text was inextricably linked to its form (hence, formal equivalence). Those who rendered more freely concentrated on what the text meant (or how it functioned) for its original audience and how we would say that in our language today.

Within this context, it might seem intuitive that authentic Jewish translations would/should exhibit features characteristic of formal rather than functional equivalence; in other words, they would fall on the literal side of the continuum. Although a theoretical argument of this sort could plausibly be constructed, the evidence showcased in this book points to a far more varied conclusion. Once again, an "either/or" bifurcation is not fair either to the myriad translators we introduce or the multilayered translations we analyze.

Overview of This Volume

Each chapter of *Jewish Bible Translations* centers on Bible versions in a single language or related languages, and the chapters generally progress chronologically. Within each chapter, I place considerable emphasis on the target audience for each translation, to the extent that we can determine it. In my view, knowing whom a translator intended to reach with his or her work is essential to evaluating the translation's level of success within its original context.

Every chapter ends with a section I call "Concluding Thoughts." In part a summary, these remarks are also intended to bring together major themes within the chapter and to offer them as a stimulus for comparisons and contrasts with other Jewish versions. In this way I highlight both distinctive and shared features of Bible translations for Jews across many cultures extending over two thousand years.

Chapter 1 delves into the first translation of the Bible, initiated in the first quarter of the third century BCE (before the Common Era). Known as the Septuagint, this translation, from Hebrew into Greek, came to serve as something of a model for subsequent Jewish translations. It is my emphasis on the Septuagint as a Jewish document that distinguishes this discussion and analysis. So, in addition to a vast store of introductory material—for example, the legendary and historical origins of this version, starting with the rendering of the Torah; the techniques used by the earliest and subsequent translators; its reception by its first and later audiences; and the transmission of its Greek text—there are ample discussions of the ways in which the Septuagint might have functioned among Jews. What does it tell us about the interpretation and application of Sacred Writ in Hellenistic Jewish communities? How and why did Jews revise these Greek renderings? What did the talmudic Rabbis think about translation in general, and the Septuagint in particular?

Another perspective on the Septuagint is offered by the observation that some Greek translators followed the Hebrew wording of their source text literally, while others fashioned their renderings more freely. We explore possible reasons for these different approaches and identify the consequences for readers in the targeted audience for each translation. In the process we discover, among other things, how elusive the term "Septuagint" is; how varied its contents; and how much we (Jews, especially) owe to Christian scribes, without whom we would have at best a few scattered fragments rather than copious collections of this Greek Bible.

The *Targums*, translations from Hebrew into Aramaic, are the focus of chapter 2. According to Jewish tradition, Aramaic translation of biblical material can be traced back to the fifth century BCE, when the scribe Ezra read the Torah at Jerusalem's Water Gate, as narrated in chapter 8 of the book of Nehemiah. However, the term *Targum* is best reserved for specific Aramaic texts that date back to the first century CE (the Common Era). So, there are distinctive Targums to the Torah, the Prophets, and most of the books that make up the Writings. We carefully examine the various approaches taken in each Targum. All together, they consistently combined literal renderings of the Hebrew text with avoidance of anthropomorphisms in relation to God, endeavored to simplify and update biblical language, and added all sorts of explanatory material that the translators presumably felt would not only be valuable to readers but, on occasion, be entertaining.

It is by no means easy to determine why the Targumists rendered their Hebrew texts in such a distinctive way. But we can fruitfully speculate on the effects such a text would likely have had on those who first heard or read it. Moreover, since portions of the *Targums* were used in synagogues in tandem with Torah and Prophetic readings in Hebrew, these Aramaic versions exerted considerable direct influence within Jewish communities for centuries, and have continued to guide biblical interpreters to this very day.

Chapter 3 introduces Jewish translation into Arabic. Special attention is paid to Saadiah Gaon, a towering intellectual figure of Judaism active in the Babylonian Jewish community of the tenth century who nonetheless remains largely unknown outside of a circle of academic specialists. He is the first Jewish translator we know a lot about. His high level of involvement within the Jewish community is something of a pattern for many who followed him. Our knowledge of Saadiah's life and activities forms the context for analyzing his translation. In an effort to engage a distinct readership (a common objective among Jewish translators), he elected to privilege the linguistic and cultural sensitivities of his Arabic-speaking audience. He also used his translation to combat those Jews (especially the Karaites) who opposed the Rabbinic interpretations and beliefs he championed.

We uncover yet another salient feature of his and many later Jewish translations: Their rendering of the Hebrew is matched, if not exceeded, by the extensive commentaries they constructed. On the basis of extant remains of Saadiah's translation-with-commentary (or perhaps more properly, commentary-with-translation), it is difficult to determine whether Saadiah produced one or more than one translation of portions of the Hebrew Bible, depending on whether a version was envisioned as a free-standing text or in tandem with commentary. Such analysis also plays a role in our discussion of German- and English-language Bibles for Jews.

There is a long and rich history of "Translation into Yiddish (Judeo-German) and German," the subject of chapter 4. From the 1200s until late in the 1700s, Central European Jews had a choice of several different styles of Yiddish-language versions. Even after the Enlightenment leader Moses Mendelssohn and his collaborators created the first translations into "proper" German, Yiddish versions were still being prepared—up until World War II. But the 1800s belonged to Jewish translators who aimed their German-language editions (texts, commentaries, introductions, sometimes illustrations) at specific segments of the population—from Reform to neo-Orthodox. These translators (including some working through the first decades of the twentieth century) varied considerably in their approach: Some allowed Semitic elements to show forth in German, while others produced a version that read smoothly in the target language; some gave pride of place (or exclusive placement) to traditional Jewish exegetes in their commentaries while others allotted space to Christian scholars at the forefront of distinctly nontraditional critical approaches; some used new technology to mass produce low-priced volumes and others enhanced their own work with illustrations, line drawings, maps, and other reader-friendly features. As we compare these German-language versions, it becomes clear that translators, along with their sponsors and publishers, were expanding the scope of what a Jewish version of the Bible could accomplish by taking into account all factors that readers would encounter, not just the translated text itself.

Chapter 5 covers Jewish translations into five European languages: Spanish, French, Italian, Hungarian, and Russian. As readers will see, there is a notably unique feature of Bible translations into Spanish:

Two of the earliest Old Testament versions owe their existence to the efforts of individual Jews as translators or benefactors. Jewish Bibles in the other four languages span the nineteenth century. We are fairly well informed about the translators of all these versions. They were well-educated leaders of their respective Jewish communities who used their translations to benefit their contemporaries in what might appear to be contradictory ways: The versions they produced (text, commentary, etc.) were intended both to educate their fellow Jews on appropriate exegetical techniques and to ease their way into fuller participation in the largely Christian societies of which they were a part.

But, as we will see, they understood these internal and external concerns as complementary means to strengthen their Jewish communities and provide for growth in the future. This analysis highlights the many goals Jewish translators set for themselves in fashioning their modern-language versions. These efforts were also in keeping with the guiding principles of the Haskalah (Jewish Enlightenment).

Chapter 6 introduces readers to Jewish translations into English. The Anglo-Jewish translations produced in Great Britain from the late eighteenth century through the end of the nineteenth century offer a fascinating window into how the Jewish community of those times adapted to an array of external and internal pressures. From there we turn to developments in the United States, beginning with Isaac Leeser in the mid-nineteenth century and ending with the latest early twenty-first century versions on the market. For much of this time Jewish translators on both sides of the Atlantic transmitted substantial portions of the Protestant King James Version (KJV), retaining its style while jettisoning its Christian interpretive framework.

Since World War II, Jews, working as individuals and on committees, have undertaken pioneering efforts to update their English-language versions to attract designated segments of the North American Jewish Bible-buying public. To an extent, these segments can be identified as traditional or nontraditional in religious belief and practice. But Jews also have a choice based on, for example, whether the Bible is for a special event or life-cycle observance, intended for use in the synagogue or home or school, and is envisioned as a Bible in and of itself or in tandem with Scripture in Hebrew. In this regard, Jewish translators and their sponsors have mirrored parallel developments in the larger Christian (mostly, Protestant) Bible industry.

Of the many options, the JPS TANAKH, or New Jewish Publication Society version (NJPS), published by The Jewish Publication Society, has come closest to establishing itself as the standard translation across North American Jewish denominations and movements. For those interested in purchasing a Jewish Bible or supplementing their current collection, the chapter concludes by acquainting readers with the various English-language Bibles currently on the market.

Chapter 7, "Non-Jewish Translations with Jewish Features," analyzes three other examples of translations. The first consists of Yiddish translations, especially of the New Testament, most of which were prepared by Jews who had converted to Christianity. These texts, from the second half of the nineteenth century through the first quarter of the twentieth, were sponsored by Protestant Bible societies and distributed by missionary societies that undertook evangelical activities within European and North American Jewish communities.

The second example is a twentieth-century "Jewish Bible" (according to its title) published by "Messianic Jews," in which their rendering of the New Testament seeks to restore Jesus to his original, Jewish context—more for evangelizing than historical reasons.[4] The last example is the work of a Christian minister who converted from the traditional Judaism into which he was born and eventually moved to China, where he produced an influential Bible translation that exhibits a number of characteristically Jewish features.

The inclusion of this material provides readers with insights beyond what we typically consider a Jewish translation of the Bible. And it encourages readers to consider where the boundaries lie between Jewish and non-Jewish biblical versions.

Taking a broad view of Jewish Bible translations as a whole, the conclusion offers three separate but interrelated analyses. First, a comparison of how Jewish translators have portrayed God and humans demonstrates that the choice of a translation really does make a difference when readers seek understanding of what the Hebrew Bible says and means on central issues. Second, an identification of seven commonalities uniting almost all the Jewish translators and translations we have brought together from over two millennia offers insight into characteristics that have typically featured in versions aimed at a Jewish audience. Finally, we consider where Jewish Bible translators are likely heading and what Jewish translations might look like in the future.

In this process, readers will come to know Jewish scholars who have made significant contributions to the study of Jewish Bible translation. Two twentieth-century giants in the field of Jewish studies, Max L. Margolis and Harry M. Orlinsky—both of whom produced volumes on Bible translation in general, with generous coverage of Jewish versions[5]—offer illuminating insights. Based on their respective experiences as editors of English-language Bibles for The Jewish Publication Society, Margolis and Orlinsky, whose paths crossed briefly in the early 1930s, had very different views on what constitutes the most effective Bible version for Jewish audiences.[6] Their contributions have stood the test of time and constitute the foundational elements upon which (or whom) I build. Others whose work I cite are Frederick Greenspahn, Edward Greenstein, Joseph H. Hertz, David H. Katz, Raphael Loewe and Everett Fox, Nahum and Jonathan Sarna, and Naomi Seidman.[7]

Using This Volume

This book has been designed to fully engage readers at all levels of Jewish knowledge, from scholars and clergy to lay leaders, participants in adult study groups, and general readers who may or may not be versed in Hebrew or other languages beyond English. Thus I have provided translations for all passages from the Hebrew Bible as well as those in languages other than English. I have also clearly explained all technical terminology. In addition, through The Jewish Publication Society (JPS), I am providing a complementary study guide that includes questions to stimulate further discussion and an extensively annotated bibliography. To use it, go to https://jps.org/books/jewish-bible-translations and click on Resources.

I hope this book (along with its guide) finds a place in adult education courses or the like. Within these settings, instructors might well consider following a different order than that presented within the volume itself, which is largely chronological within selected language groups. I recommend starting with chapter 6, "English-Language Versions," since of course these will be the most accessible for English speakers and readers. From there it might make most sense, in some contexts, to go back to chapter 4, on Judeo-German (that is, Yiddish) and German translations, followed by chapter 5, on other selected modern European versions. Next on the syllabus might be chapter 2, the Aramaic text of the *Targums*, which is likely to be more familiar to the Jewish general public than either the Greek of the Septuagint (chapter 1) or the Arabic of Saadiah Gaon's *Tafsir* (chapter 3). In short, there is something to be said for moving from the more to the less familiar.

Also, be assured that proceeding out of order will not be problematic for students. Realizing that readers might well wish to approach the material in a different order than the one fashioned for the volume, I have ensured that successive chapters, which do build on what precedes them in some ways, can also be fully comprehended and appreciated in whatever order they are read.

In other more or less informal educational contexts, leaders or teachers may wish to use select material. So, the sections on French, Italian, and Russian translations, for example, would be useful for courses that survey, or center on, developments in Jewish life throughout those cultures. Or the analysis of the Septuagint as a Jewish document or the KJV as a repository for substantial Jewish interpretation would enhance learning of Bible translations beyond the usual academic contours.

As a university professor for more than forty years (and still counting!), I can also envision this book for use in any number of courses in biblical studies, Jewish studies, and translation studies. Courses in all three of these areas are inherently interdisciplinary and largely fashioned on the basis of what professors judge to be most pedagogically relevant. Chapters 1 and 2, on the Septuagint and *Targums*, respectively, would be particularly useful for biblical studies. For classes in Jewish studies, I would recommend the chapters on Arabic translation (chapter 3) and translation into Yiddish and German (chapter 4). Those teaching courses in translation studies should find the remaining chapters—"Translations into Other Selected Languages" (chapter 5), "English-Language Versions" (chapter 6), and "Non-Jewish Translations with Jewish Features" (chapter 7)—especially beneficial.

In this connection, I would add one more point for consideration. The study guide for each chapter (again, visit https://jps.org/books/jewish-bible-translations and click on Resources) contains (1) supplementary material, including accessible books and articles, as well as reliable websites, for further study and research; (2) a listing of key terms; and (3) a variety of questions geared toward stimulating further creative thought among students.

I also encourage clergy to consider using this work as they compose sermons or otherwise address their communities more broadly. Still today, many Jews do not realize that reading an English-language Bible they have at home is not the same as reading that text in its original language. A modern-language—or even medieval-language—version of the Bible cannot supplant the text in its original language. As a supplement, however, such translations have long given value and strength to their communities. Versions in English or other languages can continue to provide this support, so long as their readers know how these texts can function.

As a practical matter, this book should help rabbis (as well as cantors, educational directors, and others) achieve their principal goals. Frequently, after reading a passage from the Hebrew Bible to the congregation, rabbis draw from different renderings of the same

Hebrew text in order to provide multiple interpretations of what is often elusive language. Similarly, rabbis basing sermons on the Torah portion of the week will usually bring together a number of passages on the same theme from several biblical books. And, as I demonstrate, even on such central concerns as the nature of God and the make-up of humanity, markedly different perspectives emerge when one version is read against another. Knowing the context in which the given translator worked enables the English wording of, say, NJPS or *The Living Torah* or Everett Fox or Robert Alter to take on its full and appropriate meaning. Simply put, this book provides the big picture. And with it, rabbis and others can more confidently and knowledgeably cite translations from other languages, going back as far as the Septuagint and the *Targums*.

Unlike many other topics within the field of Jewish studies, there is not much of a history of sustained study of Jewish Bible translations as a centuries-long, widespread phenomenon. As an unabashed advocate for the value—maybe even the necessity—of knowing about Jewish Bible versions for a full appreciation of what it has meant and continues to mean to be Jewish, I have felt obliged to plant the seeds as much as harvest the crop (if I may use agricultural metaphors). Many treasures are to be unearthed in the pages to follow. I hope that when readers encounter, and consider, *Jewish Bible Translations*, they share in the excitement I have had in researching and writing it.

Jewish Bible Translations

1

The Septuagint

The Septuagint as a Jewish Document

In mid-summer 2005 an editor charged with revision of the *Encyclopaedia Judaica* asked me to update the "Septuagint" article and its bibliography from the original 1972 edition.[1] The Septuagint is the oldest translation of the Hebrew Bible. Jews began to produce it around 275 BCE in Alexandria, Egypt. According to tradition, seventy (some say, seventy-two) Jewish scholars were responsible for the earliest portions of this translation.

The Latin word *septuāgintā* means "seventy"; hence the translation became known as either Septuagint or LXX, the number seventy using Roman numerals. When completed, the Septuagint included Greek versions of all the books of the Hebrew Bible, as well as translations of other Semitic (Hebrew or Aramaic) writings and some works originally composed in Greek.

When I discovered that the earlier *Encyclopaedia Judaica* entry had been authored by the renowned French scholar Suzanne Daniel,[2] I hesitated, wondering what I could possibly add to her work.

Upon careful review, however, I was surprised to see how "un-Jewish" the article was. It would have been equally at home in a Catholic encyclopedia or any of a number of interdenominational or nondenominational publications.

I wondered: Weren't there some things that should be especially relevant in a Jewish encyclopedia?[3]

Yes, there are.

The Septuagint originated among Jews—by Jews for Jews, we might say. It was completed at least a century before the beginnings of Christianity, used by Greek-speaking Jews, and known by Rabbis in the Talmud.

In addition, encyclopedia readers need to know that a widely held view—that Jews had abandoned the Septuagint when early Christians adopted it—is in fact false.[4] It is true that the Septuagint fell out of favor among Jews when it became the Christian Old Testament. It is also true that traditional Judaism never developed a place for the study of the Septuagint, as it did for another ancient translation, the Aramaic *Targums* (on these, see chapter 2). Still, the Septuagint was used in liturgical and classroom settings for more than five hundred years of the Christian era, and it has a distinctive role to play in modern Jewish studies.

So I closed the *Encyclopaedia Judaica* article as follows: "Today the LXX is studied by a growing number of Jewish scholars worldwide. As part of their heritage, Jews in general should not be averse to learning about the Septuagint, its development, and its distinctive features. It is a priceless reminder of a time and place, not unlike our own, when Jews struggled to varying degrees of success with issues of self-identification and accommodation within a cosmopolitan world in and of which they were a creative minority."[5]

The rest of this chapter explores what we know about the origins and early development of the Septuagint, with special emphasis on the roles Jews played in that process. Readers will also be introduced to some of the Septuagint-related controversies that attract specialists' attentions to this day.

The Letter of Aristeas

The oldest and fullest ancient account of the Septuagint's origins appears in the Letter of Aristeas,[6] purportedly a contemporary account, composed in Alexandria, Egypt, during the reign of Ptolemy II (Philadelphus), who ruled from 285 to 247 BCE. Identifying himself as Aristeas, the author addresses his remarks to his "brother," Philocrates.

Aristeas relates that the impetus for the Septuagint translation came from the royal librarian Demetrius, who wished to add "the lawbooks of the Jews" in Greek to a collection numbering more than 200,000 volumes (vv. 9–11).[7] Ptolemy agreed and sent a letter to Eleazar, the High Priest in Jerusalem, requesting seventy-two elders (six from each tribe) "of exemplary lives, with the experience of the Law and ability to translate it" (v. 39). At the same time, Ptolemy released 100,000 Jews who had been transported in servitude to Egypt by his father, the founder of the Ptolemaic dynasty. Ptolemy intended to demonstrate to the Jewish leaders in Jerusalem that he was sincere in his efforts to better both the physical and the spiritual status of the Jews in his empire.

Acceding to this request, the High Priest also sent "fine skins on which the Law had been written in letters of gold in Jewish characters" (v. 176).

The central part of the Letter describes the gifts, banqueting, and conversation between the Egyptian monarch and his Jewish guests. At the end of a week (and with only twenty-two verses left in the document), Demetrius leads the seventy-two translators across a jetty to an island identified as Pharos, where after exactly seventy-two days they complete their task. The resulting document is read to the Jewish community, which receives it with great acclaim and rejoicing, as does Ptolemy, who suitably rewards each of the seventy-two translators for his labors.

The translation procedures, as outlined in the Letter, accord well with translation-by-committee efforts to this day: "They set to completing their several tasks, reaching agreement among themselves on each by comparing versions. . . . The business of their meeting occupied them until the ninth hour [3:00 p.m.] of each day" (vv. 302–3). Only the luxury of their surroundings and their freedom from other commitments—"a magnificent building in a very quiet situation" (v. 301)—separate them from modern Bible translators. With the possible exception of the fact that seventy-two is the number of both the translators and the days of translation, a phenomenon Aristeas briefly notes (v. 307), there appears to be nothing miraculous about the process that produced the Greek Pentateuch (the first five books of the Bible).

Through the Middle Ages, the Letter of Aristeas was understood as an essentially historical account of how the first five books of the Septuagint came to be. In his *Antiquities of the Jews*, the Jewish historian Josephus (late first century CE) relies on the narrative of the Letter for his own account of how the Septuagint originated. Moreover, his paraphrase of biblical history is often based on the distinctive text the Septuagint presents. The Jewish philosopher Philo (early first century CE), himself an Alexandrian native, even adds some details, most notably that tourists of his day can visit Pharos, the site of an annual celebration to commemorate the translators' work.

Christian leaders also knew the Letter and considerably embellished it. Thus, although the earliest copies of the Letter itself date from the eleventh century CE, there is no doubt that the Letter itself is of ancient date.

But what of its historical accuracy—and in particular the veracity of its depiction of the Septuagint's creation? Because of certain discrepancies—for example, Demetrius was not the librarian at the time of Ptolemy II, and the Septuagint of the Five Books of Moses does not, on analysis, seem to represent the work of one group or individual—there is uniform agreement today that the Letter of Aristeas cannot be the eyewitness account it claims to be. In all likelihood it dates to the mid-second century BCE, at least a century later than the events it purports to recount. On the other hand, there is good linguistic evidence that the Greek version of the Pentateuch does date to the first half of the third century BCE (before 250), and the Jewish names mentioned in the Letter are also compatible with this era.

Considerable scholarly attention has been paid to the author's assertion that the Septuagint owes its origins to royal decree, as opposed to the internal needs of the Alexandrian Jewish community, where knowledge of the Hebrew language was quickly receding. Both from the historical record and historical parallels, a strong case can be made that, in this instance, internal and external needs coalesced, resulting in the Jews of Alexandria and their royal patron working together to produce this earliest written translation of the Hebrew Bible.

What was Alexandria like in the early third century BCE? Alexander the Great founded the city, which he named for himself, in 331 BCE, on the site of a town known as Rhakotis. It is said that he personally drew up the plans by which this town would be transformed into a major city in Alexander's anticipated empire. Although neither Alexander nor his biological and military heirs succeeded in turning his many conquests into a united kingdom, Alexandria did become the capital of the dynasty founded by Ptolemy I and succeeded in establishing itself as the preeminent urban center of the Hellenistic world. Alexandria was also home to leading literary scholars, scientists, philosophers, mathematicians, artists, and historians.

During the reign of Ptolemy II the building and initial collections of Alexandria's great library—projects Ptolemy I had initiated—reached completion. According to the Letter of Aristeas, Ptolemy I also directed the forcible removal of 100,000 Jews from Syria-Palestine to Egypt—they were part of the spoils of the war during which Ptolemy had established himself as ruler of Syria-Palestine as well as Egypt proper.

In connection with Ptolemy II's request to the Jerusalem High Priest for translators, the Egyptian monarch is reported to have emancipated these Jewish subjects.

Intra-Jewish Origins of the Septuagint

What internal needs did this Alexandrian Jewish community have that might have stimulated the initial rendering of the Hebrew Bible into Greek? In broad strokes, four approaches have support among modern scholars.[8]

The most pressing concern for Alexandria's Jewish community was the need to provide access to its Sacred Writ in the language that dominated Alexandrian society as well as other urban centers of the time: Greek. According to a popular scholarly view, this was accomplished in schools through the production of interlinear texts, where each line of the Hebrew was followed by a line in Greek that rendered it. This type of text typically produces a foreign-language version (here Greek) that is virtually incomprehensible without some knowledge of the base text (here Hebrew).

In certain pedagogical contexts, such as when students are learning a new language, the interlinear approach can be ideal.[9] But when in this instance the Greek ends up circulating without the accompanying lines of Hebrew, it can cause consternation and confusion for those without the requisite Hebrew background.[10]

A second view, expressed by the scholar Meleze Modrzejewski,[11] attributes the impetus for the LXX Pentateuch to the Jewish community's need for a Greek version of their law that could be included in Ptolemy II's judicial system, under whom certain groups, including the Jews, would be allowed a considerable degree of internal legal autonomy. However, to my knowledge no conclusive proof exists that the Pentateuch was ever included within the extensive judicial system established by the Ptolemies.[12] Furthermore, large sections of the Pentateuch are not legal at all and would not have been of primary interest to those compiling such an all-encompassing legal code. Nonetheless, this option, perhaps in a modified form, remains worthy of being taken seriously, because it does provide something of a rationale for official Ptolemaic interest in the law code under which Jews might govern themselves.

More recently, Sylvie Honigman, a history professor at Tel Aviv University, has advanced a third view that identifies cultural prestige more than piety as the key motivating factor in the LXX Pentateuch's production.[13] A Dutch scholar, Michael van der Meer, has extended this insight to cover the origin of Greek Joshua, which he dates to the 220s BCE.[14] As he states, promoting one's cultural heritage, especially at a difficult time, is not without parallels.[15] Van der Meer concludes, "The Greek translation of Joshua was probably meant both to strengthen the cultural position of Jews in the early Ptolemaic Period and to provide the royal court with a faithful rendering of a book concerning the history of Palestine, over which the Ptolemies and Seleucids were then fighting."[16] There is a reasonable case to be made for this position. After all, Jews in both Egypt and Palestine might well have calculated that they were in the best position to present a compelling account of themselves to their new sovereign.

Moving from the most recent to the oldest interpretation in our purview, we turn to the arguments made by British biblical scholar H. St. John Thackery (1869–1930). In this fourth view, LXX Pentateuch owes its origins to the need for vernacular readings (that is, readings in Greek) as part of religious services within the synagogue. He figured that Jews in Hellenistic Alexandria, as is true for Jews in the modern world, would made frequent use of Sacred Writ in translation for their liturgy.[17] Notably, the scholar Emanuel Tov believes that such a liturgical setting likely existed. "From the outset," he writes, "it was only natural that the Greek Pentateuch would influence the translation of the subsequent books. The reading of the Hebrew Pentateuch in the synagogue started at an early date, and although there is no sound evidence for the liturgical use of the Greek Pentateuch (nor of the later Greek Books), the Pentateuch must also have been widely known in Greek. Accordingly, it must have influenced the translation of the later books."[18]

This theory, too, may have some merit. Leading Spanish LXX scholar Natalio Fernández Marcos speaks of Thackeray's work as "the most ambitious hypothesis to try to incorporate in a coherent way the whole process of decanting the Bible from Hebrew to Greek in its different stages," even as he points to weaknesses in Thackery's reconstruction (not the least of which is that he failed to account for the translation of Joshua and Judges).[19] And, in my view, van der Meer overstates the case when he dismisses Thackeray's "option of a liturgical setting for the Greek translation of Joshua"—and by extension for the remainder of the Septuagint.[20] Given how little we know of what went on in a synagogue in third-century BCE Alexandria, we cannot altogether rule out a liturgical connection of some sort.

What *do* we know about what went on in a Ptolemaic-era synagogue or, as it would have then been known, *proseuche*? Not much. We simply do not know whether an established service existed or what role scriptural reading would have played. Some scholars posit an early practice of "lectionary" reading—the Greek in tandem with the Hebrew—that would have made the translation of the entire Pentateuch superfluous for liturgical purposes, because lectionaries display only selected verses, not entire passages. As Jennifer Dines, among others, argues, liturgical use of the Greek Pentateuch would also have necessitated some system of markers (weekly portions, etc.) or revision to make it more suitable for synagogue use.[21] This would especially be the case when considering how other translations, from the *Targums* on, were used within Jewish worship (see chapter 2).

It may well be that the Greek Bible originated in several contexts, answering to different needs of the community.[22] Moreover, these needs probably defy neat categorization as either internal or external. An explanation that broadly incorporates "both/and," rather than the narrower "either/or," is more likely to be true to the complex factors responsible for the Septuagint. This also applies to the investigations of other Jewish versions in other chapters of this book.

The Septuagint as Immutable

Near the end of the Letter of Aristeas, after the Greek text is proclaimed, the Jewish community leaders "commanded that a curse should be laid . . . on anyone who should alter the version by any addition or change to any part of the written text, or any deletion either" (v. 311). This episode brings to mind the Israelites' ratification of the Torah at Mount Sinai (as recounted in Exod. 19 and 24) and strongly suggests that this account holds the Greek Pentateuch as having equivalent authority to that of the Hebrew Torah.[23] Likely, this view reflects the author's perception of events of his own day (that is, mid-second century BCE), when rival Greek versions, in the form of revisions and fresh translations, began to challenge the unique place held until then by the Greek Pentateuch of the third century.

There is no evidence for a specific revision of the Septuagint as early as the mid-second century. Nonetheless, bilingual readers could at any time compare the Greek text with the Hebrew, revealing numerous "differences" or "deficiencies" in the Septuagint, vis-à-vis the Hebrew, that required "correction."[24]

The Alexandrian Philo, who apparently knew no Hebrew, used distinctive language to capture his understanding of the translators.[25] They were "prophets and priests of the mysteries," who, "under inspiration, wrote . . . the same word for word, as though dictated to each by an invisible prompter."[26] In the writings of Epiphanius (310–403 CE), a father of the church, the level of embellishment reached its peak with a narrative that places thirty-six pairs of translators in individual cells:

> For while they were seventy-two in number and on the Pharian island opposite Alexandria, they were in thirty-six cells, two in each cell. From morning to evening they were shut up, and in the evening they would cross over in thirty-six small boats and go again to the palace of Ptolemy Philadelphus and dine with him. And each pair slept in one of thirty-six bedchambers, so that they might not talk with one another, but might produce an unadulterated translation. Thus they conducted themselves. For, having constructed the thirty-six cells already mentioned, over on the island, and formed them into pairs, Ptolemy shut them up in them two by two, as I have said. And with them he shut up two youths to minister to them in preparing food and service, and also skilled scribes.

> Moreover, he had made no opening into these cells through the walls, but in the roof above he opened what are called roof windows. But while thus abiding from morning to evening shut in by locks, they were translating as follows. To every pair one book was given. That is to say, the book of the Genesis of the World to one pair, the Exodus of the Israelites to another pair, that of Leviticus to another, and the next book in order to the next. . . .
>
> And when they were completed, the king sat on a lofty throne; and thirty-six readers also sat below, holding thirty-six duplicates of each book, and one had a copy of the Hebrew Scriptures. Each reader read alone, and the others kept watch. No disagreement was found, but it was such an amazing work of God that it was recognized that these men possessed the gift of the Holy Spirit, because they agreed in translation. And wherever they had added a word all of them had added the same, and where they had made an omission all alike had made the omission. And there was no need for the omitted words, but for those they added there was need. Thus, it should be clear to you, how marvelously, under the guidance of God and in the harmony of the Holy Spirit, they translated harmoniously and were not at variance with one another.[27]

Only divine oversight or intervention could have produced such unanimity, Epiphanius asserted. This accorded with the elevated status the Septuagint enjoyed among early Christians.[28]

The Translators of the Greek Pentateuch

Even though we cannot place all the translators of the Greek Pentateuch on a single committee, as did the author of the Letter of Aristeas, we can still make some observations about the Greek text produced by the five (or six) individuals or groups responsible for this undertaking.

To a large extent, those responsible for the Greek Pentateuch were setting, rather than following, precedent. In general, Greek speakers did not see much reason to translate sacred texts from other languages into Greek, secure as they were in the belief that they as a people had much to offer, but very little to learn from others.

However, anyone with the talent and desire to participate in the Septuagint project would surely not have lived in total isolation from trends, movements, and other activities in the community at large.[29] For Jews in Alexandria, this would have meant some exposure to the political, civic, and intellectual life of this cosmopolitan center, especially the library and the scholars associated with it.[30]

Drawing upon these resources, the Jews responsible for the LXX Pentateuch would have learned from the experience of the dragoman, an individual in ancient Near Eastern society whose primary responsibilities involved translating governmental and business documents. To prepare renderings into Greek for these purposes, the dragoman would typically employ a literal approach, following the form, style, grammar, and vocabulary of the base text (that is, the foreign-language text being translated) as closely as possible. In general, this literal approach was quicker to produce and more straightforward to understand. Notably, it minimized the amount of interpretation that might be introduced when translators fashioned their renderings more freely.

Thus the LXX translators often employed a literal approach as the most expedient and objective way to render their Hebrew. At the same time, though, other portions of the Greek biblical text reflect a heightened interest in literary and other stylistic features of the original Hebrew—characteristics we associate with freer versions of narratives that would not typically appear in a literal translation. Moreover, many passages of both sorts in the Greek Pentateuch are very difficult to fathom for readers without knowledge of the underlying Hebrew—and they would of course constitute the majority of readers in antiquity, as in the modern world.

It is this very real amalgam of literalism and the literary, of clarity and obscurity, in the Pentateuch and elsewhere in the Septuagint, that confounds simplistic descriptions of the Septuagint. Such judgments could be the result of a modern perspective; perhaps the Septuagint's original audience would have been able to understand the problematic texts. Realistically, though, we cannot eliminate all such difficulties in this manner. Even if I characterize much of the translation that is the Greek Pentateuch as responsibly literal, I readily admit that this is not consistently the case.

Perhaps, we shouldn't be all that surprised by this. By way of analogy, consider renderings in a mainstream, popular modern English-language Bible: the New Revised Standard Version (NRSV), which first appeared in 1989. Some of its translations are also almost impossible to understand unless one knows the Hebrew that underlies them. Unlike the LXX translators, who are sometimes described as simply translating phrase-by-phrase with no interest in the larger context, we know that the NRSV translators were careful, cautious, and conservative in their approaches. Yet even these individuals, who had the additional assistance offered by modern technology, couldn't manage to maintain a consistent and intelligible style throughout their version. In short, even those who embark upon a responsible approach (literal, free, or somewhere in between) will on occasion miss their target audience.

The LXX Translators and Their *Vorlage*: Translation Technique

The reference to NRSV also points to a decisive difference in scholarly efforts to describe the ways in which the LXX translators handled their Hebrew text (often called their *Vorlage*). Whereas we know the Hebrew text the NRSV committee worked with, we do not know for certain the nature of the Hebrew underlying the Septuagint.

One question is whether this Hebrew incorporated the same consonants found in the Masoretic Text. From antiquity until the ninth or tenth centuries CE, documents in the Hebrew language, including Scripture, were written without vowels, which readers would provide based on the context. Concerned that the system of vowels (or vocalization) would be lost or misinterpreted, a group of Jewish scholars called

Masoretes began writing the vowels into Hebrew texts. The standard Hebrew version of the Bible, including consonants, vowels, and numerous marginal notations, came to be known as the Masoretic Text (MT), which was probably completed sometime in the tenth century CE.[31]

Alternatively, was another Hebrew text utilized? If two or more textual traditions were combined, were they intertwined in some way, or do stretches of one follow another? And is there consistency in this regard throughout the Hebrew text, or do circumstances differ, section-by-section, book-by-book, or even within a given book?

These very issues have divided—and, to an extent, continue to divide—LXX specialists. Prior to World War II, it was widely asserted that the Masoretic Text, or at least the consonantal text to which vowels and other annotations were later added, represented throughout antiquity the standard against which all transcribers and translators would regularly check their work. It was this text, then, that LXX translators would have had before them. From this perspective, deviations from MT would lie at the feet—or, more precisely, the hands—of scribes whose minds must have been muddled or distracted. And in this reconstruction, the original LXX can be located in those manuscripts that are closest to MT.

Not all scholars, even during the first half of the twentieth century, have been comfortable with this formulation. Surely, it can be agreed, a consonantal text very much like MT would have been available to some LXX translators, whose abilities and attention to details varied. But was it not also possible that the Hebrew that lay before the LXX translators sometimes differed extensively from MT?

An excellent and instructive example of this sort of disagreement can be found in the careers of two of the most illustrative Jewish scholars of the twentieth century: Max L. Margolis (1866–1932) and Harry M. Orlinsky (1908–92). Although the specific focus of their disagreement was the Greek book of Joshua, where LXX is 4 percent shorter than MT (or, looked at the other way, MT is 4 percent longer than LXX), their arguments were clearly intended to be applicable elsewhere in the Septuagint as well. In Margolis's analysis, differences between MT and LXX were almost always attributable to the Greek translator himself, who regularly chose not to render particular words or phrases in his Hebrew text.[32] Presumably, he did so because he felt his target audience would benefit from a shorter version without these words or phrases, which might have confused or distracted a Greek reader. Orlinsky disagreed. In his opinion, the translator responsible for LXX Joshua adopted a mostly word-for-word approach to the task of rendering the Hebrew into Greek. Thus, MT-LXX differences should be sought in the Hebrew that lay before the translator (that is, his *Vorlage*), rather than linked to any initiative on the translator's part.[33]

Intriguingly, the discovery and publication of biblical scrolls from Qumran provided primary data to support both of these views. Some of the biblical scrolls present a consonantal text that is indeed identical to MT. In many cases, all that separates these texts is the fuller orthography (or spelling) employed in the Dead Sea Scrolls—that is, the greater use of the letters *yud* and *vav* to indicate pronunciation. This demonstrates something that, in my view, should never have been contested: MT does in fact represent an ancient and authentic textual tradition.

Still, other Qumran scrolls bear witness to a Hebrew text that is close to what the LXX translators may well have had in front of them. This is true for portions of the books of Samuel and Jeremiah, in particular. And this too demonstrates something that, in my view, should always have been acknowledged: LXX translators would generally follow their Hebrew text, whether or not it happened to be consistent with what we term MT.

The biblical scrolls from Qumran do not support those who would argue that MT has always presented a better or more widely accepted version. In fact, at Qumran, varying copies of the same biblical book apparently circulated at the same time—and with seemingly equal weight and authority. This provides firsthand evidence for what is often spoken of as textual fluidity among Jews prior to the Jerusalem Temple's destruction by the Romans in 70 CE. At Qumran and elsewhere in this period, even where there was consensus as to what constituted

Sacred or Holy Writ, this applied only to books as a whole and not to the particulars or details of wording.[34] There is then no good reason to assert (as once was common to do) that the Septuagint, where it follows a Hebrew *Vorlage* at variance with MT, is presenting an aberrant or secondary tradition.

But there is another factor to consider when evaluating or explicating how particular translators work. No matter what the Hebrew wording, it is likely that ancient translators, much like their modern counterparts, sometimes strayed from that Hebrew for any number of reasons: to make theological or stylistic "improvements" for the sake of consistency, to update references likely to be obscure to the intended audience, even to radically reshape whole sections for purposes of clarity and/or relevance.

In short, the evidence, including Greek scrolls from Qumran and nearby sites, reveals a varied textual history that is as old as the oldest Greek Bible.[35] Most translators followed their Hebrew, as best they understood it, for long stretches. But sometimes they deliberately changed the obvious or likely meaning of that Hebrew.

When considering the changes enacted by individual translators, it is then helpful to distinguish between those the translators subconsciously or accidentally made and those they chose as a result of conscious effort. The former consist primarily of omissions caused by easily confused letters at the beginning or end of words, by similar wording at the beginning or end of phrases, or by other easily mistaken graphic elements. The net result of such accidents is a shortening of the text in comparison with the Hebrew being rendered. This also supports the observation that a translator's work, akin to a scribe's, involved a certain amount of drudgery, in particular when it came to rendering or transcribing long passages. The eye was constantly moving forward or downward on the page and sometimes skipped similar wording.

In contrast to unconscious editorial adjustments, which typically abridge the text, translators' conscious or deliberate interventions tend to lengthen it. When translators sought to clarify, smooth out, explain, update, or otherwise "improve upon" the Hebrew that lay before them, I refer to these as "quantitative" changes. On occasion, substituted wording did not result in any substantive change in the text's length: These I refer to as "qualitative" changes.

Naturally, there is considerable scholarly difference of opinion as to whether a given passage in the Septuagint is the result of a translator's conscious activity or is instead an accurate representation of the Hebrew *Vorlage*, which in these instances differs from MT.

Increasingly over the past half-century or so, LXX specialists have minutely analyzed the Greek text to ascertain what translation techniques each book or block of material exhibits. No matter what determination is made in a specific instance, there is complete agreement that each book or block of material must be studied on its own to determine such characteristics. This is not to say that scholars of one LXX book cannot learn from specialists in another—indeed they can, and do. For example, it has become clear that the translator of LXX Joshua had access to the earlier Greek renderings of the books of the Pentateuch.

At the same time, scholars must resist the temptation to apply globally what is the case for a given book. In the past, lack of such restraint has led to the positing of a strong anti-anthropomorphic tendency throughout the Septuagint or an equally widespread promotion of certain messianic ideas. Neither of these potentially significant assertions has withstood the careful scrutiny of later researchers.

In summary, we as modern researchers seek to distinguish between differences (vis-à-vis MT) that were due to the Septuagint translators and those that accurately reflect their Hebrew *Vorlage*, which in these instances differed from MT. But, so far as we can determine, ancient readers did not take such distinctions into consideration. Rather, those individuals who felt obliged to revise an earlier form of the Greek text were motivated by the perceived need to "correct" this text in the direction of the Hebrew text in use within their community. The assumption underlying such efforts at "correcting" is clear: The available Hebrew was the standard against which any other rendering needed to be compared. Variations from this standard were mistakes caused by translators whose faults or flaws ran from incompetence to indolence to the introduction of "improvements."

How far back did this inclination to correct the Greek on the basis of the Hebrew go? In my view, at least to the mid-second century BCE, when the Letter of Aristeas was composed.

Revisions versus the Original Version

The Letter's concluding section (described earlier in this chapter) has a tone of urgency about it, as if its author was deeply concerned about guarding what he perceived as the Septuagint's sacred status against even the slightest alteration. Such urgency most likely reflects the times and circumstances of the Letter's author, whose Greek-speaking Jewish community was faced with one or more revisions of a text upon which its tradition had bestowed the immutable status of Sacred Writ. On the basis of known revisers active at least a century after Aristeas, we can suggest that earlier, unknown revisers were likewise also concerned with differences between the established Greek text and the recognized Hebrew text of various biblical books.[36]

Even though the translators responsible for the Greek Pentateuch followed a reasonably literal rendering of the Hebrew text before them, in certain instances the Hebrew and Greek differ. For the ancient reviser, the then-current Hebrew was the standard to which any Greek text should be "revised." For the author of the Letter of Aristeas, the Greek text as passed down to his community needed no changes of any sort.

Yet the author of the Letter was not successful in establishing his community's Greek Bible as uniquely authoritative. A proliferation of revisers or new translators followed after Aristeas's time. In addition to individuals whose names we know (Theodotion, Aquila, and Symmachus), some ancient Greek manuscripts, including a few found among the Dead Sea Scrolls, exhibit revisions by anonymous translators. Moreover, close analysis of scriptural citations and allusions by New

Testament writers points to the fact that these authors occasionally relied on Greek versions we would otherwise have no knowledge of.[37] Clearly, many individuals, on their own or more likely within their communities, were not the least bit deterred by the anathema or curse threatened in the Letter of Aristeas, if they were familiar with it at all.

Modern textual scholars frequently attempt to distinguish between older and newer renderings and also between original translation and revision. However, it is unlikely that most individuals in antiquity made such distinctions. In particular, it cannot be determined with certainty whether those citing a Greek biblical text had any idea that they were dealing with a revised, reworked, or in any sense updated version of the original. In fact, I suspect, something quite the opposite was frequently at work. Their reliance on "what was written" as authoritative probably depended on an understanding of its being reliably the Word of God. Although this was especially so within the developing Christian world,[38] it is also likely that, when necessary, Jewish scholars made use of the Greek Scripture at hand without overly concerning themselves about the origins of the text.

The perseverance and power of revision can be partly gauged from the fact that sometimes the work of the revisers replaced the earlier forms of the Greek text. In the case of the book of Daniel, for example, almost all Greek manuscripts display a version that we identify with Theodotion, in place of an earlier text. For the Song of Songs (or Canticles), a literal version, similar to what we associate with the reviser Aquila, is found in all witnesses to the text. And whereas parts of the text in Samuel and Kings (books collectively known as Reigns or Kingdoms in Septuagint tradition) are original, in other sections a revision has supplanted the older wording. Although we don't know the motivations of those who collated this material, I suspect that they would, if queried, have asserted that their compilation, however uneven it might appear, was nonetheless a secure representation of what the inspired translators initially wrote down.

In his voluminous writings, the Jewish philosopher Philo added support for the view that all of the Septuagint resulted from inspiration. He expressed a reverential attitude toward the work of translators, whom he termed "prophets," and thereby allotted to the LXX the same authority possessed by the Hebrew Bible. So it is that the concept championed by the Letter of Aristeas was maintained, while the reality of an authoritative text, if it ever existed, faded further and further into the past.

The LXX beyond the Pentateuch

Were the translators of the non-Pentateuchal books aware of what their predecessors had accomplished, and did this form something of a paradigm for their efforts? When all is said and done, we are largely dependent here, as elsewhere, on the interpretations offered by the most respected and seasoned researchers.

Let us take one example: the book of Joshua, whose translator was demonstrably dependent on the Greek Pentateuch. Jacqueline Moatti-Fine, who in 1996 edited *Jesus (Josué)* in La Bible d'Alexandrie series, speaks of an intelligent faithfulness ("une fidélité intelligente") as exhibited by Joshua's translator to the political and religious vocabulary adopted in the Greek Pentateuch. In fact, she devotes almost a dozen pages of her introduction to examples supporting this aspect of the translator's profile. The scope of this faithfulness is wide: It encompasses "political [for example, institutions and their leaders] and social [e.g., tribal and family terminology] organization" and terms of "refuge," as in "cities of refuge." With respect to what she characterizes as the "great religious themes of the Pentateuch," Moatti-Fine singles out study of the Law, the presence of God in history, and the people Israel's meriting their inheritance of the land as three areas of Joshua "with a high degree of faithfulness in terms of vocabulary."[39] Within these parameters, even when there is "innovation" on the part of LXX Joshua, it can be clearly linked to distinctive Pentateuchal renderings.

Particularly suggestive are distinctions in the vocabulary of the Septuagint that do not reflect differences in the Hebrew. The most noticeable is a neologism for licit altars (see, especially, Josh. 22), in contrast to a more general term for those perceived as illicit. The Hebrew is the same for both usages. There is also the characteristic use, which links LXX Deuteronomy and Joshua, of one Greek term for the "word" when it is divine, while another term is typically used for the "words" of humans. Later research by Michael van der Meer has largely confirmed this analysis on the part of Moatti-Fine.[40]

On the other hand, a Septuagint book such as Proverbs is widely understood to contain a number of passages reflective of the translators themselves, rather than their Hebrew text. This translation was essentially independent from earlier Greek translations, such as that of the Pentateuch. In this respect, the translator of Proverbs was not unique among those responsible for the later books of the Septuagint.[41]

Given the historical and theological significance of the Pentateuch and its rendering, it is not entirely surprising that it continues to be the object of strenuous analysis and debate. Learned opinion about other LXX books is not static either. The book of Isaiah in the Septuagint is one example of the shifting of consensus. For more than fifty years, the view of Dutch-born scholar Leo Seeligmann—that the translator of Greek Isaiah engaged in wholesale updating of the Hebrew prophet's words, such that they now applied specifically to the translator's Alexandrian contemporaries—has held sway. More recent scholars are rethinking how this translator worked.[42]

The Terms "Septuagint" or "LXX"

Throughout this chapter, the terms "Septuagint" or "LXX" have been used as if the work's contents were self-evident. This is not the case in contemporary scholarly literature, nor was it true in antiquity. In ancient times, the term "LXX" had more than one meaning, sometimes as used by one and the same author, often by one and the same tradition. Furthermore, it is almost universally asserted that, strictly speaking, the term "Septuagint" (or "LXX") referred initially only to the translation of the Pentateuch, but, strictly speaking, that is not accurate either.

The evidence shows the following: Where the earliest Greek translation was limited to the Pentateuch, the term LXX was not used; where the term was used, it was generally not limited to the Pentateuch. In fact, it is possible to discern as many as six different uses for the term LXX in antiquity: (1) the earliest Greek translation of the Pentateuch (Jerome, ca. 400 CE, was virtually alone among early Christian leaders in insisting on this limitation for the term); (2) the earliest Greek translation of the entire Old Testament; (3) the Greek text, or *koine*, known to the Christian scholar Origen in the first half of the third century CE; (4) the Greek text Origen reconstructed on the basis of his comparison with the Hebrew and placed in the fifth column of his massive *Hexapla*;[43] (5) any authoritative Greek text recognized as scriptural (but not viewed as part of the New Testament); and (6) the entire Greek tradition (including revisions, recensions, various fresh translations, etc.). Although the liveliest developments in terminology arose within early Christianity, Judaism of that time was not immune to similar imprecision.[44]

The Septuagint "Canon"

Which books or parts of books did the Greek translators render—or in some cases, where original Greek composition was involved, transmit? In other words, what counted as "canon" for these translators and for the Jewish community (or communities) in which they resided?

For the period leading up to the Common Era and for the first centuries CE, we simply do not know. Only with the great codices of the third and fourth century CE were individual books or sections of the Septuagint collected into anything approaching a Bible.

And here the evidence is mixed. Codex Vaticanus (mid-fourth century CE) contains all the books of the Hebrew Bible or Protestant Old Testament and the following material that is today classified as Deuterocanonical, or apocryphal: 1 Esdras, 2 Esdras, Psalm 151, Wisdom of Solomon, Ecclesiasticus (or Ben Sirach), the additions to Esther (several of which were originally composed in a Semitic language;

others are original Greek compositions), Judith, Tobit, Baruch, Letter of Jeremiah, and the additions to Daniel (Azariah and the Three Jews, Susanna, and Bel and the Dragon). Codex Alexandrinus (fifth century CE) contains all of this and, in addition, 1–4 Maccabees and the Odes of Solomon. Although there is some uncertainty as to the original contents of Codex Sinaiticus (mid-fourth century CE), it is reliably viewed as encompassing the Old Testament according to the contours set by German Septuagint specialist Alfred Rahlfs, including the Apocrypha (or Deuterocanonicals), but without 2 and 3 Maccabees.[45] Other manuscripts and the traditions they represent include additional works or omit material contained in these uncial codices.

For modern scholars of the Septuagint, the ordering and contents as set forth by Rahlfs in his 1935 edition are generally held to be authoritative: Genesis, Exodus, Leviticus, Numbers, Deuteronomy, Joshua, Judges, Ruth, 1–4 Reigns (= 1 and 2 Sam. + 1 and 2 Kings), 1–2 Chronicles, 1 Esdras, 2 Esdras, Esther (including additions now found only in Greek), Judith, Tobit, 1–4 Maccabees, Psalms (including Ps. 151), Odes, Proverbs, Ecclesiastes, Song of Songs, Job, Wisdom of Solomon, Ben Sirach, Psalms of Solomon, the twelve Minor Prophets, Isaiah, Jeremiah, Baruch, Lamentations, the Letter of Jeremiah, Ezechiel, and Daniel (with additions). But Rahlfs and his followers did not claim that this precise ordering and contents reflect the situation in the second century CE, to say nothing of the second century BCE.

That said, we are still left wondering why, for example, Tobit, Judith, 1 and 2 Maccabees, and Ben Sirach were not part of the canon of Rabbinic Judaism, but were nonetheless accepted by some ancient Jews and later by Christians. In my view, no one has offered a fully satisfactory explanation for the process of canonization.[46] Within religious communities, various propositions have been offered to justify inclusion or exclusion, but without any sure textual or historical basis. For this reason, we cannot be certain whether any Jewish community ever held as sacred all the books listed in the great codices. Unfortunately, this gives the term "Septuagint" a degree of uncertainty or ambiguity that is difficult to ignore or overcome.

The Septuagint Not "Abandoned" by Jews

It has often been asserted that Jews abandoned the Septuagint in the first centuries CE very soon after it was adopted by early Christians. While it is certainly true that the Septuagint was ultimately pushed to the sidelines and never achieved the official status that the *Targums*, or Aramaic versions, would come to enjoy,[47] the verb "abandon" and the relatively short timeline suggested by this term do seem extreme, for a variety of reasons.

First, at least some parts of the Greek versions attributed to Theodotion and Aquila (and possibly also Symmachus) reflect revisions of an earlier Greek version. A revision, which (unlike a fresh translation) includes substantial portions of an earlier text in the same language, reflects the reviser's judgment that the earlier text retains substantial value and is valid, except where changes are required. Additionally, the first-century Jewish philosopher Philo apparently knew Scripture only from Greek texts. Moreover, the Greek Bible was used in at least some mid-sixth-century synagogues.[48] This is surely far short of total abandonment.

The "Three"

It is perhaps paradoxical that our major ancient sources for information about the Jewish revisers derives from a Christian context. In the third century, the church father Origen gathered together in his polyglot text known as the *Hexapla* as many examples as he could find of the Greek Bible. Among them were three apparently continuous Greek texts more recent than the Old Greek, all of which seem to have originated within Jewish communities.

One of these texts is attributed to Aquila, traditionally dated to the first quarter of the second century CE. It is hyperliteral, and can almost serve as a primer to the Hebrew language as well as to biblical thought and teaching for Greek speakers. For Aquila, then, the most effective foreign-language version was one that displayed its reliance on the Hebrew in the most thoroughgoing manner possible.

Another version, associated with Symmachus in the late second century CE, represents a very different approach to translation. His text reads well in Greek; at the same time, it often departs from the distinctive stylistic features of the Hebrew original. Thus Symmachus pays more attention to the needs of the Greek-speaking members of his target audience, who wanted something they could understand with relative ease.

A third version, attributed to Theodotion, mid-second century CE, strives to balance the often-competing interests of the source language (Hebrew) and the target language (Greek). This can be observed whenever he changes the earlier Greek text he was revising to accord with the Hebrew text (very much like MT) in his community or to reflect more closely Greek as it was spoken and read in his own time.

As a result, someone studying these three versions, especially when they are all rendering the same Hebrew passage, will be exposed to the major approaches to translation in antiquity as well as in the modern world: literal, free, and in-between.

Throughout his version Aquila was a reviser. That is, he started with an older form of the Greek, and changed it only when he saw a theological or linguistic reason for doing so. Theodotion was also a reviser in some instances. But in Daniel, for example, where his text supplanted the Old Greek in nearly all Septuagint manuscripts, he appears to offer a fresh translation.[49] Symmachus also combined the roles of translator and reviser.[50]

There is general agreement that Aquila, Theodotion, and Symmachus were all active in the second century CE, probably in the chronological order I've listed them here. In this regard, the case of Theodotion is particularly interesting, since some of his distinctive language found its way into the New Testament—almost two centuries earlier than the historical Theodotion is said to have lived. This has led to the supposition that a Jewish translator active in the first century BCE formulated a version that served as the basis of Theodotion's revision in the second century CE. For this reason, the anonymous earlier translator is sometimes referred to as proto-Theodotion.[51]

I hold to the view that all three individuals—Aquila, Theodotion, and Symmachus—were likely Jewish. But the ancient evidence is far from unanimous on this point. Sifting through this evidence, I contend that Aquila was born a pagan, converted to Christianity, and then to Judaism. He was probably a disciple of Akiba, one of the many rabbis with whom he studied. Theodotion was born in Ephesus. His identity as a Jew is based primarily on stories that he, like Aquila a generation or so earlier, studied with a number of Palestinian rabbis. In the ancient sources, Symmachus is often associated with the Ebionites, a Jewish-Christian sect. As such he could well have self-identified as Jewish. Moreover, another strand of tradition pictures him as a Samaritan who converted to Judaism and may have studied with Rabbi Meir.

The Septuagint among the Rabbis

The Rabbinic sources, as recorded and preserved in the Talmud, are multi-, not uni-, vocal. Some condemn the creation of a Greek version of the Torah, as in, for example, Tractate *Soferim* 1.6–7: "It is not permissible [to write the Torah] in old Hebrew, in Aramaic, in Medean, or in Greek. No language nor script shall be read from unless it be written in Hebrew." Others, such as b. Meg. 8b, present positive statements about biblical versions in languages other than Hebrew—and often specifically about the Greek text: "R. Simeon b. Gamaliel says that books [of the Scripture] also were permitted [by the sages] to be written only in Greek."[52] Passages within Rabbinic literature also cite a tradition according to which between ten and eighteen alterations were deliberately inserted into the Greek version of the Pentateuch by its Jewish translators.[53]

It is not easy to place such statements into historical, geographical, or theological contexts or categories. A suggestive chronological link may exist, pointing to increasingly negative judgments about the Septuagint as time passed. Yet, at the least, these passages are evidence of a lively and far-flung discussion among the leaders of Rabbinic Judaism about the place of the Septuagint, in particular, and translation, in general, within their communities.

Regrettably, the openness of at least some Rabbis to the study and appreciation of the Septuagint was short lived. There were several reasons for this. With the shift of the Jewish population center to Babylonia, the community moved from Greek-speaking to Aramaic- and then Arabic-speaking societies, where the Greek language was no longer dominant.[54] Moreover, the emerging Christian leadership took possession of the Septuagint, treating it as though it was a non-Jewish, even anti-Jewish document. They aggressively used the Greek text in increasingly vitriolic rhetoric against Jews and Judaism. Only among Greek-speaking Jews, a relatively small number compared to the communities in Babylonia, did a Greek-language version of the Bible continue to function as a source of prayer and study.

It was not until the early part of the nineteenth century that Jewish scholars such as Zecharias Frankel (1801–75) began to look seriously at the Septuagint as a valuable part of their heritage from the distant past. In so doing, they uncovered many places where interpretative material in the Septuagint reflected concerns found in Rabbinic discussions. Also fairly numerous are instances of what might be termed Rabbinic-like midrash.[55] These examples demonstrate that Rabbinic exegesis (or interpretation) of Scripture often drew upon earlier Jewish resources such as the Septuagint or the Hebrew texts from which LXX translators themselves derived this material.

Biblical scholar Max L. Margolis is credited with being the first academic specialist in LXX studies in the United States. His student Harry M. Orlinsky was also well known for his LXX scholarship. Today's Jewish scholars of the Septuagint include Emanuel Tov and myself.

My entry into the field was somewhat serendipitous. In 1970 I entered Harvard University as a graduate student in classics, a field in which I would earn both a BA and MA. Very soon after I started classes, I heard about the university's Department of Near Eastern Languages and Civilizations (NELC). This seemed like a perfect program for combining my ongoing enthusiasm for Greek language and culture with my fairly new interests in Hellenistic Jewish history and literature. At the end of my first year, I officially transferred into NELC.

Among my first courses in the new department was a seminar on the book of Joshua taught by renowned archaeologist and Protestant theologian G. Ernest Wright. One day I mentioned my background in classics to him, and he regaled me with stories of Max Margolis and Harry Orlinsky—two renowned Jewish scholars whose footsteps I was hoping to follow (at a respectful distance of course!)—as well as the text called Greek Joshua, which I was more excited about than either Homer or Herodotus. I was hooked. It was a marriage made on Divinity Avenue (where NELC classes literally were held), if not in heaven.

Even more today than I could have realized as a student then, I am fascinated by the industry and dedication of those individuals who thought enough of both Sacred Writ and their communities to translate the Hebrew text for the benefit of their Greek-speaking contemporaries. Just as we do today, I imagine they also wrestled with the relative merits of teaching everyone Hebrew or bringing the text to their contemporaries in the Greek language of their newly adopted culture.

The result, at least for the Pentateuch, was a Hebraic Greek version that repeatedly exhibits a linguistic dependence on Hebrew and an exegetical or interpretative independence in keeping with the Jewish community's new home in Alexandria. Many of my scholarly colleagues figure that these translators, muddled in vision, were not up to the task. But I think they achieved as much as, if not more than, anyone could have expected, given the circumstances in which they labored. And where "improvements" were possible, at least one individual, if not more, came up with revisions or corrections later on.

Final Thoughts

For the most part, Christians passed down, interpreted, and analyzed the texts of the Septuagint throughout the centuries that separate us from its initial formulation. The great codices are products of their Christian communities, as are almost all of the rest of parchment and papyrus evidence we have, in cursive as well as uncial script. Notably, evidence indicates that, on the whole, Christian scribes did not manipulate the texts they were copying to bring them into more explicit agreement with distinctively Christian concepts, especially those expressed in the New Testament. Careful analysis of myriad manuscripts has uncovered surprisingly little deliberate manipulation of this sort.[56] Thus, consciously or not, Christians transmitted, largely intact, the greatest legacy of Hellenistic Judaism: the Septuagint.

In today's academic world, Jews and Christians, along with adherents of other religions and of no religion, are full partners in the study of the origins and early development of the Septuagint. At the same time, Jews are well placed to examine unique features of the Septuagint in Judaism, especially within the rich history of Jewish biblical interpretation and application.

2

The *Targums*

Dated to approximately 275 BCE, the Septuagint, or Greek Pentateuch, or LXX, the topic of chapter 1, is the earliest recorded written version of Scripture in a language other than Hebrew. At one time scholars believed that the Hebrew Bible itself contains evidence of its translation or interpretation several centuries earlier, but academic researchers now essentially discount this view.

Early Aramaic Translations

The discredited theory focuses upon Nehemiah 8. In a scene from this chapter, dated to the mid-fifth century BCE, Ezra the scribe, having returned from Babylon, stood before an assembly of the people at Jerusalem's Water Gate, reading in Hebrew from the scroll of the Teaching, or Law.[1] As he spoke, a group of thirteen individuals, along with the Levites, "explained the Teaching to the people, while the people stood in their places. They read from the scroll of the Teaching of God, translating it and giving the sense; so they understood the reading" (Neh. 8:7–8).

Scholars disagree as to the precise meaning of the word rendered here as "translating." The third-century CE authority Rav, among others, upheld this understanding of the Hebrew root *p-r-sh*. Specifically,

Rav believed that this referred to an explanatory translation of Ezra's Hebrew text into Aramaic.

It is true that by the mid-fifth century BCE Aramaic had become the lingua franca of the Middle East, and the adult population of Jerusalem, as inhabitants of this larger world, could no longer easily understand Hebrew. If the text was being rendered into Aramaic, it would have been for their benefit.

In this scenario, interpreters were utilizing Aramaic to supplement and explain, but not replace, the Hebrew wording of the Torah—in an oral rather than a scribal context. This led Rav to postulate that Ezra was the founder of the practice whereby an Aramaic translation of the Bible was read along with the Hebrew text in synagogues. Although Rav's picture of Ezra and the synagogue is anachronistic (the first synagogues do not appear until several centuries after the time of Ezra and Nehemiah), it nonetheless contains the valuable insight that many Rabbinic interpreters of the first centuries CE traced the synagogue practice of reciting biblical passages in Aramaic, well developed in their own day, to the late biblical period.[2]

As a rule, Rabbinic traditions are considered credible witnesses to beliefs and practices contemporary with them, but they provide a far less secure foundation upon which to build a reliable understanding of events and personalities that may (or may not) have existed centuries before them. Even if we were to accept an understanding of Nehemiah 8 as portraying the act of translating from Hebrew to Aramaic, this text would not speak directly to the origins of the *Targum* as we use the term in this chapter.[3] Following the lead of specialists in this area, *Targum* refers to an Aramaic translation of a book of the Hebrew Bible undertaken by Jews during the Rabbinic period (c. 70–600 CE).[4]

Nonetheless, if we deny any conception of translation from Hebrew into Aramaic in Nehemiah, we could, in my view, be guilty of "throwing out the baby with the bathwater." In other words, it is useful both to allow for early forays into Aramaic translation and to restrict the term *Targum* to specific examples of such versions.

The same holds true for the Aramaic biblical texts from Qumran. Among the Dead Sea Scrolls, two small Leviticus fragments in Aramaic were found in Cave 4. The first consists of scattered phrases from Leviticus 16:12–15; the second contains bits and pieces from vv. 18–21 of the same chapter. By far the longest Aramaic text uncovered at Qumran is from the book of Job. From Cave 4 are two fragments, containing a few words from Job 3:5 on one and Job 4:16–5:4 on the other. And from Cave 11 are extensive portions of Job, from the middle of chapter 17 until the end of the book. Beginning around chapter 35, the extant Aramaic text is very well preserved. This find accords with a Rabbinic tradition that puts a *Targum* of Job in the hands of Gamaliel I, a Rabbinic leader early in the first century CE.[5]

Targums to the Torah

There are several important *Targums* for the Torah, the Former Prophets, the Latter Prophets, and the Writings. The most influential ones were composed in Palestine and possibly also in Babylonia. At least initially, these *Targums* functioned as supplements to the Hebrew in liturgical settings (see the relevant discussion later in this chapter).[6]

Targum Onkelos

Targum Onkelos is the best-known Aramaic rendering of the Torah, or Pentateuch. The Babylonian Talmud (b. Meg. 3a) attributes a *Targum* to Onkelos, a proselyte to Judaism, and locates him in second-century Palestine.[7] Only later, however, is the text we know as *Targum Onkelos* credited to him.[8]

In strikingly similar language, the Palestinian Talmud attributes a foreign-language rendering to Aquila, but this refers to a Greek text, not an Aramaic one.[9]

Nonetheless, there seems to be some connection between these two notices, although scholars disagree over whether two individuals, or only one, are intended. Both *Targum Onkelos* and the Greek version attributed to Aquila fall within the general characterization of literal, but with this caveat: the hyperliteral Aquila and the generally literal *Targum Onkelos* are far from identical in either approach or resultant text.

So far as we know, *Targum Onkelos* is the only *Targum* to have undergone the thorough practice of redaction. As a result of this process, subsequent scribes copied exactly what was in the text before them. They were not permitted to make any changes whatsoever. Such strict procedures grew out of, and in turn supported, the view that the text of this *Targum* was fixed and that scribes should transcribe and transmit it only in this exact form.

To ensure the scribes' complete attention to each and every form, a *masorah* (a series of marginal notes) was developed to highlight rare forms that might otherwise be "corrected." This is similar to the procedures used with the standard Hebrew text of the Bible (or MT). No other *Targums* were transcribed with such strictures. In other words, no other *Targums* were redacted.

Linguistically, *Targum Onkelos* combines elements of Western (that is, Jewish Literary) Aramaic and Eastern (that is, Babylonian) Aramaic, giving rise to several theories on its origins. What I would call the intermediate position, that the *Targum* originated in Palestine and was later redacted in Babylon, now claims a majority of scholarly adherents. This position accounts for both the predominance of distinctive Palestinian linguistic and theological expressions and the smaller amounts of characteristic Babylonian language and theology.

Analysis of the Jewish Literary Aramaic in this *Targum* would support dating its earliest portions to no later than the first half of the second century CE. Many scholars connect the initial composition of *Targum Onkelos* with the end of the Bar Kokhba Revolt in 135 CE. It is doubtless a later linguistic development than examples of this dialect in the biblical book of Daniel or in the Dead Sea Scrolls. However, it is also possible to date the earliest portions of *Targum Onkelos* to the period prior to the Jerusalem Temple's destruction in 70 CE. Only a strong and prestigious central authority like the Temple, so it is argued, could have established and maintained the standardized Aramaic that characterizes this *Targum*.

Whatever the precise date of its initial composition, it is likely that even the oldest written sections of *Targum Onkelos* contain traditions from far earlier. The original authors would have included this material and/or later editors would have added it in the period before the Aramaic text was deemed fixed. Such later editors may well have also added material from their own time that was not available to earlier authors or editors.

Of the *Targums* to the Pentateuch, Onkelos is the most literal, by which I mean that it contains the least number of interpretive additions. A careful study demonstrates that the translators worked with a Hebrew text that was, for all intents and purposes, equivalent to MT.[10] For the most part, this holds true for the rest of the *Targums* as well.

As is also the case with other *Targums*, the translators of *Targum Onkelos* parted company with their Hebrew in a number of passages. This can lead to the incorrect assertion that the *Targums* are largely paraphrases, that is, very free renderings that have little (or nothing) in common with the text they are supposedly rendering. What is actually typical—and, we might say uniquely characteristic of the *Targums*—is the combination of "literal translations of the Hebrew text with a great deal of additional and sometimes highly creative material."[11] (See examples later in this chapter.)

In this regard, Onkelos can be viewed as providing examples of the implicit rationale for such additions and the explicit form they take. For the most part, these Aramaic translators devised nonliteral sections to provide their intended audience with an accessible way to understand the Hebrew that was also consistent with the theological views being promoted by those responsible for the *Targums*. Thus, for example, they regularly replaced Hebrew place names with geographical designations more familiar to those in the Targumists' own communities. This practice, found occasionally in the Septuagint as well, can sometimes provide clues as to the time or locale in which the version was made. These translators also typically rendered figurative phrases according to sense rather than literally; more generally, they simplified difficult words, phrases, or ideas. (Examples appear later in the chapter.)

Of special notice are the many efforts to guard against what the translators saw as a potentially serious misunderstanding of the nature of God. For this reason, they restyled most Hebrew anthropomorphisms (applying human physical attributes to nonhumans) and anthropopathisms (furnishing nonhumans with human emotions) related to God so as to avoid even the possibility of thinking that God really had a human type of body or human emotions. They also avoided the suggestion that other beings could be categorized, however mistakenly, as "gods."

Alongside these efforts, the translators had no difficulty in supplementing or even contradicting biblical law, regardless of its being seen as of divine origin, when such legal passages failed to support contemporary communal practice.[12] Such changes took advantage of centuries of Rabbinic interpretation and implementation of biblical laws. In the process, Targumists made selections from existing traditions, sometimes fashioning a new approach that was presumably of particular interest to their community.

Here are some examples. All of the Targumic passages that follow are from *Pseudo-Jonathan* (see explanation to follow), but they are broadly representative of other Aramaic versions of the Torah. The translation of the traditional Hebrew comes from NJPS.

In the first examples, a general biblical term receives specific definition or description. So, Exodus 22:20: "You shall not wrong a stranger or oppress him, for you were strangers in the land of Egypt"; *Pseudo-Jonathan*: "And you shall not vex a stranger with words, nor oppress him to take his possessions." Similarly, Leviticus 25:17: "Do not wrong one another, but fear your God; for I the LORD am your God"; *Pseudo-Jonathan*: "And you shall not wrong each other with harsh words."

Where the biblical law was perceived as unclear in any way, the Targumist was ready to make what he undoubtedly perceived as necessary changes. We find this at Leviticus 18:21: "Do not allow any of your offspring to be offered up to Molech, and do not profane the name of your God: I am the LORD"; *Pseudo-Jonathan*: "And from your seed you shall not give in intercourse with a daughter of the nations, to cause them to pass to idolatry." We can detect a similar motivation in a very different context at Deuteronomy 6:9: "Inscribe them on the doorposts of your house and on your gates"; *Pseudo-Jonathan*: "Upon the doorposts you shall fix them on the third part of the lintel on the doorposts and on your gates, on the right side as you go in."

The creation of the *beit din*, or court, distinguished postbiblical Judaism from religion in biblical times. The can be observed at Exodus 22:2: "If the sun has risen on him, there is bloodguilt in that case—He [that is, the thief] must make restitution; if he lack the means, he shall be sold for his theft." *Pseudo-Jonathan*: "If he has nothing with which to pay, then the Bet Din will sell him for his theft, and until the Shemitta [or sabbatical] year." So also Numbers 30:3: "If a man makes a vow to the LORD or takes an oath imposing an obligation on himself, he shall not break his pledge; he must carry out all that has come out of his mouth" ["come . . . mouth"—noted as literal in JPS notes]. *Pseudo-Jonathan*: "A man of thirteen years . . . swears an oath to bind his soul with a bond of something that is permitted, he shall not break his word. However, the Bet Din shall release him, and if they do not release him, he shall do according to all which comes out of his mouth."

Sometimes the Targumist expanded the application of biblical law, as at Deuteronomy 22:10: "You shall not plow with an ox and an ass together." *Pseudo-Jonathan*: ". . . with an ox and ass or with any creature, two species connected together." On other occasions, he lessened the extent to which a law could be applied. So, Deuteronomy 19:15: "A single witness may not validate against a person any guilt or blame for any offense that may be committed; a case can be valid only on the testimony of two witnesses or more." *Pseudo-Jonathan*: "One witness shall not arise against a man for any capital offence or for any monetary crime."

Occasionally the Targumist took the opportunity to introduce a related matter not mentioned in the Torah text. Deuteronomy 24:4: "Then the first husband who divorced her shall not take her to wife again, since she has been defiled—for that would be abhorrent to the LORD. You must not bring sin upon the land that the LORD your God is giving you as a heritage." *Pseudo-Jonathan*: "for it is an abomination before the Lord, and her children who are born from her are not an abomination." Or, he expounded a general principle of wide application. Deuteronomy 19:21: "Nor must you show pity: life for life, eye for eye, tooth for tooth, hand for hand, foot for foot." *Pseudo-Jonathan*: "And your eye shall have no pity—a soul for a soul, the value of an eye in exchange for an eye, the value of a tooth in exchange for a tooth, the value of a hand in exchange for a hand, the value of a foot in exchange for a foot."[13]

Targum Pseudo-Jonathan

In addition to Onkelos, there are four other *Targums* to the Pentateuch. Three of them, it is generally agreed, are of Palestinian (specifically Galilean) origin.[14] Probably the best known of the four, *Targum Pseudo-Jonathan*, contains a rendering of all but fifteen verses from the Pentateuch. Its name resulted from a misreading by a fourteenth-century commentator. In abbreviated form this *Targum Jerushalmi* (or *Targum* to the Pentateuch) was known as TJ. Knowing that Jonathan ben Uzziel was widely believed to be the author of the major *Targum* to the Prophets, a Jewish scholar misinterpreted this J as a reference to the same Jonathan, although there are no scholarly or even traditional links between the two *Targums*. The ensuing title, "Pseudo-Jonathan," can be considered something of a compromise that honors the Jonathan to whom this work was attributed while at the same time acknowledging that this attribution is not correct.

Scholars have dated this *Targum* to no earlier than the seventh century CE, if its references to Muhammad (c. 580–632 CE) and possibly to Byzantium are integral parts of the original text. However, if a copyist added these references, as some scholars now contend,

Targum Pseudo-Jonathan may be dated to the mid- or late fourth century CE. Even with this earlier date, *Targum Pseudo-Jonathan* is still the latest of the four *Targum* types based on the Palestinian *Targum*.

The most evident characteristic of this *Targum* is its expansiveness. Even a rough calculation yields that it is nearly twice as long as the Hebrew text upon which it is based. It is an infinitely rich source for teachings of the talmudic period.

The Fragment *Targum*

The second of the Palestinian *Targums*, popularly referred to as the Fragment *Targum*, contains just a bit more than 900 verses from the approximately 5,500 verses that make up the Pentateuch; most of these Aramaic verses cover the historical rather than the legal sections. In actuality there are two Fragment *Targums*: FT (V = Vatican Codex 440), the earlier and longer one (with selections from 908 verses); and FT (P = Paris Codex 110), containing additional material from *Targum Onkelos*. FT (P) may also be seen as a prototype to sections in *maḥzorim* (festival prayer books) that contain consecutive passages for recitation on specific holidays. The selections found in both Fragment *Targums* were taken from a version of the original Palestinian *Targum* written in the late second or early third century.

The wording of some passages in the Fragment *Targum* is older than Pseudo-Jonathan. Other passages contain references to events in the mid-fifteenth century. In its current form, then, the Fragment *Targum* is very much a compendium of Aramaic texts from a vast chronological expanse encompassing perhaps a millennium.

Although the term "Fragment" or "Fragmentary" within the name of this *Targum* is conventional, it is a misnomer. As Paul Flesher and Bruce Chilton observe: "These Targums do not contain *fragments* of *Targums* but rather *selections* of *Targums*. . . . Even though they do not have the entire Pentateuch, they are 'complete' manuscripts in that they were intentionally created in their present form."[15]

It is not certain how these *Targums*, which in their original state contained some verses from each of the five books of the Pentateuch, came to be constituted. Why would someone have selected these particular verses from a complete Palestinian *Targum* and circulated them in this form?

Codex Neofiti I

Codex Neofiti I contains the third Palestinian *Targum*. An instructive story is associated with the correct identification of this manuscript. In 1949 the Spanish scholar A. Díez Macho saw the name Codex Neofiti I listed in the Vatican Library under the entries for Codex Onkelos.[16] This Aramaic text was copied at the beginning of the sixteenth century. Even a cursory sampling of the text of this manuscript led Díez Macho to doubt that it could be a version of Onkelos. After a careful examination of the manuscript in 1956 Díez Macho discovered that it was in fact a version of the Jerusalem *Targum* to the Pentateuch.

Codex Neofiti I covers every verse in the Pentateuch. It is the only extant exemplar of the Palestinian *Targum* to do so. As such, it offers scholars the most extensive continuous text available for a *Targum* to the Pentateuch.

In several respects it differs from the other *Targums* identified with Galilee or Palestine, including the greater frequency with which it displays variant readings in its margins or between its lines. These variant readings are invaluable sources of alternative texts that scribes wished to transmit to readers of their manuscripts.

Cairo Genizah Fragments

Fragments from the Cairo Genizah (a huge repository of Hebrew, Arabic, and Aramaic documents, including biblical material, dating from the ninth to the nineteenth century CE) constitute the fourth category of Pentateuchal *Targums* from Palestine. Some of these fragments originally belonged to continuous *Targums* to the entire Pentateuch; others apparently came from smaller compositions used as part of the liturgy for festivals and special Sabbaths.

As codified in the Mishnah (third century CE) and later Rabbinic writings, an oral translation, or *Targum*, in Aramaic was to be provided after every verse of Torah read in the Hebrew during a synagogue service.[17] These sources attribute considerable emphasis to the oral nature of these Aramaic translations, on occasion forbidding the use of a written Aramaic text in the synagogue. This was to ensure that congregants would not confuse the Aramaic version, which was only recited, with the original text in Hebrew, which was uniquely read from sacred scrolls. Written Aramaic texts could be used solely for classroom purposes or for private study. Thus, both of these environments, the synagogue and the school, likely played important roles in the development of these Pentateuchal *Targums*.[18]

Targums to the Prophets

For the most part, the same synagogal practice held true for *Targums* to the Prophets (Former and Latter). A prophetic portion in Hebrew, linked by Rabbinic exegesis to the Torah reading, also became part of the service.[19] In this case, the Aramaic explanation was also orally rendered, but only after every third verse.

The primary *Targum* to the Prophets is *Targum Jonathan*. Its date of initial composition is generally accepted to be in the third century, and its final editing is usually set in the seventh century.[20] As is true for the *Targums* to the Pentateuch, the date of completion is by no means the sole determinant of the varying dates of the contents.

The talmudic text (b. Meg. 3a) also holds that Hillel's student Jonathan ben Uzziel produced this *Targum* "at the dictation of Haggai, Zechariah, and Malachi," the last three prophets in Jewish tradition. Their linkage with the *Targum* and its human author is intended to provide something of a direct link from the Hebrew Bible to its Aramaic rendering.

Targum Jonathan holds together as a unified composition based on similar stylistic features throughout.[21] This *Targum* also exhibits noteworthy points of affinity with *Targum Onkelos*. Both are in the same Aramaic dialect, avoid humanlike language in relation to God, include the periodic updating of place names, add explanatory narrative, and demonstrate efforts to simplify what were apparently taken as difficult passages. Where the *Targum* rendering is literal, sometimes the translator appears to be working with a Hebrew that varied, if only slightly, from MT. The second portion of *Targum Jonathan*, covering the Latter Prophets, has noticeably more additions than the earlier portion, covering the Former Prophets.

Evidence for the existence of a Palestinian *Targum* to the Prophets derives from two sources: citations from well-respected exegetes such as Rashi (eleventh century CE) and David Kimchi (twelfth and thirteenth centuries CE) and fragments collected in an early eleventh-century manuscript. Taken as a whole, these sources yield an Aramaic text that is Palestinian in character, but with additions that show the influence of the Babylonian Talmud.

Targums to the Writings

In the Jewish tradition, the third part of the Hebrew Bible is known as the Kethuvim (Writings), or Hagiographa. The contents of this rather miscellaneous collection of books was probably established by the first century BCE. Yet the order in which these books appeared fluctuated considerably in different editions of the Hebrew Bible, and several of them received little attention in traditional Jewish learning. Moreover, with few exceptions (as noted in the discussion that follows) they did not play a role in the synagogue liturgy.

Because of their lesser status in both the synagogue and the classroom, it is not surprising that most of the *Targums* to the Writings are later in composition than the *Targums* to the Torah and the Prophets.[22] For similar reasons, no author or compiler devoted sufficient time and effort to produce a single *Targum* to cover the entire set of books that make up the Writings. Different authors composed the *Targums* to this portion of the Bible, book by book.[23]

In fact, the only biblical books for which we lack even one *Targum* are among the Writings: Daniel and Ezra-Nehemiah. This omission may be the result of minimal communal interest in these two books (with Ezra and Nehemiah constituting a single composition), or it may have to do with the fact that these are the only books of the Hebrew Bible with extensive sections in Aramaic.

In an early period, the reading of the book of Esther arose as a primary constituent of the public celebration of Purim. At later dates, four other books from the Writings found their way into public worship: Song of Songs, Ruth, Lamentations, and Ecclesiastes. For the most part, as we'll observe in the next section of this chapter, the *Targums* to these books, collectively spoken of as the Five Scrolls (*megillot*), are filled with midrashic or homiletical additions; literal renderings are comparatively rare. Possibly, the Aramaic translators felt more freedom in rendering these books because their wide use for teaching and entertainment suggested a concentrated emphasis on the expectations of the target audience, which included women and children in addition to men.

In connection with other *Targums* to the Writings, some interesting patterns emerge with regard to literal (more or less word-for-word renderings of the original) versus free (renderings connected only loosely with the original) translations. In Job, for example, there are between forty and fifty double renderings (that is, two translations of the same word or phrase) of the Hebrew appearing within the Aramaic text: one literal, the other free.[24] Similarly, some renderings of the *Targum* to Psalms are literal, while others are much freer. This has led scholars to hypothesize that at least two translators are responsible for the material.[25] And the renderings of the Hebrew in the *Targum* to Chronicles, whether they reflect the work of two translators or one translator and a reviser, are predominately literal, but with some paraphrastic portions.[26]

Examples

Up until now, this chapter has largely consisted of discussion and analysis of *Targum* as a type of biblical translation, and of specific

Targums within their cultural, historical, linguistic, stylistic, and exegetical contexts.

The examples below, with at least one from each of the traditional Jewish divisions of the Bible—Torah, Prophets, and Writings—allow us to examine in greater detail extended biblical texts as they appear in MT and in the *Targums*. For each passage, the Hebrew and Aramaic are juxtaposed in English versions that facilitate comparison. Significant features or elements of each are highlighted and compared.

Where possible, one or more explanations are offered to help shed light on how the Targumists handled their Hebrew text, which (as observed earlier in the chapter) was almost always close, if not identitcal, to the consonants of MT.

The five selected passages, taken individually or as a whole, help us to accomplish several goals. First, we gain a sense of how scholars of the Targum plied their craft: a largely comparative process. Second, working conscientiously through these passages allows us to substantiate the claim that the *Targums* are substantially literal renderings of the Hebrew when the Targumists were engaged in the process of translation. We can see how close the English wording of the Hebrew and the Aramaic are in such sections. And, third, we can discern one of the defining characteristics of a *Targum*: its combining literal renderings with Aramaic material that the Targumist has added to clarify, modify, or otherwise revise MT to accord with theological, geographical, historical, or cultural features he wished to emphasize. It is, I think, safe to surmise that the Targumists did so for the benefit of their communities as they best determined.

I encourage readers to use their own best judgment in evaluating this material. In doing so, they should feel free to accept or modify some of my views—or, as they see fit, to reject them in favor of their own.

Exodus 6:8–9

MT: 8. "I will bring you into the land which I swore to give to Abraham, Isaac, and Jacob, and I will give it to you for a possession, I the LORD."

9. But when Moses told this to the Israelites, they would not listen to Moses, their spirits crushed by cruel bondage.

***Targum Onkelos*:** 8. "And I will bring you into the land which I swore with My Memra to give it to Abraham, to Isaac, and to Jacob; and I will give it to you as a possession; I am the Lord." 9. So Moses spoke accordingly with the Israelites, but they did not listen to Moses because of the mental anguish and from the labor which bore down upon them.[27]

Commentary: The Hebrew text that NJPS translates as "I swore" is literally "I raised My hand."[28] *Targum Onkelos* avoids the anthropomorphism of this Hebrew by using an Aramaic verb that is identical in meaning to the English word in NJPS. Moreover, *Targum Onkelos* introduces the term "Memra" (literally, "word"), frequently used in all the *Targums*, as a way of deflecting direct reference to the Divine. In verse 9 the verb translated in both *Targum Onkelos* and NJPS as "listen to" is literally "accept from." *Targum Onkelos* also rephrases the final clause of this verse so as to present "mental anguish" as a separate item alongside "cruel bondage" or "labor."

***Targum Neofiti I*:** 8. "And I will bring you into the land which I raised my hand in oath to give to Abraham, to Isaac and to Jacob, and I will give it to you as an inheritance and a possession. I the Lord." 9. And Moses spoke thus with the children of Israel, but they did not listen to the words of Moses because of broken spirits and harsh bondage.[29]

Commentary: Unlike *Targum Onkelos, Targum Neofiti I* retains the anthropomorphism with the use of "my hand." Immediately thereafter it adds the basically tautological phrase "in oath"—after all, what does raising the hand mean here except that God is taking/swearing an oath? In verse 9, the Aramaic expression rendered "broken spirits" literally means "shortness of breath."

***Targum Pseudo-Jonathan*:** 8. "And I will bring you into the land which I swore by my Memra to give to Abraham, Isaac, and Jacob, and I will give it to you as a possession, I the Lord." 9. Moses spoke thus to the people of Israel, but they did not listen to Moses, because their spirits were crushed, and because of the terrible idolatry they practiced.[30]

Commentary: At verse 8, *Targum Pseudo-Jonathan* uses the same strategy as *Targum Onkelos* to avoid an anthropomorphism connected with God. Unique in this *Targum* is the phrase "the terrible idolatry they practiced" (lit., "the hard idolatry that was in their hands")—taking a general word for labor and applying it specifically to worship. This concept—that the Israelites practiced idolatry as slaves in Egypt and were therefore at least partially complicit in the period of extended bondage that was their punishment—is also found elsewhere.[31]

Ezekiel 34:7–10

MT: 7. Hear then, O shepherds, the word of the LORD! 8. As I live—declares the Lord GOD: Because My flock has been a spoil—My flock has been a prey for all the wild beasts, for want of anyone to tend them since My shepherds have not taken thought of My flock, for the shepherds tended themselves instead of tending the flock—9. Hear indeed, O shepherds, the word of the LORD: 10. Thus said the Lord GOD: I am going to deal with the shepherds! I will demand a reckoning of them for My flock, and I will dismiss them from tending the flock. The shepherds shall not tend themselves any more; for I will rescue My flock from their mouths, and it shall not be their prey.

Targum Jonathan: 7. Therefore, O leaders, hear the word of the Lord: 8. As I live, says the Lord God, because My people have become a prey, and have been handed over for destruction to all the kingdoms of the nations for want of a leader, and My leaders have not searched for My people, and the leaders provided for themselves but did not provide for My people; 9. therefore, O leaders, hear the word of the Lord. 10. Thus says the Lord God: Behold I am sending My wrath against the leaders, and I will demand an accounting for My people at their hand; and I will put a stop to their leadership of the people, and the leaders shall no longer provide for themselves. I will rescue My people from their hand, and they shall not be handed over to them for destruction.[32]

Commentary: Throughout this section, the Targumist abandons imagery of "shepherds" and "sheep" in favor of its direct application as "leaders" and "people"—a fairly common procedure. This modification also leads to considerable difference in wording between the MT and the *Targum* in verses 8 and 10.

Ṇahum 3:5–8

MT:

5. I am going to deal with you—
   declares the LORD of Hosts.
   I will lift up your skirts over your face
   And display your nakedness to the nations
   And your shame to kingdoms.
6. I will throw loathsome things over you
   And disfigure you. And make a spectacle of you.
7. All who see you will recoil from you
   And will say,
   "Nineveh has been ravaged!"
   Who will console her?
   Where shall I look for
   Anyone to comfort you?
8. Were you any better than No-amon,
   Which sat by the Nile,
   Surrounded by water—
   Its rampart a river,
   Its wall consisting of sea?

***Targum Jonathan*:** 5. "Behold. I am sending my wrath upon you," says the Lord of hosts, "and I will reveal the shame of your sins upon your face, and I will show the nations your shame and the kingdoms your disgrace. 6. And I will cast abominations upon you and will treat you with contempt, and I will make you repugnant in the eyes of all who see you. 7. And it shall come to pass that everyone who sees you will withdraw from you and say, 'Nineveh has been plundered!' Who will mourn for you? Where shall I find those who will comfort you? 8. Are you better than the great Alexandria which is situated between the rivers, with water all about her, whose wall is the sea, the waters of the sea her wall?"[33]

Commentary: The graphic Hebrew expression whereby God lifts Israel's skirts over its face (v. 5) is both simplified and possibly clarified in the *Targum*'s less dramatic wording, "I will reveal the shame of your sins upon your face." Here, No-amon of MT verse 8 has become Alexandria—a substitution found elsewhere in the *Targum* to the Prophets. Perhaps the Targumist was unfamiliar with the location of No-amon; equally likely, however, the reference to Alexandria is deliberate, because of the city's substantial Jewish population and geographical location in connection with the sea.

Zechariah 2:1–4

MT: 1. I looked up, and I saw four horns. 2. I asked the angel who talked with me, "What are those?" "Those," he replied, "are the horns that tossed Judah, Israel, and Jerusalem." 3. Then the LORD showed me four smiths. 4. "What are they coming to do?" I asked. He replied: "Those are the horns that tossed Judah, so that no man could raise his head; and these men have come to throw them into a panic, to hew down the horns of the nations that raise a horn against the land of Judah, to toss it."

Targum Jonathan: 1. And I lifted up my eyes and saw, and behold, four kingdoms. 2. And I said to the angel who was speaking with me, "What are these?" And he said to me, "These are the kingdoms which scattered the people of Judah, Israel, and the inhabitants of Jerusalem." 3. And the Lord showed me four artisans. 4. And I said, "What are these coming to do?" And he answered saying, "These are the four kingdoms which scattered the people of Judah and did not permit anyone to walk with erect posture, and these have come to frighten them, to destroy the kingdoms of the nations which took up arms against the land of the house of Judah to drive it into exile."[34]

Commentary: The "horns" of MT, here and elsewhere, are clear references to nations of the world. In keeping with other examples, such as "leaders" for "shepherds" in Ezekiel 34, the Targumist in this passage has made the real-world connection explicit through his use of the term "kingdoms." Apparently those responsible for the *Targums* wanted to insure that their audience understood, immediately and unequivocally, exactly what the text was saying. The Aramaic here also shares the expression "to walk with erect posture" with other *Targums* to the Prophets.

Esther 2:1

MT: Some time afterward, when the anger of King Ahasuerus subsided, he thought of Vashti and what she had done and what had been decreed against her.

Targum Rishon: After all these things, when he relaxed and calmed down from the intoxication of his wine and when the power of King Xerxes' anger had receded, he began to remember Vashti. Whereupon his princes addressed him and said as follows: Were you not the one who pronounced upon her a guilty verdict of execution for what she had done? The king then replied to them, I did not decree for her to be executed but rather than she come before me. I ordered that her kingdom be removed from her. They replied to him: No, but did you not decree the death penalty upon her on the advice of the seven princes? Immediately, thereupon, the anger of the king became powerful, and he decreed to have the seven princes hung upon the gallows.[35]

Commentary: This is an exception to the general style of *Targum Rishon* to Esther as a rather straightforward rendering of the Hebrew text. Here the Targumist has made extensive and elaborative additions to Esther 2:1. The subsiding of the king's anger is closely connected with a process we might speak of as sobering up from a hangover. As MT and *Targums* to Esther 1 attest, everyone—the monarch definitely included—had been drinking a lot. In the course of the debate between king and courtiers, we also learn that Vashti had been sentenced to the death penalty—something the king wishes to distance himself from now by casting the blame on his primary advisers, who unsuccessfully argue in their own defense.

Targum Sheni: After these matters, when the great anger of King Xerxes subsided, he summoned all his princes and said to them: "I am not angry at Queen Vashti but I am angry at you. As for myself, I said thing(s) under the influence of wine, (but) as for yourselves, why did you make me decree to execute Queen Vashti and that I should remove her name from the kingdom? Now I will kill you, too, and remove your names from the kingdom."[36]

Commentary: Story-wise the additions in *Targum Sheni* are comparable to those found in *Targum Rishon*. But they are notably less extensive in *Targum Sheni*, since here the king's advisers are not given the opportunity to plead, even if ultimately in vain, for their lives.

Esther 5:8

MT: "—if Your Majesty will do me the favor, if it please Your Majesty to grant my wish and accede to my request—let Your Majesty and Haman come to the feast which I will prepare for them; and tomorrow I will do Your Majesty's bidding."

Targum Rishon: If I have found compassion in the sight of the king, and if it please the king to grant my request and to fulfill my plea, then let the king and Haman come to the meal which I prepared for them in the evening and tomorrow I will do so according to the ordered decree of the king.[37]

Commentary: *Targum Rishon* renders this verse in a manner that stays quite close to the Hebrew. The only noteworthy addition is the specification that the feast or meal Esther is preparing will take place in the evening—information, found also in the LXX, which helps to clarify the timeline for Esther's subsequent activities.

Targum Sheni: Then Esther replied, saying, "You are king! If I have found favor and sympathy before you, and if it pleases the king to grant my request and to fulfill my petition, let the king and Haman come to the meal that I will make for you, and tomorrow I will do according to the word of the king." On account of three matters did Esther invite Haman to the meal. First matter, because Esther knew that Haman had slain Hathakh on account of his errand, [i.e.,] running mission between Esther and Mordekhai; so Esther thought: "I will invite Haman to the meal (in order to appease him)." Second matter, because she thought to uproot the hatred from his heart and (furthermore, to cast) jealousy between Xerxes and Haman so that the king should say: "What is this thing? Of all my governors Esther only invited Haman to the meal?" Third matter, Esther thought: "The eyes of all the House of Israel are directed toward me that I petition King Xerxes that he should execute Haman; I will therefore invite him to the meal in order that the heart of the Israelites will be changed, and they would direct themselves toward their Father in Heaven and pray for mercy from Him."[38]

Commentary: The initial portion of *Targum Sheni*'s rendering of this verse is, like *Targum Rishon*'s, a fairly literal reflection of the Hebrew. *Targum Sheni* then expands considerably to provide three reasons (or "matters") for Esther's actions. As is often the case in *Targum Sheni*, these aggadic additions have parallels elsewhere in Rabbinic literature. The reference to Esther's casting jealousy between the king and Haman helps give readers some context for understanding the king's actions at 7:8, which might otherwise appear somewhat overwrought.[39]

Final Thoughts

Most people have some idea of what a translation, especially a Bible translation, should look like. Their range may be narrow—literal only, free (or freer) only—or their horizon might be wide enough to include any and everything from hyperliteral, or interlinear, to hyperfree, or paraphrastic.

Yet few conceive of a literal rendering interspersed with miscellaneous additional material. Nonetheless, as we've seen, this is in fact an apt and accurate description of a *Targum*. Although we might speculate that two different groups or schools of individuals were responsible for these two very different styles, almost all scholars today affirm that the individuals responsible for the literal approach to the Hebrew are the same persons responsible for the additions.

For all these translators, the goals would have been the same: to provide an easy-to-understand and updated version of the Bible for their audience and to ensure that this version was consistent with the practices and beliefs of their Jewish community. Some Targumists made greater use of literal renderings, while other found more opportunities for expansion. But these are not separate or antithetical approaches to their tasks.[40]

We would be in a far better position to appreciate the Targumists' efforts if we possessed reliable information about where they worked, at what historical periods, and for which audiences. Regrettably, all we know about these crucial issues is what little the text itself provides. And so, we must work with imperfect tools to arrive at conclusions that in many respects are tentative at best. But this is the nature of the task we have set for ourselves.

3

Bible Translation into Arabic

By the end of the ninth century CE, the Jews of Babylonia had long formed communal organizations that epitomized their cultural, political, and religious achievements. The community's basic structure—including the exilarch, the leader of the Jewish people in exile—may have been established as early as the mid-second century CE, when the Parthians ruled the area.

Fast-forward some five centuries. In the seventh century, when Omar, the second caliph of Islam, took over Babylonia, he ratified and enhanced Jewish self-governance. The Jews continued to be led by an exilarch—in recognition of the fact that no matter how prosperous they were or how much they achieved, the people were not in the Land of Israel, but in the Diaspora, in exile.

The Babylonian Context for Saadiah's Translation into Arabic

Two great academies, one at Sura and the other at Pumbedita (the latter replacing an earlier academy in Nehardea, which had been destroyed in the mid-third century CE), then dominated the religious life of the Babylonian Jews—and their influence often extended well beyond their borders to farthest Spain. The rabbi charged with leadership of each academy was given the honorific title of gaon (the origin and exact meaning of this term are not certain. One explanation is that it references Psalm 47:4, where the expression "pride of Jacob" appears. In biblical Hebrew, one meaning of the root *g-w-n* is "pride"). As we will see, the two reigning gaonim did not always agree with each other; nor did they consistently agree with the exilarch. Nonetheless, this system flourished, producing such seminal works as the Talmud and midrashim, as well as countless other commentaries, collections, and codes.[1]

Even with considerable self-autonomy, the Jewish community was not free from the demands of whatever political power conquered and subsequently ruled over the territory that then encompassed Babylonia. By the ninth century, that power belonged to Muslims, and their language was Arabic.

As had been true earlier on, when Greek speakers, and then Aramaic speakers, governed them, the Jews of the ninth century also adopted the language of their rulers. And, as was true of Greek and to a lesser extent of Aramaic, their adopting or adapting another language entailed far more than simply learning a new vocabulary and different syntax. At least as much, it involved an introduction to, and possibly an immersion in, a new culture with its own ideas. Some of these were compatible with traditional beliefs and practices, but others would confound and even confuse long-held patterns of thought and action. And, as was true before (and would be countless times in the future), translation was the means by which the distance—in this case from Hebrew or Aramaic to Arabic—would be bridged.

Of the primary figures involved in the translation of the Bible into Arabic, one individual takes center stage: Saadiah ben Yosef (882–942). When he was born in the undistinguished portion of lower Egypt known as the Fayyum, it is unlikely that anyone would have predicted his illustrious career—of which Bible translation was only a part.[2] Nor was he unique among Jewish Bible translators in this regard (as we shall have occasion to see in the chapters that follow).

What follows is a selection of readings from Saadiah's Arabic version, along with a rendering of the traditional Hebrew, or Masoretic

Text (MT as rendered in NJPS). In this way, readers will have direct contact with characteristic features of Saadiah's methods and goals prior to a further discussion and analysis of these and other examples.

Avoiding Anthropomorphism and Anthropopathism

God Has No Mouth. Genesis 1:3 and parallels—MT: "God said, 'Let there be light'; and there was light"; **Saadiah:** "And God wished [or willed] that there be light and there was light."

Nor Eyes. Job 28:10—MT: "His [that is, God's] eyes behold every precious thing"; **Saadiah:** "Every mighty act was foreknown to him."

Nor Hands. Exodus 9:3—MT: "Then the hand of the LORD will strike [your livestock in the fields]"; **Saadiah:** "Behold God's affliction is striking."

Nor Feet. Exodus 24:10—MT: "Under His [that is, God's] feet [there was the likeness of a pavement of sapphire]"; **Saadiah:** "Beneath his Light."

Nor Emotions (Heart). Genesis 6:6—MT: "[And the LORD regretted that He had made man on earth,] and His heart was saddened"; **Saadiah:** "And he made pain enter their hearts."

Nor Emotions (Laughter). Psalm 2:4—MT: "He who is enthroned in heaven laughs"; **Saadiah:** "He Who dwells in heaven makes [people] laugh."

God Doesn't Travel to Earth to Know What's Going On. Genesis 11:5—MT: "The LORD came down to look at the city and tower that man had built"; **Saadiah:** "And God caused something hidden to descend [or, brought down an instruction of intimidation] to see the city and the tower that the people built."

Nor Can God Be Compared in Station to a Human. Exodus 15:3—MT: "The LORD, the Warrior [literally, the LORD is a man of war]"; **Saadiah:** "God controls war."

Nor Does God Change. Deuteronomy 4:24—MT: "For the LORD your God is a consuming fire"; Saadiah: "God's punishment is a consuming fire."

Avoiding Contradiction

TANAKH Cannot Contradict Itself. Genesis 2:17—MT: "[But as for the tree of knowledge of good and bad, you must not eat of it;] for as soon as you eat of it, you shall die"; Saadiah: "For in the day that you eat of it you shall deserve to die." **Genesis 9:2—MT:** "He [that is, Noah] said, 'Cursed be Canaan; the lowest of slaves shall he be to his brothers'"; **Saadiah:** "He said, 'Cursed is Canaan's father, an enslaved slave he shall be to his brothers.'"

Or Contradict Logic. Genesis 3:20—MT: "The man named his wife Eve, because she was the mother of all the living"; **Saadiah:** "And he named his wife Eve for she was the mother of all the living that are rational and mortal."

Avoiding Ambiguity

TANAKH Is Not Ambiguous Halakhically (that is, according to Rabbinic halakhah). Exodus 23:19; 34:26; Deuteronomy 14:21—MT: "You shall not boil a kid in its mother's milk"; **Saadiah:** "You shall not eat meat with milk."

Or Aggadically (that is, as found in nonlegal or narrative passages in the Hebrew Bible). Genesis 6:2 (see also Job 1:6)—MT: "The divine beings [or, the sons of God] saw how beautiful the daughters of men were and took wives from among those that pleased them"; **Saadiah:** "The sons of the nobles saw the daughters of the commoners [or, the daughters of the masses] that they are nice and took for themselves wives of all that they chose." **Genesis 21:14—MT:** "And she [that is, Hagar] wandered about in the wilderness of Beer-sheba"; **Saadiah:** "And she went and lost her way in the 'well of Seven' in the desert." **Genesis 23:2—MT:** "Sarah died in Kiriath-arba—now Hebron"; **Saadiah:** "And Sarah died in the City of Four, which is Hebron."

A Brief Overview: The Life and Achievements of Saadiah Gaon

Saadiah was born in 882. We know few details of his upbringing and early life in Egypt. It appears that from a relatively young age he profited from an education that combined traditional Jewish learning with secular studies such as philosophy and grammar, in which Islamic scholars excelled. In fact, Saadiah may have begun his first attempts at Bible translation while still living in Egypt.

At some point, not later than 915, Saadiah moved to Palestine, where he appears to have come into contact with many of the leading Rabbinic (or Rabbinate) figures residing there.[3] In 921–22, while Saadiah was moving again, now from Palestine to Babylonia, a controversy over the Jewish calendar was coming to a head and threatening to upset the status quo of Jewish communities worldwide. Since the mid-fourth century CE, the calendar had been based on a series of rules that Palestinian rabbis had felt empowered to interpret. In 922, the leading Palestinian decider, Aaron ben Meir, set the first day of Passover on a Sunday, and a number of other Jewish communities followed suit. The Babylonian Jewish community, and those who accepted its authority, however, were intent on beginning the holiday on a Tuesday. This resulted, in 922, with the observance of Jewish holidays on different dates in different Jewish communities. For example, Passover was Sunday in Palestine and Tuesday in Babylonia, and the New Year was Tuesday in Palestine and Thursday in Babylonia. This practice was hardly conducive to the maintenance of a unified system of beliefs and practices among Jews worldwide.

When Saadiah learned of this dispute, he took the side of Babylonian Jewry, whose calculations agreed with his own. On his own authority, but in full agreement with the Babylonian Jewish leadership, Saadiah issued a written appeal to ben Meir, whom Saadiah viewed as "the offending Palestinian rabbi," to back down. Ben Meir refused to budge. A protracted correspondence ensued, the exchange growing increasingly extensive and bitter on both sides.

Upon his arrival in Babylonia, Saadiah continued to offer his full support and considerable erudition to the Babylonian lay and religious leaders engaged in this dispute. It was widely judged a Babylonian success that this community, and those who followed it, observed the Passover and New Year according to their (and not ben Meir's) calculations in 922.

Eventually, Saadiah, now hailed as a major authority on the Jewish calendar, authored his *Book of Festivals* (*Sefer ha-Mo'adim*) to buttress opposition to the Palestinian rabbinical leadership on this matter. It was one of the reasons for Saadiah's immediate—but not necessarily enduring—popularity among the Jews of Babylonia.

In 928 Saadiah was selected as gaon of the Sura Academy, a singular honor for an outsider.[4] Four years later, however, he was again involved in controversy, and this one of his own making: He refused to sign a verdict of the exilarch, David ben Zakkai, that would have settled a will from which the exilarch would have personally benefited by a substantial amount. Even though his fellow gaon in Pumbedita had signed off on it, Saadiah thought it was unjust (see, for example, Deut. 1:17: "You shall not be partial in judgment: hear out low and high alike"). Although we lack evidence, it is fairly certain that this was not the first disagreement between Saadiah and the incumbent exilarch.

The dispute soon escalated from threats of violence to acts of violence, which in turn incited Saadiah the gaon and David b. Zakkai the exilarch to excommunicate one other and appoint new leaders to the other's respective positions. A battle of pamphlets ensued, the level of rhetoric often sinking below what we might expect from such learned individuals. The former gaon and exilarch were no longer in power.

The opponents eventually reconciled in 937. Saadiah, for his part, was reinstated as gaon, a position he would continue to hold in relative peace until his death in 942.

All in all, the altercation did not have a negative impact on Saadiah's work as a scholar. In fact, although his years away from leadership of the Sura Academy were forced upon him, they were among his most productive, both in terms of the quantity and quality of his output.

Especially relevant to this chapter, specialists agree that the majority of Saadiah's Bible translation took place during these always busy, often tumultuous years of his residence in Babylonia.[5]

Saadiah's activities mark him as a man who took stands decisively and in a thoroughgoing manner. He was not about to compromise core beliefs because of an assumed deference to a leading Palestinian rabbi or a major Babylonian administrator. He challenged the practitioners of the existing communal system—but at the same time, he continued to work within the system. In the process, he drew upon his own knowledge of tradition and his equally perceptive sense of what was best for his contemporaries. These traits are also in evidence from his work as a translator.

In addition, the brief biography here provides a context in which to analyze and evaluate the samples of Saadiah's translation (provided above). For Saadiah, it was important that the three major intellectual emphases of his life—the Bible, Rabbanite exegesis and interpretation of the biblical text, and philosophy—stand together, such that the insights from one branch of learning would not contradict those obtained through the other two. Among the major goals of Saadiah's Arabic version of the Bible, then, was to demonstrate that, when properly understood, no passage of the Bible contradicted any other passage, any element of traditional Rabbinic exegesis, or any tenet of the philosophical system that Saadiah had constructed.[6] His method of translation also included other features, such as the incorporation of Arabic terms and Islamic thought, as well as the rejection of any human characteristics (physical or emotional) associated with God and a fixation on avoiding any ambiguity in rendering the Hebrew text.

Given the many goals Saadiah set for himself when rendering Scripture into Arabic, it is not surprising that the examples selected above, while reasonably representative of Saadiah's approach, are not exhaustive as a demonstration of the unique value of Saadiah's Bible translation. But they do represent a worthy beginning to the task of fully understanding Saadiah's Arabic version.

Saadiah as Champion of Rabbanite (Rabbinic) Exegesis

Of all the examples from Saadiah presented earlier in this chapter, perhaps the one that immediately attracts attention is his inclusion of the explicit prohibition against eating meat with milk—Exodus 23:19, 34:26; Deuteronomy 14:21: "You shall not boil a kid in its mother's milk" (MT); "You shall not eat meat with milk" (Saadiah). Of course, this accords with long-standing Rabbinic exegesis and practice.[7] The placement of this interpretation in the Bible itself was, then, undoubtedly a carefully considered effort to thwart the exegesis and practice of a prime opponent of the Rabbis: the Karaites.

The Karaites, whom Saadiah first encountered in Palestine, were a schismatic group (from the Rabbinate perspective) that did not accept the authority or the interpretations of Rabbanite Judaism. They preferred to rely on their own understanding of the Hebrew Bible—an understanding based on the careful reading of the text by each individual in the group.

At the time, a Karaite would simply have responded that the prohibition against consuming milk with meat was a result of Rabbanite (mis-) understanding and, as such, one of many practices and rituals that lacked biblical support from the plain reading of the text. Saadiah's response, as it were, was his Arabic text itself, because Saadiah intended for his rendering to become the standard Arabic version for all Jews. For their part, the Karaites actively supported numerous Arabic versions produced by other Karaites, apparently viewing every one of them as a supplement to the Hebrew Bible.[8] Saadiah, however, consciously shaped his work as *the* Bible for his and succeeding generations of Arabic-speaking Jews, who would (or at least should) be completely confident in their reliance on his version for the authoritative explication of the plain sense of the text. In this context, Saadiah would not admit alternative renderings and interpretations into the discussion.

Saadiah's Translation as *Tafsir*

With this in mind, we can tease out the motives for Saadiah's rendering at Genesis 2:17. The Hebrew text "for as soon as you eat of it, you shall die"—implying that eating forbidden fruit will result in the immediate death of the perpetrators—stood contradicted by the immediately subsequent verses, in which Adam and Eve remain distinctly alive after their rebellion against God. Generations of conscientious exegetes have resolved this apparent contradiction in a variety of ways—and consigned their solutions to marginal notes or commentaries. For Saadiah, however, there was only one way to deal with such concerns: Surely, Adam and Eve deserved to die, but in his graciousness God allowed them to live—"for in the day that you eat of it you shall deserve to die." Rather than leave it to the reader to consider alternatives, Saadiah resolved the problem and placed his solution in the text itself.[9]

It is notable that Saadiah referred to his own work using the Arabic term *tafsir*, which aligns more closely to our word "commentary" than to "translation."[10] And indeed Saadiah had initially composed his translation as the starting point for his often extensive and digressive commentary. It appears that, even during his lifetime, the translation part of his commentary began to appear separately (either in its original or in a revised form) for purposes of popular consumption, inasmuch as the translation with commentary would have been a bulky work—both physically and intellectually. In fact, even the general reader had considerable access to Saadiah's exegetical prowess, since interpretive renderings found their way into the text itself.[11]

Another example of Saadiah's introduction of an interpretive rendering is found at Genesis 6:2. This is part of a challenging passage (Gen. 6:1–4, which comes just before the extended narrative[s] of Noah and the flood) that would stimulate all sorts of speculation over the ages. Genesis 6:1–2 (as rendered by NRSV; for NJPS, see below) reads, "When people began to multiply on the face of the ground, and daughters were born to them, the sons of God saw that they were fair; and they took wives for themselves of all that they chose."

Were these "sons of God" divine or human? Either is possible, and both have support from diverse exegetical traditions. NJPS resolves the ambiguity in one way, using "divine beings," while in the notes, the translators/editors alert readers to the alternative rendering. For Saadiah, however, such speculation was not (or, at least, was no longer) necessary; nor would those whose Bible was his Arabic text be likely to engage in similar speculation.[12] In his rendering of Genesis 6:2, the "sons of God" become "sons of nobles." The coupling, then (for him and his readers), was not a matter of divine beings/angels and humans, but rather a mixture of human classes.

Indeed, for Saadiah, the role of angels (especially their intermingling with humans) was limited, particularly in comparison with other, more expansive interpretive traditions. In like manner, Saadiah portrayed Job's adversary (not Adversary, as in NJPS) as a mere mortal. His rendering of Job 1:6, "When it was the day that God's beloved came and presented themselves before Him, Job's adversary was present along with them,"[13] was in keeping with Saadiah's view that all occurrences of the Hebrew term "satan" referred not to an angel, but to a human.[14]

In making such judgments about the meanings of Hebrew words, Saadiah was drawing upon the deep knowledge he had acquired in preparing a Hebrew-Arabic dictionary—just one of his numerous achievements in the field of lexicography and, more broadly, language studies.[15] At times, however, we may wonder whether Saadiah was a bit too clever for his own good, as in Genesis 3:24, where he substituted "Healing Tree" for the well-known phrase, "the Tree of Knowledge" (see above). But he did so consciously, based on the multiple meanings that in his opinion the Hebrew root could take.[16]

His search for the meaning of words, coupled with his demonstrable eagerness to produce a text that his intended audience could easily apprehend, led Saadiah to provide translations for many proper nouns, where other translators and commentators (both ancient and modern) would transliterate. Two examples of this phenomenon—

namely, the "well of Seven" and the "City of Four"—appear earlier in this chapter. Transliteration (beer-Sheba) appears in MT at Genesis 21:24: "And she [that is, Hagar] wandered about in the wilderness of Beer-sheba"; and in Saadiah: "And she went and lost her way in the 'well of Seven' in the desert." Transliteration (Kiriath-arba) also appears in MT at 23:2: "Sarah died in Kiriath-arba—now Hebron"; and in Saadiah: "And Sarah died in the City of Four which is Hebron."

Although we cannot be certain about the impact such renderings had on their original audience, it is tempting to speculate that they were part of Saadiah's efforts to make the text immediately accessible and to avoid ambiguity. In this light, Saadiah probably reckoned that his readers would benefit from the translation of at least some place names rather than their having to wonder what the name meant—after all, the name was in Hebrew, a language they presumably didn't know. So, at Genesis 21:14 and elsewhere, readers would not have had to wrestle with the meaning of *sheba* (did it mean "seven" or "oath"?) in the place name Beer-sheba.

Already in his lifetime or shortly thereafter, Saadiah's practice of providing translations instead of transliterations was commented upon, generally without favor. The acclaimed biblical exegete and author of the classic Hebrew grammar *Moznayim*, Abraham Ibn Ezra (1089–1164), who lived about a century later than Saadiah, was among the earliest of such critics whose work survives. While expressing negative views about Saadiah's practice of offering translations of many place names, Ibn Ezra partially excused Saadiah on the grounds that his predecessor had sought to make sure that both his Jewish and non-Jewish readers alike would easily understand what might otherwise be unclear or uncertain. In his reproach of Saadiah, Ibn Ezra was likely echoing earlier criticisms of this practice.

Islamic Influence on Saadiah

For the most part, Saadiah's interpretive readings were consistent with Rabbinic exegesis. But this was not always true.

Take Genesis 3:5 as an initial example. NRSV presents one way of reading the Hebrew of this verse: "for God knows that when you eat of it your eyes will be opened, and you will be like God, knowing good and evil." NJPS offers another interpretation: "but God knows that as soon as you eat of it your eyes will be opened and you will be like divine beings who know good and bad." In a note, JPS editors/translators acknowledge that their rendering, "divine beings who know," is not the only one.

Saadiah, though, glosses "divine beings" using "angels," a reading not found in any Jewish sources, including those in the mystical tradition, prior to Saadiah. But this understanding is not his own construction, for it was already in the Qur'an.[17] So we have to reckon with the fact that Saadiah must have had deep familiarity with Islamic religious and philosophical argumentation, and that he willingly made use of it when it seemed appropriate—even, sometimes, when it differed from the Jewish traditions of which he was an heir.

Further instances of Saadiah's reliance upon Islamic sources abound. Here are two others.

Throughout Genesis 39 Saadiah uses a relatively rare Arabic word meaning "tunic" to reflect the rather general Hebrew word for Joseph's garment. That very same word is used throughout the sura in the Qur'an that speaks of Joseph.[18]

At Numbers 19:2 the Hebrew text identifies the color of the heifer unequivocally: It is red. This identification elicits little, if any, animated discussion among the Rabbis. However, among Islamic scholars of Saadiah's time there was discussion, much of it quite animated, about the possibility—or rather, the impossibility—of breeding a heifer of that color. Taking his cue from these musings of his Muslim contemporaries, Saadiah initially included in his text an Arabic word that generally means "yellow." Based on further considerations, however, Saadiah probably intended the term to signify "black" in this context. In either case, the "black (or yellow) heifer" failed to make an appearance in later revisions of Saadiah's work or in translations that generally followed his wording.[19] Thus, in addition to its connection with Islamic thought, this example also demonstrates that those who came after Saadiah did not follow him consistently or uncritically.

We can also see Saadiah's reliance upon Arabic sources—or, perhaps, simply upon common sense—in Genesis 3:20. Attentive readers of the Hebrew text may have recognized that its characterization of Eve as the mother "of all the living" is a bit of a misstatement or overstatement. For his part as well, Saadiah could not imagine that the biblical text would contain an image inconsistent with common knowledge. Thus, Saadiah's text, intended as the standard Arabic version, does not have this image: "And he named his wife Eve, for she was the mother of all the living that are rational and mortal."[20]

The Consistency of Saadiah's Translation

Biblical expressions Saadiah deemed apt for "correction" often exhibited a mixture between failure to adhere to rational observation and intrabiblical inconsistency. As an example, we can look at Numbers 22:22. An alert reader might express uncertainty, if not exasperation, at the divine displeasure with Balaam—after all, just two verses earlier God had assented to Balaam's request to accompany the Moabite emissaries if they invited him. Well, they did invite him; he went—and now God was "incensed" ("But God was incensed at his [that is, Balaam's] going" [MT]). On this occasion (as on so many others), Saadiah's readers would have no reason even to pause: yes, God had allowed Balaam to go with the Moabites, but it was Balaam's choice to go enthusiastically ("because he [that is, Balaam] went enthusiastically" [Saadiah])![21]

In the Hebrew of Psalm 120:5, the alleged inconsistency is not between one biblical passage and another, but is located in a single circumstance that Saadiah apparently viewed as improbable and possibly illogical—that the Psalmist had been literally forced by his enemies to live among one distant group (Meshek; see also Ezek. 38:2 and 39:1) and then another (Kedar; see also Isa. 21:17 and 42:11): "Woe is me, that I live with Meshech, that I dwell among the clans of Kedar."

In Saadiah's more nuanced reading—"Woe is me that I sojourned with people who resemble the inhabitants of Meshek, dwelt with men who are like the inhabitants of the tents of Kedar"—these particular names (Meshek and Kedar) are meant to be representative of a far wider range of unpleasant living conditions to which the Psalmist had been subjected.[22]

The nature of these living conditions, whether understood literally or more broadly, is noted in Psalm 120:6–7: "Too long have I dwelt with those who hate peace. I am all peace; but when I speak, they are for war" (MT). Saadiah did not think that either the place names or the living conditions were intended to be specific, especially since his readers wouldn't know where these places were. But they wouldn't need to know. Taking their cue from Saadiah, they would understand these references, however obscure geographically, as sure signs of the plight of the Psalmist's embattled and embittered experience.

Other instances of this concern for consistency abound. At Genesis 27:12–13, Jacob and his mother are in the final stages of formulating the plot whereby Jacob, pretending to be Esau, will wrest his father's "innermost blessing" from his brother. Concerned about the chances of paternal detection, Jacob expresses the fear that, with all of this plotting, he will end up with his father's curse rather than the anticipated blessing. In the Hebrew text, Rebekah appears to be seeking to assuage her son's fears by preemptively taking Jacob's possible future curse upon herself: "'and I [that is, Jacob] shall bring upon myself a curse, not a blessing.' But his mother said to him, 'Your curse, my son, be upon me!'" Saadiah seems to bristle at this image of Rebekah's willingness to assume someone else's curse. This does not accord with his sense of justice. So Saadiah writes: "and I [Jacob] shall bring upon myself a curse not a blessing. 13) His mother said to him: Warding off your sin is upon me!"[23]

To my knowledge, this passage from Genesis 27 has not elicited any substantial comment from biblical exegetes or scholars. On the other hand, our next example is the much-discussed curse uttered by Noah in Genesis 9. As recorded in MT, Noah curses Canaan (Gen.

9:25: "Cursed be Canaan / The lowest of slaves / Shall he be to his brothers"). But why is Canaan cursed, when Canaan's father Ham is the one who failed to observe proper decorum when confronted with his father's (that is, Noah's) naked body? As Genesis 9:20–24 tells us: "Noah, the tiller of the soil, was the first to plant a vineyard. He drank of the wine and became drunk, and he uncovered himself within his tent. Ham, the father of Canaan, saw his father's nakedness and told his two brothers outside. But Shem and Japheth took a cloth, placed it against both their backs and, walking backward, they covered their father's nakedness; their faces were turned the other way, so that they did not see their father's nakedness. . . . Noah woke up from his wine and learned what his youngest son had done to him."

Saadiah neatly bypasses this interpretive difficulty by having Noah curse Canaan's father Ham—who was the guilty party—instead of Canaan. But, Saadiah being Saadiah, he could not simply pull this solution out of his exegetical hat. He notes that each time Ham is mentioned earlier in chapter 9, he is identified as the father of Canaan. In effect, Saadiah surmised, "father of Canaan" functioned as Ham's surname. And so, Noah's cursing of Canaan was not aimed at Noah's seemingly blameless grandson, but rather at his completely guilty son, here referred to solely through the surname by which he was known.[24] As is true in other cases as well, we may be intrigued by Saadiah's reasoning even when we are not convinced by his logic.

One further example is especially useful in providing concrete evidence of how Saadiah dealt with certain types of internal inconsistency. At Deuteronomy 6:16, the Hebrew text offers this admonition: "Do not try the LORD your God, as you did at Massah." This seems to be in tension with the divine invitation offered at Malachi 3:10: "Bring the full tithe into the storehouse, and let there be food in My House, and thus put Me to the test—said the LORD of Hosts." In the first instance, at Deuteronomy 6:16, God commands the Israelites not to "test" (NJPS, "try") him. At Malachi 3:10, God encourages, even invites, Israel, to "test" him (NJPS, "put to the test"), using the same verb as in Deuteronomy 6:16.

For Saadiah, such tension between one biblical passage and another could not be allowed to stand. Basing himself on a third biblical text, "To test God was in their mind" (Ps. 78:18), he determined that the distinguishing feature in judging whether it was acceptable to "test" God or not was the people's intention. It was permissible to test the powers of God (as at Mal. 3:10, in Saadiah's view), but not to challenge God as an expression of doubt or denial (as at Deut. 6:16).

The use of a third passage to explicate apparent inconsistencies between two others was a long-standing Rabbinic approach to matters of law, or *halakhah*. Saadiah expanded this practice to include all of the biblical text, halakhic and narrative (aggadic) alike. In this way, he produced a biblical text that incorporated his insistence on the thoroughgoing coherence and integration of all Scripture.[25]

Saadiah's Representations of the Divine

Quantitatively, and perhaps also qualitatively, one of the most characteristic features of Saadiah's translating is his consistent sidestepping of anthropomorphic and anthropopathic references to God. Like those who produced the *Targums*, Saadiah sought to avoid the attribution of human characteristics—physical and emotional alike—to Israel's deity. As we saw in the previous chapter, the Targumists typically handled such expressions by deflecting them from God himself to the "word" or "presence" of God.[26] Although Saadiah sometimes makes do with similar Arabic expressions, he most often follows different strategies.

At Genesis 11:5 and 18:21, where God is the subject of the verb meaning "to go down" or "descend" in the Hebrew, in Saadiah's version God remains the subject—but the verb is in the causative. That is, God causes something to go down or descend. The idea that God would somehow physically lower the Divine self—or, probably even worse, need to lower the Divine self—in order to determine what was happening on earth was anathema to Saadiah's understanding of the plain sense of the biblical text.[27]

In like manner, Saadiah could not accept the imagery of God, or God's heart, as being sad (as at Gen. 6:6) or, at the opposite end of the emotional scale, of God's laughing (as at Ps. 2:4). Once again, Saadiah retains God as subject and then makes use of the causative form and meaning of the Hebrew verb. In these cases, Saadiah does rather decisively change the basic understanding of the clause, especially at Psalm 2:4: "He who is enthroned in heaven laughs" (MT); "He Who dwells in heaven makes [people] laugh" (Saadiah). Shielding his readers from a serious flaw in their understanding of God appears to be Saadiah's far more pressing concern than mechanically rendering the source text.[28]

Saadiah also takes pains to ensure that his readers do not falsely associate human body parts with God on the basis of biblical descriptions. Here are some representative examples among those cited earlier in this chapter. God does not have a mouth (Gen. 1:3 and parallels)—MT: "God said, 'Let there be light,' and there was light"; Saadiah: "And God wished [or willed] that there be light and there was light." God does not have eyes (Job 28:10)—MT: "His [that is, God's] eyes behold every precious thing"; Saadiah: "Every mighty act was foreknown to him." God does not have hands (Exod. 9:3)—MT: "Then the hand of the LORD will strike [your livestock in the fields]"; Saadiah: "Behold God's affliction is striking." God does not have feet (Exod. 24:10)—MT: "Under His [that is, God's] feet [there was the likeness of a pavement of sapphire]"; Saadiah: "Beneath his Light."

In these and other cases, Saadiah exercises extraordinary care to avoid any possible misunderstanding of the nature of God. Thus, throughout most of Genesis 1, God "wills" creation rather than "speaks" it. This rendering allows for a clearer understanding that creation was solely the result of divine volition, without any external pressures or constraints.[29] And at Exodus 15:3, Saadiah renders the Hebrew expression, literally, God "is a man of war," as God "controls war," thus acknowledging his decisive role in this human endeavor while at the same time keeping God above the fray, as it were.[30]

At Deuteronomy 4:24 the MT description of God as a consuming fire is at odds with what reason, as well as revelation, tell us about the nature of the Divine. Fires must be started and tended by someone, and at some point in the natural course of events they will burn out. But an eternal God does not depend on any power outside of the Divine for God's origins or actions. Saadiah thus rather deftly sidesteps what he perceives as a possible breach of theology and reason by associating the fire not with God but with Divine punishment ("God's punishment is a consuming fire").[31] This description does in fact conform to a proper understanding of punishment as initiated, defined, and brought to an end solely by God, on God's terms.

Even when there was no direct mention of God by name, Saadiah sought to protect Israel's deity from readers' misapprehensions. Looking once more at the Hebrew text of Numbers 22:22, we perceive something amiss when God appears to be upset with Balaam's doing exactly what God gave him allowance to do. Saadiah's addition of the adverb "enthusiastically" allows us to discern the problem: While there was nothing inherently wrong with Balaam's action, the fault lay with his unwarranted "enthusiasm."

For the most part, Saadiah's rendering of the Psalms remains quite close to the Hebrew.[32] In this context, his deviations from the Hebrew assume an added significance. This is certainly the case in Psalm 22:2. The interrogative of the Hebrew text, "why have You abandoned me?," presupposes a prior act, real or perceived, of abandonment by God with respect to the Psalmist. This presents the troubling image of a deity who might have failed to provide support for a worshiper in dire straits. Admittedly, Saadiah's rendering, with its imperative, "do not abandon me," leaves open some doubt in the Psalmist's mind about God's possible abandonment of him.[33] However, this doubt can be resolved through the expressions of divine praise and protection found later in this psalm and in other poetic compositions elsewhere in the Psalms.

In his pursuit of as ideal a delineation of the perfect God as humanly possible, Saadiah also made use of distinctively Muslim formulations.

For example, at Psalm 18:32, Saadiah used a traditional Islamic formula, *la ilah illa* ("there is no god but Allah"), for the Hebrew text rendered in NJPS as "who is a god except the LORD."[34] At Leviticus 19, MT frequently exhibits a phrase in which the Hebrew wording *ani YHWH* ("I am the LORD") appears. About half the time, "I am the Lord" appears alone; in the other places it is expanded to include "your God" (so, "I am the LORD your God"). This is undoubtedly the Hebrew text Saadiah also read. However, in his *Tafsir*, Saadiah always introduced the Arabic equivalent of "your God," which was common after the parallel Arabic phrase, *ana allah* ("I am God"), in Islamic liturgical and other texts.[35] In these as well as other examples, Saadiah emphasized connecting with his readers (who, even if they were Jews, would certainly have known these common Islamic phrases) over providing readers with a translation containing each and every nuance of the Hebrew.

Islamic influence can also be detected in Saadiah's rendering of at least two terms through which humans are closely associated with God. The Hebrew priest, or *Kohen*, becomes imam in Saadiah's text, and Saadiah regularly uses *rasul allah*, a phrase restricted in Islamic texts to Muhammad as the "messenger of God," as an epithet for Moses.

The *Tafsir* as a Free, Functional Equivalence Translation

For the most part, the examples we have seen thus far pertain to Saadiah's goals with respect to individual words and phrases. We've seen that Saadiah sought to produce a text in conformity with the Hebrew Bible, Rabbinic exegetical traditions, and reason. In his view, any Hebrew word or phrase that as much as hinted at a rift in this unified structure required modification through addition, omission, or replacement.

In earlier sections we also adduced examples to demonstrate that Saadiah was frequently guided in his revisions by Muslim religious texts and Islamic philosophy. This turns out to be true even when a cognate phrase would more closely join Saadiah's Arabic version with the biblical Hebrew he was translating.

In all of this, Saadiah was self-consciously constructing a rendering of the plain sense of the text, as he understood it, that would be easily accessible for his intended audience: individuals who had at best a sketchy appreciation for the Bible in Hebrew but at the same time enjoyed a rather full immersion in the Islamic culture of their day. To use an image that has currency among contemporary translation scholars, Saadiah brought his source text to the reader rather than bringing the reader to the source text.[36] To put it another way, Saadiah placed primary importance on conveying the message of the text in Arabic rather than on maintaining distinctive features of the Hebrew at the expense of a free-flowing Arabic.[37]

In today's parlance, we can speak of Saadiah's translation in terms of functional rather than formal equivalence. In other words, Saadiah sought to determine how a given phrase or unit of text functioned in the Hebrew Bible and then to fashion an Arabic that would express the same thing for his audience.[38] In the process, Saadiah jettisoned characteristic forms of biblical Hebrew in favor of structures that were native to written and spoken Arabic.[39] On a continuum of translations, with "literal" being at one end and "free" at the other, Saadiah's rendering clearly occupies a place among the free versions.[40]

We reach the same conclusion when looking at passages that constitute what we would call a sentence (in biblical Hebrew a "sentence" may be part of a verse, an entire verse, or extend to two or more verses). Here there are two distinguishing styles. The largely paratactic style, featured in biblical Hebrew, is constructed mainly of coordinate clauses (e.g., "And Moses came, and he saw the bush, and the bush burned without being consumed"). The syntactic style, favored by many other languages, is characterized by the regular use of subordinate clauses (e.g., "When Moses came, he saw the bush that burned without being consumed"). Saadiah's approach to translation favored subordination over coordination. In using this approach, Saadiah failed to retain a characteristic feature of biblical narrative, but his version does present a more readable text for his target audience.

Saadiah's preference for a contemporary literary style is already on display in Genesis 1. Whereas most versions, even functionally equivalent ones, have "And there was evening and there was morning, a x day [or day x]," modeled on the Hebrew, Saadiah writes, "And after the evening and morning of the day x passed. . . ."[41] And whereas in Genesis 3:24 MT reads paratactically, "He drove the man out, and stationed east of the garden of Eden the cherubim and the fiery ever-turning sword, to guard the way to the tree of life," Saadiah offers us this syntactic rendering: "And when He expelled the man, He set in the East of the Garden angels and flashes of an inverting sword to guard the Healing tree."[42]

Saadiah's Goal: *The* Standard Arabic Version

It was in the nature of Saadiah's position as gaon and, for a period of time, ex-gaon (and, I suspect, also in keeping with his forceful personality) that Saadiah set out to establish his text as the standard Arabic version rather than as one of many provisional renderings.[43] As we discussed, in keeping with this sought-after status, he sought to rid the biblical text of ambiguities, offering a single explanation and leaving no room for dissenting views.[44]

The Cairo Genizah has yielded some fragments of Judeo-Arabic translations prior to Saadiah.[45] Saadiah made use of some elements of "the popular tradition reflected in these translations," while at the same time, as the contemporary scholar Meira Polliack notes, "he changed some of their popular traits, particularly, their verbal echoing of the Hebrew source text. In doing so, he produced a standard Arabic version which had canonizing force and so could be used across different Jewish communities in various contexts."[46]

In some ways, his efforts were parallel to those of Jerome, who in the late 300s CE was initially presented with the task of bringing order and consistency into the older Latin renderings of the Bible circulating during his lifetime. As was true with Saadiah's *Tafsir*, so too was Jerome's translation, eventually called the Vulgate, intended to supplant as well as correct earlier versions. Saadiah and those who followed him largely achieved their goal (see especially the discussion in the subsequent section). As augmented and "corrected" by later editors and copyists, Jerome's version ultimately swept away all other Latin texts and achieved a unique status as *the* Bible of the Roman Catholic Church well into the twentieth century.

At the same time, Saadiah's eyes were focused primarily on his present circumstances, and probably also on the future. Here his principal adversaries were the Karaites, who denied to the Rabbis a monopoly on biblical interpretation (as well as much else). They were producing their own versions that promoted their understanding of the "uninterpreted" biblical text in a style that combined salient features of the Hebrew with familiar characteristics of the Arabic.

Undoubtedly, Saadiah found staunch, if not uncritical, allies among his fellow Rabbanites, but he would also have drawn strength from Islamic philosophers and theologians, at least some of whom were his contemporaries.

Measuring Saadiah's Success

Was Saadiah successful in his efforts? Yes.

After all, Saadiah's rendering of the Bible was the object of sometimes vitriolic attack by his Karaite opponents. Generations of Karaites saw Saadiah as *the Enemy*. Even if they were acquainted with other translations, they did not bother to refute them. If we can gauge someone's prominence (or notoriety) by their notoriety (or prominence) in the eyes of the opposition, Saadiah was indeed successful in establishing his version of the Bible as the one to contest.

Among Rabbanite leaders, there must have been something of a collective sigh of relief, for Saadiah's erudition and industry ultimately established a vernacular Bible that could withstand attacks from Karaite "insiders" as well as opposing Muslim "outsiders."

That said, neither Saadiah nor his *Tafsir* were immune to criticism. Some critics were unhappy with his overall approach. Others singled out a particular practice, such as his translating rather than transliterating proper names or his using Islamic terminology when a Hebrew cognate was readily available. Still others were opposed to specific readings he championed (several of which we examined above).

Beyond Saadiah's lifetime, the *Tafsir* did indeed maintain the preeminent place among Arabic-speaking Jews that Saadiah had sought for it. It was frequently copied, in whole or in part, for a considerable period of time.[47] To this day, there has been a steady trickle, if not torrent, of editions of portions of the *Tafsir*, especially the Five Books of Moses, with translations into French, English, or another modern language.

During the process, mistakes of omission as well as addition surely occurred. According to some scholars, wherever an alternative rendering appears in the text, this is a sure sign of a copyist's activity, for Saadiah himself sought to present solely one understanding of *the* Bible in Arabic, not just one among many.[48]

Some accounts report that the *Tafsir* was introduced into the synagogue liturgy in some Arabic-speaking areas, notably Yemen, where it functioned as the *Targum* had functioned—being recited verse-by-verse after a section of Scripture was read in Hebrew. But this view is not uncontested.[49] At the same time, Arabic-speaking Jews almost certainly used it for their personal study of the Torah.

Extant Evidence for Saadiah's Translation

Those who seek extant evidence in order to research Saadiah's Bible version(s) are presented with a formidable task. Saadiah may well have produced two different translations of the books of the Torah, and some speculate that he followed the same practice with many, if not all, of the remaining books of the Bible.[50] If this is so, then portions of the two biblical versions were likely mixed together early on in their transmission history.

One of the two distinct versions (if they indeed existed as such) was intended to form part of a commentary. Today scholars possess sections of Saadiah's translation both without and with commentary—and those commentary notes are always learned, usually complicated, and frequently lengthy, sometimes obscuring the translation itself. The two versions were apparently aimed at different audiences: the latter to attract the intellectual elite.[51]

In some respects, Saadiah's ability to multitask (to use a modern term) was not unlike that of Maimonides (1135–1204 CE), who produced extensive exegetical and philosophical works while serving as court physician and communal leader to Jews in Egypt and elsewhere. We have no account, by Saadiah himself or by any of his contemporaries, of how Saadiah structured his life. With due regard for their differences (for example, Maimonides was a physician, Saadiah was not; Saadiah held a formal bureaucratic post in the Babylonian Jewish hierarchy; Maimonides' position seems less structured if no less prominent), I think we can penetrate this absence of evidence regarding Saadiah by looking at Maimonides' self-description (in a letter to a friend who is thinking of visiting him) of a hectic and tiring life:

> The Lord God Himself knows how I am able to write you this letter. I have had to run away from people, isolating myself in a hidden place. Sometimes, I have had to lean against the wall, and at others, I've had to write lying down because I am so ill and weak. . . . I will write you my daily schedule:
>
> I live in Fostat, and the Sultan lives in Cairo. The distance between them is 4000 cubits [a mile and a half]. My duties to the Sultan are very heavy. I must see him every morning to check on his health. If one day he doesn't feel well, or one of the princes or the women of his harem doesn't feel well, I cannot leave Cairo that day. . . .
>
> It often happens that there is an officer or two who needs me, and I have to attend to healing them all day. Therefore, as a rule, I am in Cairo early each day, and even if nothing unusual happens, by the time I come back to Fostat, half the day is gone. Under no circumstances do I come earlier. And I am ravenously

hungry by then. When I come home, my foyer is always full of people—Jews and non-Jews, important people and not, judges and policemen, people who love me and people who hate me, a mixture of people, all of whom have been waiting for me to come home.

I get off of my donkey, wash my hands, and go out into the hall to see them. I apologize and ask that they should be kind enough to give me a few minutes to eat. That is the only meal I take in twenty-four hours. . . .

Because of all this, no Jew can come and speak with me in wisdom or have a private audience with me because I have no time, except on Shabbat. On Shabbat, the whole congregation, or at least the majority of it, comes to my house after morning services, and I instruct the members of the community as to what they should do during the entire week. We learn together in a weak fashion until the afternoon. Then they all go home. Some of them come back and I teach more deeply between the afternoon and evening prayers.

That is my daily schedule.[52]

Complicating researchers' efforts to know the real Saadiah and his work, certain translations have been falsely attributed to Saadiah. After careful scrutiny, scholars have demonstrated that various Arabic translations or commentaries circulating under Saadiah's name—particularly, editions of Daniel, Ezra, and Nehemiah—were wrongly ascribed to him in the process of transmission.[53]

Meanwhile, substantial portions of the Torah, Isaiah, the Five Scrolls, Psalms, Proverbs, and Job are extant. Researchers may yet find other fragments of his work, along with additional evidence of pre-Saadiah Jewish Arabic translations, in remains from the Cairo Genizah. Collating and interpreting this material is an ongoing task. We are grateful beneficiaries of the results of this process.

There is a delightful story about the discovery of this material in the Cairo Genizah:

> In 1896, Agnes Smith Lewis and Margaret Dunlop Gibson, identical-twin daughters of a Scottish widower, returned to Cambridge . . . bearing pages from several ancient Hebrew manuscripts they had purchased from a Cairo bookseller. They showed the parchment leaves to a Cambridge University scholar named Solomon Schechter, who was startled to discover among them an original copy of the Hebrew proverbs of Ben Sira. . . . Schechter set off to Fostat (Old Cairo), where the manuscripts had been found, eventually making his way to the Ben Ezra synagogue—the site, according to legend, where baby Moses had been found in the reeds. Deep within the building, in a hidden repository called a *genizah* (from the Hebrew word *ganaz*, meaning to hide or set aside), Schechter uncovered more than 1,700 Hebrew and Arabic manuscripts. He and his patron Charles Taylor, master of St. John's College, donated the fragments to Cambridge in 1898. They published their account of the discovery in 1899 and facsimiles of the documents in 1901.[54]

Saadiah's Intended Audience

If it is correct that Saadiah envisioned his likely readers as individuals who were unable to consult the Bible in Hebrew, he surely had the vast majority of contemporary Jews in mind. But did he also envision substantial numbers of Muslims among his readers?

The answer to this question is tied to an issue discussed primarily by specialists: What script did Saadiah initially use to create his Arabic version? Although we might well conjecture, "He used Arabic script, of course," today's experts generally conclude (based on painstakingly careful analysis of the manuscript evidence, as well as reports by individuals such as Ibn Ezra, who may have been acquainted with such texts in Hebrew script) that Saadiah wrote his Arabic-language *Tafsir* in Hebrew script. If this assessment is correct, Saadiah would have been intentionally excluding a sizable number of Muslims, for only a highly educated Muslim elite would have had the ability or the inclination to tackle a work not written in Arabic script.

In this practice, as in many others (including a preference for functional equivalence, as we saw earlier in this chapter), Saadiah contributes significantly to any serious discussion of Jewish Bible translation.

Final Thoughts

This discussion of Saadiah's Bible translation should serve to caution us against making any facile generalizations about Jews as translators. While most translators of the Septuagint privileged the Hebrew in their often odd-sounding Greek, and the translators of the *Targums* managed to be both very literal and quite free in adjacent passages, Saadiah very consciously followed the policy of bringing the text to the reader. His Arabic masked many distinctive features of the Hebrew in the process of becoming easily accessible to his readers. Thus, characterizing a particular approach to translation as distinctively, to say nothing of uniquely, Jewish simply will not do.

Still, the LXX, the *Targums*, and Saadiah do appear to share certain features. In all three cases, great effort was made to carefully reflect every nuance of the Hebrew text. Admittedly, different translators used divergent means to accomplish this goal, but nonetheless, there is nothing slovenly about these versions.

Moreover, they all take into account the Jewish community in which the Hebrew Bible originated and for whom these versions were primarily intended. All of these translators, working as individuals or as members of a committee, recognized that they had an obligation to past exegetes as well as to members of the Jewish community, present and future.

The Jewish exegetical tradition was never antiseptic or monolithic. It follows that biblical translations produced within this tradition are likewise varied—and exciting.

4

Bible Translation into Yiddish and German

In addition to studying and writing about Bible translations, I have another scholarly passion: religion, especially Jews and Judaism, in popular culture, especially in comic strips. I could make the case that this is another example of "translation": here from the primarily textual to the primarily visual. I could also make the case, as with Bible translations, that comic strips are for me a source of enjoyment and, yes, education—features I wish to share through writing and speaking.

Early Yiddish Translations

Among the many types of comic strips I collect are those that feature Yiddish words. This is a surprisingly widespread phenomenon—comprising examples from "bupkes" to "tushie," from "goniff" to "schlub," and showing up in a range of mainstream strips online and in print.[1] Similarly, given the close connection between Yiddish and humor in the modern world,[2] many comedians of prior generations delivered their monologues or punch lines in Yiddish. Even today, hit performers (not all of whom are Jewish) continue to pepper their routines with Yiddish phrases or allusions.

With all of this, it may be difficult to remember that, historically, Yiddish was not predominantly a language of entertainment. Rather, it was the primary spoken language of millions of Ashkenazi Jews from the tenth century through the mid-twentieth century.[3] A combination of German, Hebrew, Aramaic, and Slavic, with smatterings of Romance languages, Yiddish, also known as Judeo-German, served every function imaginable.[4] Among these functions was Bible translation, although early on this was not a high priority.

For this reason, the first translations of the Hebrew Bible into a Yiddish dialect did not occur until the 1200s. These early Yiddish exemplars of the Bible tended to be very literal renderings of the Hebrew. They were intended principally for the home and primary school (or *heder*), the two domains that women directed. In this light, a printer of Yiddish Bible texts from as late as the sixteenth century observed that the texts he produced could be read by women and children without any formal instruction.

This observation encourages us to wonder about the intended audience for any given translation, which would have varied considerably and, in turn, affected its function. For example, the Septuagint (chapter 1) came to function independently of the Hebrew as the Bible for Greek-speaking Jews and, later, for Christian communities. The *Targums* (chapter 2), by contrast, were constructed to accompany rather than replace the Hebrew text. The Arabic translation Saadiah produced (chapter 3) was meant both to replace the Hebrew it reflected and interpreted and also to supplant any earlier Arabic versions. The sixteenth-century printer's observation suggests that Yiddish versions of the Bible were aimed primarily at two groups—women and children—who did not or could not have direct access to the Hebrew.

The Classic Yiddish Bible: *Tsena Ureena*

The wooden renderings of the earliest Yiddish Bibles slowly gave way to a new version that incorporated enormous amounts of extra-biblical, primarily aggadic (that is, narrative) material into selected biblical passages.

By far the best known of these works is the *Tsena Ureena,* a phrase taken from Song 3:1, meaning "come out and see."[5] Its author, Yaakov (or Jacob) ben Isaac Ashenazi of Yarnow, was an itinerant teacher living from 1550 to the mid-1620s. His work is an example of a *Teutsch Humash* (that is, a Bible translated into Yiddish). Because of its emphasis on biblical characters who are female, as well as the fact that the two verbs in its title are feminine, *Tsena Ureena* has often been referred to as "the Women's Bible."[6]

While this text did in fact occupy a special place in the lives of Yiddish-speaking women for centuries, its author (or perhaps someone not far removed from his time) had envisioned a larger audience. The title page of the oldest extant edition, from 1622, explicitly speaks of the production of this work "in order to enable men and women to find a balm for their souls, and to understand the words of the Living God in simple language."[7]

Such a characterization undoubtedly reflected the reality of that time. Despite protestations to the contrary, it is unlikely that all adult Jewish males were sufficiently conversant with Hebrew to be able to consult the Bible knowledgeably in the original.

Although facility in Hebrew was a prime goal of the *heder,* which only boys attended, it is farfetched to imagine that all male youth achieved this goal or retained this knowledge throughout their lifetimes.

Ben Isaac's expectations for a broad audience were largely realized. Although some potential readers may have taken offense at his frequent intermingling of assorted midrashic elaboration with the biblical text, its overall reception among both the Jewish populace and religious leaders was positive.

Its publication history also demonstrates its immediate and abiding popularity. The original was published sometime between 1608 and 1610.[8] Three editions published prior to 1622 were already out of print by that date. In all, more than two hundred editions of *Tsena Ureena* appeared from the mid-seventeenth century until the first half of the twentieth century.[9] It continued to be oft-used in almost all Eastern European Jewish homes from the early 1600s to the first half of the 1900s.[10] Furthermore, this translation was itself translated (in part or in its entirety) into Latin, French, German, and English.[11]

A modern researcher penned this admiring appraisal of the *Tsena Ureena*:

> [Its author] orchestrated a charmingly informal medley of Biblical paraphrase, Midrashic exegesis, illustrative narrative—and unabashedly moral instruction. . . . He drew freely on the expositions of *Rashi, Ramban* . . . and other classical commentators. . . . What a blessing, then, for the thirsting masses who had neither the leisure nor the sophistication to seek out the original sources for themselves.[12]

Undoubtedly, generations of Yiddish speakers and readers, male and female, would have echoed these sentiments.

A sampling of a few passages from the *Tsena Ureena* reveals its distinctive "medley." Each of the three passages that follow begins with a reference to a specific biblical passage for which I have provided an English translation. Then come the midrashic elaborations that are the distinctive feature of this version.

First consider Leviticus 9:1—"On the eighth day Moses called Aaron and his sons, and the elders of Israel"—which introduces several offerings made in front of the Tent of Meeting:

> *It was on the eighth day*. King Shlomo says in the Book of Proverbs: *The Wisdom of women builds her house* (Prov. 14:1), which teaches us that the Torah is likened to a wise woman. The verse speaks of her wisdom in the plural form of the word because the Torah is replete with wisdom. It is like a clever woman who builds her home upon strong foundations and guards it well, bringing into it all that is needed, and cooking good food, preparing pleasant drink, setting her table and inviting her friends.

So too is the Torah. It is as full of wisdom as a table set with delicious food; and it invites everyone and says, "Whoever is a fool and lacks wisdom, come to me and I will teach you," as the verse states, *Come, eat of my bread, and drink of the wine which I have mixed* (Prov. 9:5). The Torah invites all to share in its food and drink, to discard their old ways and take its wisdom, and in this way live long.[13]

Let's turn now to Numbers 23:23:

NJPS:

> Lo, there is no augury in Jacob,
> No divining in Israel:
> Jacob is told at once,
> Yea Israel, what God has planned.

These translators note that their renderings of the second and fourth lines of this verse are uncertain. This forms part of the non-Israelite prophet Balaam's second address:

> *For there is no magic in Yaakov.* "They deserve blessings because they do not engage in magic. They know all without magic, for God reveals all through the *Urim VeTumim*. God Himself is the master and guardian of Israel, so magic has no effect on them, and they have no need of it. God knows all that will be and lets them know, even though the angels do not know all that will be."
>
> Bilaam saw how Israel will sit before God as a student sits before his teacher, and they shall study Torah, while the angels outside ask Israel: "What did God study with you?" Then Israel will say: "*Behold, a nation shall rise up like a lion* (Num. 23:24). Israel rises up early to put on *tallis* (prayer shawl) and *tefillin* (phylacteries), says the prayers of *Shema* and *Shemoneh Esreh*. And when they go to bed at night, they first recite the *Shema*, and all harmful beings fly away. How can one use magic against them?"[14]

Finally, let's see how Jacob ben Isaac handles Deuteronomy 12:5, which can be understood only within its immediate context:

NJPS:

> 2. You must destroy all the sites at which the nations you are to dispossess worshiped their gods, whether on lofty mountains and on hills or under any luxuriant tree. 3. Tear down their altars, smash their pillars, put their sacred posts to the fire, and cut down the images of their gods, obliterating their name from that site.
>
> 4. Do not worship the LORD your God in like manner, 5. but look only to the site that the LORD your God will choose amidst all your tribes as His habitation, to establish His name there. There you are to go, 6. and there you are to bring your burnt offerings and other sacrifices, your tithes and contributions, your votive and freewill offerings, and the firstlings of your herds and flocks. 7. Together with your households, you shall feast there before the LORD your God, happy in all the undertakings in which the LORD your God has blessed you.

Tsena Ureena:

> *Only to the place* which *the Lord, your God, shall choose*. God says: "You shall not bring a sacrifice, except at the place which God shall choose."
>
> God did not reveal immediately that the place was Mt. Moriah in Yerushalayim, for three reasons. First, if the nations knew the place they would have fought each other over it, because it is holy; second, the nations would have laid waste to the land, had they known that Israel would there bring sacrifices; and third, if Israel had known the place they would have quarreled with one another, each wishing to have the holy place, just as they quarreled, during the incident of Korach, over the priesthood. Therefore, even Israel did not know where the place to bring sacrifices would be.[15]

These three passages vary considerably in the degree to which the extensive elaboration is connected to the particular biblical passage. This connection is loosest in the first example about how Torah is similar to a wise woman; here the only text shared by the Bible and the elaboration is "on the eighth day." The connection is closest in the third, which explains why God did not choose to immediately reveal that Mount Moriah in Jerusalem was to be the sole site for licit sacrificial worship and associated rituals. In the second example, the Numbers 23 passage, Jacob ben Isaac creatively combines verses 23 and 24 to convey the image of God as teacher and Israel as his pupils, which then leads to a partial enumeration of ritual items and significant prayers.

The commentary to the first passage is one of many that would have been especially appealing to women of that time. Here they are praised for dutifully carrying out their role as providers of food and hospitality—a role also assumed for them, we are told, by the Torah.

The First Complete Bibles in Yiddish

The popularity of the *Tsena Ureena* did not preclude the publication of other Yiddish editions of the Bible. For one thing, its text-with-midrash approach was not deemed appropriate for all contexts and audiences.

Moreover, this work contained only a part of the Hebrew Bible: all of the Prophets and most of the third portion of the Hebrew Bible (Kethuvim, or Writings) were absent. In fact, Yiddish translations of the entire Hebrew Bible were not published until the end of the seventeenth century.

The very first such version was printed in Amsterdam in 1676–78. Jekuthiel Ben Isaac Blitz, who was employed in the printing office of Uri Phoebus, created it for Polish Jews who had fled to Amsterdam after the Chmielnicki Massacre (1648–49, during which Cossack hordes, led by Bohdan Chmielnicki, murdered as many as 100,000 Jews).

Additionally, Blitz, on behalf of his employer, wanted to open up Poland itself for sales. Toward this end, he obtained privileges to do so (essentially, a virtual monopoly for his Yiddish translation of the Hebrew

Bible) from the Polish Council of the Four Lands (the central body of Jewish authority in Poland at the time) as well as the Polish king, John III Sobieski; furthermore, leading Portuguese and German rabbis in Amsterdam and elsewhere confirmed these privileges. Nonetheless, at least according to one source, Blitz's work met with only limited success: "This translation exercised very little influence, as the Judeo-German [Yiddish] in which it was written contained many Dutch words and expressions."[16]

Even before Blitz had completed his edition, one of the compositors at Phoebus, Joseph Witzenhausen, decided to produce a translation of his own. A rival printing establishment, headed by Joseph Athias, agreed to publish Witzenhausen's Yiddish text of the Bible, for which it obtained privileges similar (and in some ways superior) to what Blitz had received.[17] The complete Phoebus edition appeared in 1678; in its final form, Athias's version was published the year after.

The full range of motivating factors for these dueling editions is uncertain. Nonetheless, it is not difficult to discern elements of personal and institutional rivalry, desire for prestige, and monetary considerations.[18] On the other hand, the quality of the translations themselves does not seem to have played a central role.

Interestingly, the third edition of Witzenhausen's translation, published in 1711, was written in German, rather than Hebrew script.[19] Perhaps the author and his publisher envisioned attracting an even wider audience by this means. In any event, this helped set the stage for the period in which many German-language versions of the Hebrew Bible appeared: the eighteenth, nineteenth, and early twentieth centuries.

Yiddish Bibles for Christian Missionaries

Meanwhile, several other historic developments carried forward new Yiddish translations of the Bible.

The first of these was the creation—by Christian organizations such as the British and Foreign Bible Society (BFBS)—of Yiddish translations of both the Old and the New Testaments. Although BFBS itself, like other Bible societies, did not proselytize, one of its primary goals was to mass-produce Bibles in many languages that could be used by missionaries who sought to convert non-Christians, including Jews.

The westward movement of Eastern European Jews in the latter quarter of the nineteenth century had intensified Christian efforts to reach out to Jews. Because Yiddish was the spoken language of millions of these individuals, the perceived need for Yiddish Bibles in missionaries' hands dramatically increased.

Christians, typically Jews who had recently converted to Christianity, were pressed into service. Not surprisingly, the resulting Yiddish-language Old Testaments were fully compatible with Christian theology. Yiddish versions of the New Testament were prepared under similar auspices.

At first, missionary societies distributed these Yiddish Bibles, mass-produced at low cost, throughout Eastern Europe. Later, these Yiddish Bible–carrying missionaries sought out Jews aboard ships, in harbors, and in their newly settled communities in the West. (For an expanded discussion of these Bibles, see the first part of chapter 7.)

Notably, BFBS leaders and Jewish leaders of the time did have one goal in common: enhancing the reputation of Yiddish as a legitimate language. As chronicled in BFBS records, beyond theological concerns, the Christian leaders overseeing the publication of Yiddish Bibles were deeply interested in raising the quality of Yiddish from "jargon" to a standardized, recognized language. Around this same time, in early September 1908, Jewish groups gathered together in the Ukrainian city of Czernowitz for a similar purpose: the Conference for the Yiddish Language.[20]

The Yiddish Bible in the Twentieth Century

A decade or so later, during the first quarter of the twentieth century, the acclaimed poet and stylist Solomon Bloomgarden (1870–1927), better known as Yehoash, composed and published what is possibly the best-known Jewish translation of the Bible into Yiddish—and, alas, the last undertaking of this sort.

The year 1910 saw the publication of the first part of his version: the book of Isaiah in one volume, and Job, Song of Songs, Ruth, and Ecclesiastes in another.

Not satisfied with his knowledge of Hebrew or his initial renderings into Yiddish, Yehoash spent January 1914 through the summer of 1916 in Palestine studying everything he could find that related to the Bible and its translation, including ancient languages. Then, from 1916, when he returned to New York City, until his death in 1927, he continuously worked on and revised his translation, in spite of poor health (he suffered from tuberculosis).[21]

Beginning in 1922, he published portions of his translation, at the rate of several chapters per week, in the New York Yiddish daily, *Der Tog*. This afforded him a small income and the opportunity to interest potential investors in a full-scale publication of his efforts. After almost three years, more than half of his rendering of the Hebrew Bible had been serialized in this way.

Finally he succeeded in raising sufficient funds to publish all of his work as a book, or rather a series of books. Before he died, the first two volumes of his translation, which contained the Torah, appeared in print. Between 1926 and 1936, The Jewish Publication Society (JPS) published the remainder of his translation. In all, this edition comprised eight elegant volumes of Yehoash's version, the culmination of sustained efforts by the translator, his family, and the publisher. In 1938, a pared down, popular edition was printed in two volumes, followed in 1941 by a diglot (that is, in two languages) edition in which Yehoash's Yiddish appeared alongside the Hebrew of the Masoretic Text.[22] By then, Yiddish as a living language—and, more tragically, large numbers of Yiddish speakers—was already on the road to destruction.

Yehoash's Yiddish Bible, however, remained beautifully resonant. As the distinguished Bible scholar and translator Harry M. Orlinsky wrote: "The translation . . . is as much a literary masterpiece in its own right as any translation of the Bible could be. It not only captures the Jewish feeling and rhythm of the original, but it is a delight to read for its own sake."[23]

Fortunately, the events leading up to World War II did not foreclose the production of Yiddish-language literature. Noteworthy are the poems and plays by Itzik Manger (1901–69), who was born in Czernowitz (then in Austria-Hungary, now in Ukraine). Especially active during the 1930s, he composed a series of poetic works that reflected creatively and sensitively on the text of the Hebrew Bible. Two brief excerpts from Manger's poetry exhibit its distinctive characteristics.[24]

The first is from a poem titled "Abishag Writes a Letter Home":

> David, the king is pious and old
> As for her, life isn't bad . . .
> She [Abishag] is the royal warming-flask
> And warms the old man's bed.[25]

To this we may compare 1 Kings 1:1–4 from the Hebrew Bible:

> King David was now old, advanced in years; and though they covered him with bedclothes, he never felt warm. His courtiers said to him, "Let a young virgin be sought for my lord the king, to wait upon Your Majesty and be his attendant; and let her lie in your bosom, and my lord the king will be warm." So they looked for a beautiful girl throughout the territory of Israel. They found Abishag the Shunammite and brought her to the king. The girl was exceedingly beautiful. She became the king's attendant and waited upon him; but the king was not intimate with her.

The second comes from "The Patriarch Jacob Meets Rachel." Rachel is speaking:

> "And you are Jacob, *mon cousin*"
> She's embarrassed with shame
> As Jacob, in his secret heart
> Thinks, "Wow, oh what a dame."[26]

In this case, the following verses from Genesis 29:10–11 are the apparent inspiration for Manger's scene: "And when Jacob saw Rachel, the daughter of his uncle Laban, and the flock of his uncle Laban, Jacob went up and rolled the stone off the mouth of the well, and watered the flock of his uncle Laban. Then Jacob kissed Rachel, and broke into tears."

Readers may ask whether these and other biblically based poems by Manger (who also composed updated versions of patriarchal stories and expanded the narrative of the book of Esther) properly belong in a volume on Bible translation. The inclusion of these delightful excerpts is intended to raise this very question.

Surely we have referenced and analyzed a number of "translations" that are far from literal or formal equivalences. We can view the Yiddish *Tsena Ureena*, where midrash freely mixes with what might more exactly be termed "biblical" renderings, in this light. The *Targums* often incorporate as many nonbiblical exegetical and explanatory verses as literal ones. Saadiah Gaon readily abandoned the Hebrew biblical text for expressions and concepts more at home with his Arabic-speaking (and reading) audience. And depending on how we understand the translation technique of some LXX "translators," they frequently jettisoned the Hebrew that lay before them in favor of a Greek that spoke directly to historical or theological/philosophical concerns of contemporary Hellenistic Jews.

We know some things about how Saadiah as well as the author of *Tseena Ureena* viewed their respective texts. In the other examples mentioned above, we don't have any sure sense of how specific Aramaic or Greek "translators" would have characterized their efforts.

To return to our inquiry: Are Manger's poems translations or adaptations or reflections or something else? We can address such matters only if we are aware of them—hence my inclusion of Manger in this volume.

Moses Mendelssohn and the First Translation into German

As a medium of communication between and among Jews, Yiddish served the people well. Indeed, Yiddish renderings of the Bible had a long and colorful history.

By the mid-eighteenth century, however, when Jews in German-speaking lands were finally granted long-denied access to the higher realms of cultural, political, social, and literary society, some Jewish leaders felt the need to have Sacred Writ rendered in German (the language of the dominant society), instead of Yiddish (the language they associated with an insular and increasingly outmoded stance).

Less than a century before Jacob ben Isaac, Martin Luther had produced his landmark German version of the Bible. While he labored on the Old Testament from 1522 to 1534, it would take about another 250 years, until the last quarter of the eighteenth century, for the Jewish community to have its own translation of the Bible in German.

As part of Luther's efforts to reform Christianity, he shaped a German text characterized by forceful language and direct diction. A literary masterpiece against which all subsequent German Bibles would be measured, Luther's version reflected some elements of the Jewish interpretive tradition. A prime example is the medieval exegete Rashi, as refracted through Christian sources (primarily, Nicholas de Lyra), who wielded considerable influence upon Luther.[27]

Approximately two and a half centuries after Luther, the Jewish intellectual and Enlightenment leader Moses Mendelssohn (1729–86) sought to remedy what he saw as the deplorably low status of Bible versions available to his fellow German-speaking Jews.[28] Elite cultural and social circles were at last opening up to them. But how, he asked, could members of this burgeoning bourgeoisie gain admittance, if they remained unacquainted with the High German style spoken and written by the Christian leadership of his day? Mendelssohn's version of the Bible and the accompanying commentary—the first Jewish translation into the German language (rather than Judeo-German)—

produced by himself and others whom he inspired, served as one of his responses to this issue.[29]

The publication of Mendelssohn's translations of the Bible began with his version of Ecclesiastes (1770). His Pentateuch followed (1783), then Psalms (1785–91) and Song of Songs (1788). Various scholars collaborated with Mendelssohn on the other biblical books while he was alive and continued in his style and with his goals after his death. A complete edition of the Bible by Mendelssohn and his followers appeared in the mid-1830s. It was often reprinted thereafter.

Mendelssohn accepted much of the language of the by-then classic formulations of Martin Luther, while at the same time excluding all of the specifically Christian renderings Luther had formulated. In support of his Jewish renderings, Mendelssohn marshaled an array of Jewish commentators. This was in keeping with the other major goal of Mendelssohn and his collaborators: to familiarize fellow Jews with the richness and authenticity of their own exegetical traditions.

As Saadiah's Arabic translations had initially appeared in Hebrew script (as far as scholars have been able to determine; see chapter 3), so the first editions of Mendelssohn's version, called the *Biur*, were printed in Hebrew characters. In a sense, then, Mendelssohn sought broadly to increase knowledge among Jews about Judaism as much as to enhance social, cultural, and political opportunities for Jews in the larger world. In this regard, Max L. Margolis perceptively observed: "[Mendelssohn's work] served as a text-book for acquiring the language of the educated, which led naturally to familiarity with the German literature and German culture. Then again inwardly it wrought a change by luring away the youth from the narrower occupation with codes and casuistry to the wider field of biblical interpretation and to the appreciation of the Scriptures as literature demanding and creating an aesthetic taste."[30]

As with Saadiah's *Tafsir*, the primary meaning of the term *Biur* is "commentary" rather than "translation." Even though Mendelssohn's work (translation and commentary in German, sometimes accompanied by the Masoretic Text) became known as the *Biur*, it bore a title,

Book of the Paths of Peace—an allusion to Proverbs 3:17: "Her [wisdom's] ways are ways of pleasantness, and all her paths are peace" (KJV).[31] In addition, its introduction, called "Light for the Path," recalled Psalm 119:105: "Thy word is a lamp unto my feet, and a light unto my path" (KJV).[32] By means of these two designations, Mendelssohn situated his work as translator within the biblical image of all-encompassing divine wisdom. This was the way ("path") toward enlightened understanding and practice of God's word. Jews, he believed, could not attain a full and authentic understanding of and appreciation for the direction of this path by relying on non-Jewish interpretations or even on Jewish sources, when these were constricted through a narrow preoccupation with "codes and casuistry" (to use Margolis's fine alliterative phrase; see above).

In his extensive writings, Mendelssohn bemoaned the fact that since the proliferation of Judeo-German versions, "no-one has taken to heart to emend this perversion and to translate the Holy Torah into the proper and accustomed language generally used in our generation. Jewish children who desire 'to perceive words of understanding' 'run to and fro seeking the word of the Lord' [see Prov. 1:2 and Amos 8:12, respectively] from Christian Scholars."[33] Note the pedagogical interest on Mendelssohn's part. He had initially undertaken the translation project to instruct his sons.[34]

Mendelssohn also contended that both Jewish children and adults who expected to find spiritual sustenance in Christian Bible sources would imbibe little, if anything, of value:

> Christian translators—who do not have the traditions of our Sages, and who do not heed the words of the Masorah, not even accepting the vowel points and accents that we have—make the words of the Torah into a broken wall. Everyone goes out against [the Masorah] and does with it as he pleases [for this expression, see Dan. 11:16]; they add and delete and change the divine Torah. [This affects] not only the points and the accents, but sometimes even letters and words (for who will stop their

> vanity?) according to what they think and feel. As a result, they occasionally do not read what is written in the Torah, but that which occurs to them.[35]

As harshly critical as Mendelssohn was in his suggestion that Christian scholars were prone to far-fetched and random emendation of the biblical text, he ultimately realized that differing methodologies were not the primary distinction between Jewish and Christian translators (and translations) of the Bible. Rather, Jews and Christians read and interpreted the Bible in fundamentally different ways. He noted: "I do not censure those scholars [for their critical approaches], for what should compel them to heed the tradition which they did not receive from their forefathers or the Masorah which was not transmitted to them from trustworthy men? They do not accept the words of the Torah to preserve and fulfill all that is written there."[36]

That sacred task, he avowed, could be undertaken only by Jews:

> For us, the Torah is an inheritance . . . to know the commandments that God commanded us to learn and teach, to preserve and fulfill, for it is our life and length of our days [see Deut. 30:20]. In order that our lives not be hanging on the hairbreadth of conjecture or the thread of reflection alone, our Sages decreed for us the Masorah and erected a fence for the Torah and for the commandments, for decrees and laws, in order that we not grope like the blind in the dark [for this image, see Isa. 59:10]. . . . We do not live from the mouth [of . . . an emendator], but from that which our trustworthy masters of the Masorah transmitted to us.[37]

Yet even though Mendelssohn had firmly planted his work in Jewish teachings, from its inception, his *Biur* was controversial within some segments of the Jewish community. A number of Jewish leaders feared that once their students were introduced to High German through Mendelssohn's rendering, they would abandon the Jewish texts they had traditionally studied in favor of works that formed part of the German literary canon. The example of Mendelssohn's own family demonstrates that there may have been some truth in this concern. Although he remained true to his understanding of Judaism, within two generations almost all of Mendelssohn's direct descendants became Christians.

Throughout the nineteenth century, successive editions of Mendelssohn's translation, printed in German characters, sold well. Moreover, Mendelssohn's translation, which aimed to educate its target audience in the dominant language of its world while maintaining fidelity to authentic Jewish exegetical traditions, would go on to serve as a role model for later translators rendering the Bible into other languages, most notably Max L. Margolis, editor-in-chief of The Jewish Publication Society's influential 1917 translation. In addition to sharing Mendelssohn's conviction that only Jews could produce a Bible translation fully appropriate for Jews, Margolis, working in Philadelphia, also made use of an elevated form of the target language of English. In this way, he believed he could ease the passage of his fellow immigrant Jews from outsider status to eloquent communicators ready to partake of the broader society America had to offer. From the first decades of the nineteenth century, the audience for German-language Bible versions among Jews grew. Partly this was the result of increased proficiency in the German language, something Mendelssohn had predicted and promoted. As a result, translators grappled with issues of formal or functional equivalence, renderings of key terminology such as divine names, the level of German linguistic and cultural awareness on the part of intended readers, and the need to market a specific edition in an ever-more crowded field of competing Bible versions. In this light, publishers discovered that they could enhance sales by packaging some editions as family Bibles.

The market also became increasingly diverse, with the rise of Reform and neo-Orthodox communities among German-speaking Jews.[38] Versions that sought to appeal to Reform Jews typically made a place, especially in their introductions and commentaries, for the critical nontraditional scholarship then being developed by Protestant researchers (for example, their presentations of the Documentary Hypothesis, arguments against Mosaic authorship of the Torah, and expressions of doubt about early dates for the composition of books such as Ruth, Daniel, Esther, and Ecclesiastes). Among the neo-Orthodox, Rabbinic interpretations of the biblical text were expounded. At the same time, translators who sought to engage Jews in these versions effectively doubled down on their adherence to tradition by shaping parts of their commentaries as defenses (implicit or explicit) against the critical stances then in vogue among many Reform Jewish and Protestant thinkers.

In the remaining sections of this chapter, each Bible version is introduced in chronological order, beginning in the 1830s and ending in the 1960s. This arrangement should not obscure features that link these versions, as well as those that distinguish them. Based on observations made in the previous paragraphs, readers are encouraged to be especially attentive to issues related to the style of German used in the translations and the theological/ideological positions put forth in the introductions and commentaries.

The German Translations of Zunz and Philippson

In 1837, Leopold Zunz (1794–1886), along with several co-translators, produced the first new German version of the entire Bible for Jews in the nineteenth century. (Recall that Mendelssohn's *Biur*, begun in the eighteenth century, continued to be available in expanded forms and formats.)

A pioneer (one observer spoke of him as "the savant") of modern Jewish religious scholarship, or Wissenschaft des Judentums,[39] Zunz was influenced by, but never identified with, the Reform movement in Judaism. As a result, he was familiar with the critical scholarship that was being formulated at many German-speaking universities and other centers of learning. When judged appropriate, Zunz allowed for the introduction of language and insights that challenged traditional Jewish exegetical traditions.

At the same time, he and his coworkers adhered strictly to the Masoretic Text, including the system of accents associated with it. Zunz would characteristically work through all available Hebrew manuscripts to assure this strict adherence.

In addition, Zunz was far more attuned to characteristics of the source language than Mendelssohn had been. For instance, whenever possible, he maintained in his German the regular absence of the verb "to be," as is characteristic of biblical Hebrew. Zunz also tried to preserve as much of the Hebrew word order as possible. Furthermore, he insisted on retaining the Hebrew form of place names and personal names through transliteration.

As a result, Zunz's version differed considerably from Mendelssohn's. Unlike Mendelssohn's, it did not aim to present an idiomatic, grammatically correct, free-flowing German text. Zunz's translation consistently reminded his readers that they were looking at a German version of a Hebrew original—or, as one scholar put it, "it proclaimed . . . that the Bible, even its German garment, was essentially a Hebraic document."[40]

These two features—the inclusion of nontraditional, non-Jewish biblical scholarship and the conscious effort to take the reader closer to the original text through the privileging of the source text—offended some of Zunz's contemporaries; he did not escape their criticisms or the negative comments of some later observers. The marketplace, however, which represented a broader consensus, was far more favorable. Over the course of more than a century—at least until 1935—seventeen editions of his work appeared.

Starting two years after the publication of Zunz's first edition, in 1839, and continuing for almost a decade and a half (until 1853), Ludwig Philippson (1811–89) published his rendering of the entire Hebrew Bible with commentary. In one sense, Philippson directly challenged Zunz, whose German syntax he and other critics had found awkward. By design, Philippson's German rendering thus read much more smoothly and easily than Zunz's. At another level, Philippson went considerably further than Zunz in biblical interpretation, for he was far more receptive than his predecessor to the critical scholarship of the day. For example, each of Philippson's biblical books contained an introduction that presented a concise history of interpretation: contemporary Protestant scholars shared these pages with Jewish commentators. These introductions, like the biblical text itself, were constructed with a general audience in mind. And Philippson's Bible was popular.

Another feature adding to the popularity of Philippson's Bibles was the inclusion of illustrations—and not just a few of them or works by lesser-known artists. To this day he is perhaps best known for his use of engravings by the famed French artist Gustav Doré, although he also incorporated the works of a great many other artists. The 1844 edition of his Pentateuch translation displayed more than five hundred woodcuts, many of them based on the findings of archaeological excavations of his time.[41] The 1858 edition featured more than seven hundred woodcuts.

This 1858 edition had at least one famous reader—Sigmund Freud. His father gave him this illustrated Philippson Bible when he was seven years old. Freud's enduring interest in the Bible most likely dates from this early period in his life.

The German Translation of Samson Raphael Hirsch

For many, Philippson's Bible, with its numerous "reader-friendly" features (e.g., a smooth German text, extensive introductions and commentaries aimed at an intelligent lay audience, illustrations), represented a marked advance over anything else available on the market. Yet his open inclusion of critical scholarship in addition to traditional Jewish exegesis was highly unpopular among traditional Jews and vocally denounced by their rabbinic and lay leadership. In their view, critical approaches, which Philippson regularly featured in both his introductions and commentaries, were antithetical to traditional methods of biblical exegesis as practiced at least since Rabbinical times. Although rabbis had typically allowed for, and even encouraged, a variety of interpretive viewpoints, all of these discussions and disagreements took as their starting point the divine origin of the biblical text and the basic truths about God and humans it propounded. It was precisely these "truths" that critical scholarship was challenging.

The time was ripe, both theologically and marketing-wise, for a German-language version of the Bible envisioned solely within the contours of traditional Judaism. And, as circumstances would have it, an individual arose who was ideally suited for the task at hand: Samson Raphael Hirsch (1808–88).

As one historian would put it, the counterpart to Reform "came forth through the profound and powerful personality, and through [the] strong religious fervour [of Hirsch], the creator and leader of the neo-orthodoxy. . . . As the progenitor of neo-orthodoxy in western countries, [Hirsch] was aspiring to fuse European culture with unqualified loyalty to rigourously observed traditional Judaism."[42] In this sense, Hirsch viewed his task as the means by which traditional Jews could strictly maintain their religiously determined lifestyles, while at the same time selectively participating in the general culture of their day.

As part of this ambitious process, Hirsch translated the Pentateuch, the Psalms, and prayer books. At the heart of this work was his German-language version of the Pentateuch, or Torah. As Hirsch himself expressed it, both the rationale for and the goal of his Pentateuch translation were to derive the explanation of the text from the words themselves; to pay close attention to the nuances of particular expressions; to make use of traditional Jewish halakhic (legal) and aggadic (narrative) exegesis; and to use all of this to explore and establish the Jewish outlook and the norms of Jewish life. Hirsch emphasized "the living interdependence and authenticity of the written and oral Law."[43] On this affirmation, which was crucial to the development of Rabbinic Judaism, he built his translations and commentary.

Hirsch's "endeavour to explain the Biblical text . . . out of itself . . . and on the basis of our own tradition, [was] in keeping with [his] general principles of Jewish research."[44] In his view, those who espoused Reform Judaism had preconceived notions of what the biblical text ought to say. Not surprisingly, they read those ideas into the text—a procedure that was out of alignment not only with traditional Judaism but also with the procedures of scientific investigation that were being developed in Hirsch's own time. Thus, in the appreciative words of Isidor Grunfeld, one of his editors and translators: "Samson Raphael Hirsch, true scientist that he was, objectively investigated the sources of Judaism as *given phenomena*. . . . Instead of construing theories *a priori* as the philosophers of the pre-scientific era did, the modern scientist [of whom Hirsch is one] first watches the facts . . . and it is from his observations that he arrives at a theory by way of generalization."[45] And, Grunfeld continued: "Any theory concerning Judaism . . . must be checked by and out of the classical sources of Judaism, i.e., the Written Text of the Torah and the Talmud which contains its authentic interpretation. Both together form what is known as the Torah in the wider sense of the word."[46]

Hirsch's "scientific approach" was then contrasted with the supposedly modern outlook of the principal exemplars of Reform Judaism. This was Hirsch's great merit, said Grunfeld, "to have applied to Judaism these improved methods of reasoning which modern science imposes . . . with the only difference that legal facts took the place of natural facts. It was strange that Hirsch, the representative of strict orthodoxy, was much more up-to-date in his method of research and presentation than the Reformers who prided themselves on being 'modern' and 'enlightened.'"[47] This appeal to science in the overturning of a basic tenet of Reform—namely, that Orthodoxy was woefully out of keeping with modern times—was characteristic of Hirsch's project of constructing neo-Orthodoxy as the only valid approach to Judaism in the Age of Enlightenment.

Hirsch had systematically studied comparative Semitic philology, but did not bring that study to bear in his translation and interpretation of biblical Hebrew. Instead, his approach toward Hebrew was based on his understanding of its uniqueness. For him, "Hebrew was not only the language in which God created the world. . . . It was also the original language . . . of mankind, and might have remained the universal language uniting all humanity but for the great revolt against God at the time of the 'Generation of the Dispersion' [Gen. 11]."[48] As Hirsch himself maintained, "We must read the Torah *in Hebrew*—that is to say, in accordance with the spirit of that language. It describes but little, but through the rich significance of its verbal roots it paints in the word a picture of the thing."[49]

In Hirsch's view, a key component to the correct understanding of biblical Hebrew was a "view of etymology based on the interrelationship of sounds." Consider his commentary on the root *b-r-'* (to create), which forms the first verb in the Bible, at Genesis 1:1:

> [This and cognate roots] which all have the meaning of striving to get out, or getting out of a state of being constrained or bound, give this root the underlying concept of bringing something out into the open. . . . So this root means bringing something into reality which hitherto had only existed inwardly, in the mind. It is creating something purely out of one's mind and will and out of nothing else. It is . . . accordingly used only for creation by God. Before the world existed materially it existed only as a thought—to speak in terms of human beings—in the mind of the Creator. The act of creation gave this thought an external concrete existence. The whole world, in toto and in detail, is accordingly nothing but a materialised thought of God.[50]

As to the word *'-l-o-h-i-m* (here, God), which occurs first in Genesis 1:1, Hirsch wrote:

> The root '-l-h occurs in the demonstrative pronoun '-l-h "these." But the demonstrative plural "these" always looks at a plurality of things as being in some way joined together to form a unit. And so, whereas '-l-h in general points to the visible plurality of objects in the world, the name of God '-l-v-h could designate the

> One Whose might and will encompasses all those objects together in unity. The One through Whom all the plurality, by everything being related to Him, becomes one union, one whole, one world. Hence '-l-v-h really means: the One Who is ruler, director, law-giver, judge of the world. . . . From this underlying conception of the root '-l-h as world-director, law-giver, judge, the same root is also used to designate an oath '-l-h. An oath, according to the Jewish idea, is not merely an appellation to the God-head, but is an actual placing of the whole of the material world of the one who swears under the verdict of the One Who has power to deal with them . . . and the curse by which the destroying power of the Director of the world will proclaim the falsity of a false oath.[51]

Finally, commenting on the word order, by which "God" appears after—rather than before—the verb "create," Hirsch wrote: "In the way we have believed this name of God to be derived from '-l-h, God can be called '-l-o-h-i-m only after the creation of the world, as it refers to His relation to the world."[52]

Here is one further example, also taken from Genesis 1:1, elucidating Hirsch's understanding of the concept expressed by *sh-ma-yim* (sky) as having developed from the root of the word:

> [Sh-ma-yim is] the designation of the whole extra-terrestrial world, as the double "shem," as the above and below, "there," the immeasurable double space, above and beneath the earth,[53] or rather—from the root "shum," directing, fixing the place—as the whole complex of extra-terrestrial bodies through whose mutually attracting and repelling forces the earth, like every other point in the universe, keeps to its appointed place. For every point in the universe, the whole of the rest of space with all its bodies, would be sh-ma-yim. In any case the word sh-ma-yim already tells us that we have not to expect here any super-terrestrial cosmogonic revelations. The extra-terrestrial is only mentioned and considered in its relation to the earth.[54]

The close relationship between text and commentary, also evident in many other Jewish Bibles, is likewise crucial to a proper evaluation of Hirsch's efforts. As Rabbi W. Gunther Plaut, editor of the Reform Movement's *The Torah: A Modern Commentary*, would later observe, for Hirsch:

> the translation was only the necessary backdrop to the commentary, not the other way around. To be sure, one started with the text, but what Tradition made of it was the important matter that needed to be communicated to the Jewish reader. And his exhaustive and brilliant commentary was thoroughly traditional. Talmud, Midrash and the great commentaries of the past were his constant reference. His translations of Torah and Psalms were nothing more than a medium by which the eternal truth and beauty of the original could be made known.[55]

And that medium owed its very existence to Hirsch's certainty about the unity and unique sanctity of the Written and Oral Law.

From this vantage point, Hirsch absolutely rejected all critical approaches to the Hebrew Bible.[56] He also foresaw an even more deleterious aspect of Bible criticism: "its anti-Semitic origin and character, and its consequent threat to the preservation of the spiritual and human values of mankind."[57] As Hirsch undoubtedly recognized, a number of critical biblical scholars in Germany, all of them Christian, used their redating, rearrangement, and reassessment of the Old Testament to demean ancient Judaism and denounce Jews contemporary with them. Jews who adopted critical stances were apparently able to separate what they saw as suitable results from their unsavory proponents. In so doing, these Jewish scholars broke with the framework and exegetical stances of Rabbinic Judaism. This, Hirsch was obviously unwilling to do. For him, not only Jews but also all mankind was dependent for their spiritual and corporeal well-being on the preservation and enhancement of the Bible as traditionally viewed.[58]

Hirsch's translation of the Torah, printed in Frankfurt, first appeared in 1867. His rendering of the Psalms was published in 1882; a German-language version of the Minor Prophets, produced by his son Mendel, came out in 1900.

We might expect that Hirsch and his son would have favored a "Hebraizing" style like that of Zunz over against the smoother German of Philippson or Mendelssohn. However, Hirsch's translation falls squarely within the parameters set by Mendelssohn and Philippson, although he did retain Hebrew personal names.[59] Apparently, Hirsch calculated that his translation should be fairly straightforward to appeal to as wide an audience as possible (as opposed to the often convoluted argumentation of his commentary). Moreover, given his indisputable credentials as a leader of traditional Judaism, Hirsch presumably felt that he would be exempt from any of the criticisms leveled at earlier translators in this regard. And, so far as I know, he was correct in this calculation.

Of all the Jewish renderings of the Bible into German, only Hirsch's version of the Bible was subsequently translated into English. This has opened up his work to a far larger audience of scholars and general readers than would otherwise have been possible. In English, the Hirsch Torah continues to exert significant influence within Orthodox circles worldwide.[60]

The German Translation of Simon Bernfeld

The translator Simon Bernfeld (1860–1940) had served as chief rabbi of the Sephardi community in Belgrade before returning in 1894 to Berlin, where he had earlier studied. In Berlin, Bernfeld labored on his version of the Bible, along with many other historical and philosophical works.

Unlike many other Jewish translators of the Bible, Bernfeld felt that his major achievement was the translation itself rather than the creation or compilation of an extensive commentary to accompany the text. As one appreciative observer has written: "[Bernfeld's] main principle is clearly formulated: the Bible has to speak to us without any commentary, i.e., the translation has to be understandable, easy and useful, and to avoid lengthy commentary, diverting the reader from the text."[61] Bernfeld did include short explanations bracketed within the text itself or located in brief footnotes. But he placed all other commentary, including an extended discussion of general issues, in his introduction.

It is there, for example, that he wrote vigorously against Zunz's and other translators' efforts to Hebraize the German. By contrast, his translation was expressed in the commonly accepted German of his day. This stylistic choice furthered his goal of producing a translation that would be as widely accepted among Jews as Luther's version was among Christians. His audience, he explained, consisted of German Jews who "became middle class, increasingly well-educated and, most important, convinced that the best of German culture was thoroughly hospitable and even parallel to Jewish ideals."[62]

To advance his objective, Bernfeld also judiciously cited recent authorities—some Jewish, such as Samuel David Luzzatto, others Christian[63]—in addition to traditional Jewish commentators. Furthermore, he appears to have consciously chosen *Herr* (Lord) for YHVH, in keeping with Luther, although he was said to have preferred Hirsch's *Hashem* (The Name). His primary concession to Hebrew as the source language was his decision to follow biblical word order in a number of passages, even when this practice violated German norms.

From some vantage points, Bernfeld's translation appeared to stand out among the competition. As Plaut asserted, Bernfeld's version of the Bible was "a work of serious scholarly and linguistic merit: [it] represent[ed] a high point of German Jewry's adaptation to German civilization, yet it was Jewish without apology."[64] As such, it may be said to reflect some of the major goals Mendelssohn had set out for his translation more than a hundred years earlier.

Another scholar, S. Belligheimer, personally attested to "the popularity of this translation." Yet he also noted that "the co-existence of several translations at the time of the publication of Bernfeld's made an overruling popularity of [any] one translation very difficult." Thus, Bernfeld's prodigious efforts were not sufficient to produce a translation that would "belong to [all of] the people."[65]

The German Translation of Buber and Rosenzweig

Also prior to World War I, two Jewish philosophers, Martin Buber (1878–1965) and Franz Rosenzweig (1886–1929), began to work on their own ambitious Bible translation. Their overall goal, which indeed had been a guiding force for some Bible translators since the third century BCE, was to transport their readers back to a time, place, and society far different than their own. More specifically, they aimed to introduce readers to important features in the original Hebrew, such as wordplays and repetitions, that up until then were largely inaccessible to those who could not read the Hebrew text. Only in this way, they believed, would readers be able to experience the Hebrew Bible authentically.

To accomplish this goal, they created something unique in German literature. They stretched the German language to (or even beyond) the breaking point—in such passages, those unfamiliar with Hebrew would have to labor to comprehend the meaning of what they were reading. This seeming paradox was exactly what Buber and Rosenzweig sought. As they saw it, the struggle would be worth it: Readers would finally be able to engage in a face-to-face encounter with the many exciting literary and theological features of the Hebrew text that, up until then, only those who read the Hebrew had ever experienced.

When Rosenzweig died in 1929, their project was far from finished. It would take Buber three more decades, after World War II and the Holocaust, to complete the work. Buber finally finished it in 1961 while living in Israel, to which he had moved in 1938. In addition to the translation's impact within German-speaking Jewish communities, it also inspired at least one modern English-language version (see chapter 6).

In accompanying essays (which, unlike the Bible translation itself, have since been translated into English), Buber expounded on the two creators' intentions in producing their version. In "On Word Choice in Translating the Bible," for example, Buber offers as eloquent a defense of formal equivalence as I have ever read:

> Even the most significant translations of the Bible that we possess . . . do not aim principally at maintaining the original character of the book, as manifested in word choice, in syntax, and in rhythmical articulation. . . . They accordingly carry over the "content" of the text itself into another language. They do not *a priori* ignore the peculiarities of its constituent elements, of its structure, of its dynamic; but they easily enough sacrifice those peculiarities when stubborn "form" seems to hinder the rendering of "content." It is for them as if genuine tidings, genuine speech, genuine song contained a What easily detached from their How.[66]

Buber and Rosenzweig also emphasized the need to give appropriate emphasis to the oral and foreign nature of the biblical text (vis-à-vis what the modern reader of a translation usually experiences):

> The holy text is for all uninterrupted antiquity an orally transmitted text. . . . What originates in speaking can live again only in speaking. . . . The auditory form of the German translation should then correspond to spokenness thus understood—not for silent reading but for accurate recitation, drawing out the full auditory value.
>
> The Germanization of the Bible must also be "called out." Only then will its unfamiliarity not become merely an alienating oddness. But its unfamiliarity is itself necessary, is indeed the one necessity, if, with all our false expertise about the Bible, all our condescending solidarity with it, a translation is to produce an encounter between the Bible and people today.[67]

The result was far removed from the process of bringing the text to the reader inherent in functional equivalence translations. Rather, Buber maintained that "readers who read in earnest will have to face the task of working themselves—living themselves—into the text, a task that will inevitably bear fruit."[68]

Elsewhere, Buber described in some detail a feature of biblical Hebrew that he and Rosenzweig were especially concerned with replicating in their German version. Called *Leitwort* in German, this term, Buber explained, referred to "a word or word root that is meaningfully repeated within a text or sequence of texts."[69] The repetitions created a "dynamic [effect] because what takes place between the verbal configurations thus related is in a way a *movement*."[70] Moreover, this was "probably the strongest of all techniques for making a meaning available without articulating it explicitly."[71] Many, perhaps most, Bible translations obscure this technique by intentionally translating the same word or word root differently when the word or root appears two or more times in proximity. By contrast, Buber and Rosenzweig exposed German readers to this technique, which Hebrew speakers would immediately recognize.

Paronomasia (punning and wordplay) often occupied a significant role in this type of repetition. Thus, for example, in the story of Jacob and Esau, Buber identified "four motivic words—'deceit,' 'birthright,' 'blessing,' and 'name.'"[72] The interplay of language, sound, and judgment between these words in Hebrew becomes evident in the Buber-Rosenzweig rendering of Genesis 27:35–36: "To Esau's 'exceedingly great and bitter cry' Isaac answers, 'your brother came with deceit and took away your blessing.' And then Esau: 'is this why his name was called Yaakov/Heel-Sneak? For he has now sneaked against me twice;/ my first-born right [*bekhorati*] he took, and now he has taken my blessing [*birkhati*]!'"[73]

Final Thoughts

Within the context of Jewish Bible translations, few if any other languages can match the richness exhibited by the array of Judeo-German and German-language versions we surveyed in this chapter. On its own terms, the chronological scope of these translations is impressive: more than 450 years separate the first edition of the *Tsena Ureena* from the completion and final publication of Buber and Rosenzweig's version. As products of their own time, each translation reflected the conditions of the Jewish community for whom/in which it was produced as well as major developments in the dominant Christian societies where Jews were resident.

These translators also eyed different segments of the Jewish community in shaping the style of their translations and the ideological/theological stance of their commentaries. For some, adherence to the source text, in Hebrew, necessitated the presentation of a Yiddish or German version that was out of synch with what readers were familiar with from contemporary literature or speech, that is, the formal equivalence translation style.

Other translators, both traditional and Reform, paid far closer attention to the preparation of a translation that more or less seamlessly meshed with the Yiddish or German then in use, thus taking the text to the reader, that is, the functional equivalence approach to translation.

What is perhaps most elusive is our inability to tie different translation approaches to the theological/ideological stance of those who produced them. It is, I think, intuitive to associate a more formal equivalence version with translations produced by, and aimed at, traditional communities. In like manner, we might almost automatically place functional equivalence texts within Reformist contexts. But, as we've seen, it doesn't work out that way.

With his goal of expressing traditional Jewish exegesis in precise and proper German, Mendelssohn and his colleagues typically focused on the perceived needs of their contemporary target audience rather than transmitting Semitic, that is, non-German, nuances and syntax. In spite of his intense interest in Hebrew etymology as evinced in extended notes, Samuel Raphael Hirsch fashioned a German version that was notably straightforward for his contemporaries. Between these two giants was Ludwig Philippson, whose readers were introduced to Reform Jewish and critical Protestant scholarship through a version that, like Mendelssohn and Hirsch, smoothly presented biblical narrative and law in contemporary-sounding language.

A slightly older contemporary of Philippson, Leopold Zunz, was also a proponent of Reform in nineteenth-century Germany. In fashioning his text, however, he paid exceedingly close attention to the grammar, word order, and idiom of the Semitic texts he was translating. In common with other formal equivalence versions, readers of Zunz's translation consistently felt the geographical and chronological distance between themselves and the biblical text.

Similarly, in nineteenth-century and early twentieth-century Germany, both traditional and nontraditional Jewish translators—or more likely their publishers or distributors—experimented with different modes of packaging their versions. Among the questions they asked and sought to answer were what should a typical page look like, approximately how many notes should appear and where should they be placed, what sorts of introductions (if any) are best suited for the intended audience, should illustrations be included, what fonts should be used (on occasion, new ones were invented), how should the volume (or volumes) be bound, whose endorsements would be most persuasive, and so on. Generally, these deliberations reflected the enhancements made possible by new technology of the times as well as the increasing size—and fragmentation—of the potential audiences.

Only in chapter 6, on English-language versions, do we have a time frame approximating the four-and-a-half centuries of Yiddish and German translations we've been exploring in this chapter. And even there, the chronological expanse is only half as long. Nonetheless, as we'll see, there are parallels as well as distinctly unique features when we compare relevant translations and translators.

5

Translations into Other Selected Languages

Among the many notable Jewish Bibles are versions that were translated into five other languages—Spanish, French, Italian, Hungarian, and Russian.

My choice to focus first on Spanish, French, and Italian arises from the recognition that many readers of this book are familiar with one or more of these languages. But there are issues of greater substance as well.

As it turns out, Spanish is the first Western European language to which Jews turned in their efforts to produce vernacular versions (that is, versions in the language spoken by members of the majority culture in which they lived). As we will see, the first two of these versions are remarkable not only for their origins but also for the impact they had on later, non-Jewish translations of the Bible into Spanish.

The two French versions we explore are from the mid-nineteenth century and the last years of the same century, respectively. By the time of the first version, French Jews already enjoyed a personal and institutional status equal to all other French citizens—yet social and legal prejudice always lurked just beneath the surface, memorably and horrifically protruding in the century's last decade. The versions French Jews produced reflect these factors, among others.

Although Italian Jews had Bible translation options both before and after the first half of the nineteenth century, when the scholar and poet Samuel David Luzzatto lived, his Italian-language translations, with commentaries, would prove to be the most influential. Luzzatto represented a measured engagement between traditional Jewish exegesis and Haskalah (Enlightenment) approaches to the Bible. Because of his integrity and erudition, Luzzatto's texts were read and studied widely beyond the world of Italian-speaking Jews.

From there we examine Bible translations for Eastern European Jews through the lenses of Hungarian- and Russian-language versions. Although the millions of Russian speakers dwarfed the relatively modest number of Hungarians, the Jewish versions produced in these societies have remarkable parallels. In all cases (one in Hungarian, two in Russian), the translators, much influenced by Enlightenment thought and practice, conceived of their versions as central to efforts to make Jews in their respective societies more Hungarian or Russian. This was not seen as pushing their fellow Jews away from their Judaism, but rather enhancing the opportunities for authentic Jewish beliefs and rituals. It was hoped that when Jews became more completely Hungarian or Russian, it would then be possible for them to also be more fully Jewish.

Clearly, many of these translators were deeply enmeshed in the historical and social ferments sweeping through Europe during the first half of the nineteenth century. The Bibles they produced would be unique by-products of their reactions to changing political, religious, and cultural circumstances.

Indeed, throughout history and in many lands, Jewish translators of the Bible were rarely unacquainted with external as well as internal trends that affected their own communities. Distinctive circumstances within a given society would then lead to unique or at least unusual characteristics in each version of the Bible.

In essence, this chapter provides rich context for comparing and contrasting various translators' efforts during the same or similar time spans, as they operated within distinct, yet interconnected, cultures.

Spanish

In Western Europe, Jewish involvement in Bible translation occurred earliest in Spain.[1] Jews would produce two influential versions: the Alba Bible, in the third decade of the fifteenth century; and the Ferrara Bible, in the mid-sixteenth century. Interestingly, both reflected Jewish exegetical viewpoints and concerns, even though they had different audiences in mind.

The Alba Bible

In 1422 Don Luis de Guzman was grand master of the Order of Calatrava, a Roman Catholic military order founded in Castile and confirmed by papal bull in 1164. Having apparently tired of waging war, Don Luis determined that he would sponsor a translation of the Bible into Spanish, accompanied by a commentary. He requested that a rabbi, Moses Arragel, who lived in a small Castilian town, undertake this task: "Know, O Raby Moses! that we desire to possess a Bible with glosses and comments; and we are told that you can do the work well."[2]

Two primary concerns motivated Don Luis to make this admittedly surprising request. First, he sought to heal a rift between Jews and Christians that had ignited antisemitic riots in 1422 in Madrid. At the same time, the Spanish nobleman recognized the value of an Old Testament translation by someone who knew Hebrew well and would judiciously select commentaries from Jews and other exegetes. On the basis of the finished product, we can affirm that "Raby Moses" was an excellent choice for this project.

Arragel, about whom we know little beyond his participation in this project, sensed the difficulty of producing a Castilian/Spanish version that would be satisfactory for Roman Catholics and thus was initially reluctant to participate. Eventually, however, he acceded to Don Luis's insistent requests.

Don Luis assigned a Franciscan friar, Arias de Enciena, to convey his expectations for this version to Arragel and to work with him, although the rabbi, not the friar, was charged with preparation of the text. This collaboration between a rabbi and a Roman Catholic points to a rare moment of relative religious tolerance in this era.

Arragel had deep knowledge of Hebrew. He also made extensive use of Jerome's Latin translation, the Vulgate, which served as the official Bible of the Roman Catholic Church at the time.[3] When the two texts agreed, Arragel had little difficulty arriving at an appropriate rendering. When they differed, he felt no hesitation in following the Hebrew.[4] In like manner, he arranged the biblical books in accordance with the traditional ordering of the Jewish Bible.

Arragel also took advantage of this relative freedom in his glosses and more extended commentaries. Sometimes he espoused views that differed from church teachings, invariably acknowledging these with statements such as, "This is the opinion of the Christians, but the Jews hold just the opposite view." At other times, he differed from the dominant viewpoint of Jewish exegetes, declaring, for example, that many expressions are best understood in a figurative sense. Through Friar Arias, Arragel was sufficiently conversant with the views of Don Luis to cite them on numerous occasions; he was sufficiently diplomatic never to disagree with the grand master.[5]

All in all, Arragel exhibited a remarkable breadth and depth of erudition. Among Jewish sources he explicitly drew upon the Talmud, the Midrash, Rashi, Ibn Ezra, and Kimchi. His glosses also contained Jewish tales and proverbs not found in the Hebrew Bible. Furthermore, he knew Christian scholarship well, as is evident through his references to Bernard of Clairvaux and Nicholas de Lyra, among others. His expertise also extended to classical authors such as Aristotle, Euclid, and Pliny.[6] Don Luis, so it appears, had chosen very wisely.

Arragel completed his primary responsibilities on the "Bible of Olivares," including the glosses, in 1430. (Don Luis belonged to the noble House of Olivares.) It consisted of 515 folios.[7] Glosses, written in small script, surrounded the text, which was elegantly laid out in two columns. The ceremony of presentation to Don Luis was a grand occasion featuring laudatory evaluations from the head of the Franciscans, among others.[8]

But the Bible was not yet considered complete. It was sent to Toledo, where Franciscan censors carefully examined the text, word by word, making whatever changes they deemed necessary. This took three years. The illustrations were also selected and inserted during this time.

Truly, the work was beautiful. According to most counts, there were 334 illustrations, of which either four or six filled an entire page.[9] A considerable number of the images reflected a distinctly Christian perspective, though many others incorporated what appeared to be Jewish imagery. Perhaps Arragel played a role in selecting the illustrations or, by that time, these "Jewish" themes may have already been incorporated into Christian art.[10] This is a still unresolved question for art historians and others.[11]

From 1433 until almost two hundred years later (1624) the whereabouts of this manuscript are unknown. It probably escaped the fires of the Inquisition (in which both people and books were burned) through the ingenuity and bravery of the few Spanish humanists who recognized its unique value.

When the manuscript reappeared, it was returned to a descendant of Don Luis in the House of Olivares, probably as a result of Count-Duke Olivares's donations to the Catholic Church. Sometime thereafter, the manuscript came into the possession of the fifth duke of Alba, who was also viceroy of Naples. Either he or one of his successors attached his family name to the version, hence the "Alba Bible." It became, as it were, one of the prized acquisitions of this family.

We can gauge the Alba Bible's abiding importance to Spanish culture by the care with which artists and scholars produced a limited facsimile edition of it in 1992—in commemoration of King Juan Carlos's retraction that year of the five-hundred-year-old order to expel Jews from Spain.[12]

The Ferrara Bible

The period between 1430, when the Alba Bible was completed, and 1553, when a new Bible translation known as the Ferrara Bible would be printed, was momentous in many ways.

From the vantage point of Bible production, two developments stand out. The first was technological: Johannes Gutenberg's development of moveable type, in 1453. The second was historical and of immediate impact to the Jews of the Iberian Peninsula: In 1492, upon the union of the Christian rulers Isabella of Castile and Ferdinand II of Aragon, Jews were expelled from Spain. One of the places that welcomed fleeing Jews was the northern Italian city of Ferrara—and among the rather liberal attractions fostered by the ruling family of this region was ready access to printing presses. Jews from Spain and Portugal, whose freedom to enjoy open, unfettered religious self-expression had been increasingly limited in their homeland, were among those who took fullest advantage of the opportunities this presented.

In 1553 in Ferrara, the first Spanish—or, more properly, Judeo-Spanish (Ladino)—translation of the entire Hebrew Bible was published, for use by Sephardi Jews. In particular, there was concern for Conversos (Spanish and Portuguese Jews who had become Roman Catholics, typically as a result of threats) and their descendants, who were returning to Judaism after leaving the Iberian Peninsula. These individuals were not (or no longer) able to read biblical and liturgical texts in Hebrew. Unlike earlier Ladino versions, which usually covered only portions of the Bible, the Ferrara Bible was printed in Roman rather than Hebrew script. This feature decisively enlarged the audience for this version to encompass both Jews and non-Jews who had no knowledge of Hebrew.

The Ferrara Bible also differed in language and style from previous versions in Ladino. In particular, this translation closely followed the grammar and syntax of the original Hebrew. As is true for formal equivalence versions in general, so the language of the Ferrara Bible, while incorporating Spanish vocabulary, had a distinctly non-Spanish—in this case Hebrew—structure to it. Possibly, those responsible for this Bible consciously used this approach to acquaint their target audience with features of the Hebrew language without requiring them to actually learn any Hebrew.[13]

This Bible also appeared in two formats—a larger, or tall, format, in which the biblical text occupied 802 double-columned pages with 44 lines in each full column, and another format with much smaller pages—but with seemingly identical texts.[14]

Other variations also surfaced. For example, depending on the version, readers would see either a longer or a shorter dedicatory statement on the verso (right page) of the title page. The expansive dedication—signed by two men with Spanish-sounding (that is, Christian) names, Alvaro de Vargas and Duarte Pinhel—was to Ercole d'Este II, fourth duke of Ferrara, "without whose sanction publication of Scripture in Spanish would have been impossible." The shorter dedication was to Dona Gracia Nasi, a well-to-do philanthropist whose many benefactions for the Jewish community included substantial aid to Jews forced to leave the Iberian Peninsula and support for rabbinic scholars and Jewish institutions such as hospitals, synagogues, and yeshivot. Without her generous support, we may surmise, the Ferrara Bible would never have appeared. This dedication was also signed by two individuals—in this case, men with Jewish names, Yom Tob Atias and Abraham Usque. As it turns out, the signatories to the longer dedication and the shorter dedication were in fact the same individuals.[15] Both were ex-Conversos who had adopted Spanish names when they lived as Christians, but presumably reverted to their earlier Hebrew appellations when they returned to Judaism.

In addition, there are two versions of the colophon (inscription at the end of a book). In one, dated May 1, 1553, the same two individuals named in the longer dedication to the fourth duke of Ferrara are credited with printing the work and assuming the production costs. In the other, the same two individuals named in the shorter dedication to Dona Gracia Nasi receive credit for the same activities. This colophon is dated "14 Adar, the sixth month, *Anno Mundi* [since the creation of the world] 5313."[16] This is equivalent to March 10, 1553.

For years, the vast majority of specialists assumed that these differences originated in two distinct editions of the Ferrara Bible: one aimed at the ruling family of Ferrara and more generally at a supportive Christian audience, and the other at Sephardi Jews. However, more recent examination of extant copies of the Ferrara Bible does not bear out this admittedly attractive solution. In fact, the longer dedication to the duke is frequently found in volumes that conclude with the Jewish dating, and vice-versa. Moreover, there does not appear to be any correlation between the size of the folio and its intended audience.[17]

Efforts to explicate the initial publishing strategies for the Ferrara Bible have also focused on variations in the wording at Isaiah 7:14. Up until the twentieth century, Christian versions of this text invariably spoke of "a virgin" who would conceive. In Jewish versions, "young woman" or "maiden" was the consistent rendering. Seemingly along these lines, some copies of the Ferrara Bible contain the translation *virgen* (virgin) and others *moca* (maiden) in this passage. But there are also copies of the Ferrara Bible that have a transliteration of the Hebrew word for young woman/maiden, *ALMA* (always all caps), rather than either of the two Spanish translations. This would have been meaningful only for Jews (or others) who knew Hebrew pretty well, since only Hebrew speakers would have been able to make sense out of this transliteration.

For a long time, the preferred explanation for these variants was that *virgen* was substituted for *moca* or *ALMA* in some copies that were being prepared for Jews when they needed to submit them to Christian censors or Inquisition authorities. But further close examination does not support this explanation. The latest hypothesis offers *ALMA* as the original rendering, replaced first by *virgen* and then by *moca*, as a compromise.[18] According to this view, the transliteration *ALMA* was the initial way the Bible's translators sought to avoid the thorny, potentially explosive question of interpretation and identification in Isaiah 7:14. But precisely because *ALMA*, as a transliteration, didn't mean anything, the translators opted for "virgin" in some subsequent editions. That, however, didn't sit well with many Jews who were part of the target audience. For them, and then for all subsequent readers (Jewish and Christian) of later editions, it was to be a "young woman" of whom the prophet Isaiah spoke.

Whether or not this hypothesis wins the day, it is clear that we can no longer speak assuredly of separate "Jewish" and "Christian" editions of the 1553 Ferrara Bible.[19] At the same time, we can continue to affirm the significance of the Ferrara Bible, and its undoubted Jewish origins, for a full understanding of Jewish Bible translations.

We can also say with certainty that the Ferrara Bible enjoyed great success. It was reprinted a number of times wherever Jews of the Iberian Peninsula settled after their expulsion. It became a staple for the large number of Sephardi Jews who moved to the Netherlands. As late as the mid-eighteenth century, Amsterdam publishers were bringing out new editions.

Beyond this, the Ferrara Bible served as a model for the first classical Spanish translation of Scripture: the Santa Biblia, prepared by Casiodoro de Reina and published in Switzerland in 1569.[20] What is more, one of the leading translators of the Old Testament in KJV, Lancelot Andrewes (1555–1626), had a personal copy of the Ferrara Bible, which he was known to copiously annotate.

French

By the fourth decade of the nineteenth century, French Jews were well on their way to full participation in the political, economic, and cultural spheres of their country. Almost all impediments to the practice of Judaism had also been removed. Judaism was a recognized religion, with the same legal standing as Roman Catholicism and several Protestant denominations. Such recognition carried with it financial support from the state as well. Overall, it was a period of growing prosperity and prominence for French Jewry.

In this context, a large-scale project was undertaken: to provide French-speaking Jews with a version of the Hebrew Bible.

Samuel Cahen's *La Bible, Traduction Nouvelle*

The major proponent of this project was Samuel Cahen (1796–1862). Born in Northeast France, in the city of Metz, he was brought up and educated in Mainz (or Mayence), a city that was much contested between the French and the Germans at the end of the eighteenth and the beginning of the nineteenth centuries. Nonetheless, it offered a congenial environment for Cahen, who was able to follow a traditional Jewish education in rabbinical studies and become fully acquainted with the pedagogical methods and materials associated with modern languages and literatures. In 1822, after his graduation and a brief stint as a tutor in Germany, he moved to Paris, which was to be the center of his intellectual and institutional efforts for the rest of his life.[21]

During his first decade in Paris Cahen served as director of the Jewish Consistorial School and published instructional material on teaching Hebrew, a short Hebrew-French dictionary, and a new French translation of the Passover Haggadah.[22] In 1840 he considerably expanded his horizons to found the *Archives Israélites*, a monthly literary journal devoted to Jewish writers and their works; it evolved into one of the most prominent publications of its type.[23]

During this same period he undertook what was to be the major achievement of his life: the translation of the Bible into French, with the Hebrew on facing pages, accompanied by critical notes and extended essays by himself and others. For two decades he devoted himself to this project. His goal was to produce in French a version that followed MT closely in terms of grammar, syntax, and vocabulary (the latter through the use of Hebraisms). His audience consisted of fellow Jews and also those Christians who sought the immediacy of contact with the Hebrew language that no French version had yet offered.

Finally, in 1851, all eighteen volumes of his magnum opus, *La Bible, traduction nouvelle* (The Bible: A new translation), were published. It was widely recognized as a major advance for French speakers, both Jewish and non-Jewish.[24]

Still, the Bible had its critics. Some took issue with Cahen's uncritical handling of certain material in the notes and essays. In view of the fact that he had assembled critical scholarship, including the latest archaeological and philological research, in addition to a wide range of Jewish sources, including the Septuagint, it is not altogether surprising that his grasp of the material was sometimes uncertain. Others found it difficult to understand some of his renderings, especially when his desire to reproduce characteristic features of Hebrew led to opaque French.

In my view, such criticism—some of it valid, other aspects at variance with his stated goals—should not detract from the overall value of Cahen's contribution to Jewish Bible translations.[25] *La Bible, traduction nouvelle* remained the unrivaled standard version of the Bible for both Jews and Christians until the very end of the nineteenth century. Even today it is readily available in updated paperback editions.[26]

Zadoc Kahn and *La Bible du Rabbinat Français*

The second major Bible for French-speaking Jews was published nearly fifty years after Cahen's first translation.

While the Jewish community had experienced vibrant growth during much of this period, antisemitism was becoming a growing and increasingly public issue, with reactionaries accelerating their verbal attacks and concocting plots to discredit individual Jews or Judaism in general. All of this activity culminated in the mid-1890s with false accusations of treason against the young Jewish military officer Captain Alfred Dreyfus. Although credible evidence of his innocence on all charges of collusion with the Germans was brought to light, he was still forced to undergo years of hardship in a penal colony before he was at last exonerated. His plight captured national and international attention—and brought to the fore the tenuous nature of Jewish life in Europe even under what were then the best of circumstances.[27]

The recognized and respected leader of the Jewish community during this difficult period was Zadoc Kahn (1839–1905), the chief rabbi of France as of March 1890.

Born in the town of Mommenheim in the Alsace region, Kahn entered the rabbinical school of Metz (coincidentally, Metz was Samuel Cahen's hometown) at age seventeen. When the school moved to Paris as the renamed Séminaire Israélite, Kahn continued his studies there. Upon graduation he was appointed director of the seminary's preparatory school. In 1867 he became assistant to the chief rabbi of Paris, Lazare Isidor.

The following year, Isidor became chief rabbi of France, and Kahn was elected to succeed him as chief rabbi of Paris, thereby filling the now open position. To allow this to happen, the rules had to be relaxed because at that point Kahn had not yet reached the prescribed age of thirty. Crucial to Kahn's election to this office was the acclaim accorded to the thesis he wrote at the Séminaire Israélite, "L'Esclavage selon la Bible et le Talmud" (Slavery according to the Bible and the Talmud), in which he assembled and analyzed a massive amount of ancient Jewish and non-Jewish material.[28]

During the two decades of Kahn's leadership, the Jewish community of Paris greatly prospered, economically and intellectually. Kahn cofounded and served as an early leader of the Société des Études Juives (society of Jewish studies), a scholarly group devoted to research and publication in the fields of religion, culture, and history of the Jewish people as well as biblical exegesis. Beyond such academic endeavors, Kahn was a central figure in raising and administering funds for Jewish hospitals, schools, and other community institutions.

When Lazare Isidor died in 1889, Zadoc Kahn was unanimously elected to take his place as chief rabbi of France. He would hold the position until his own death in 1905.

Kahn officially assumed his new office in March 1890. He then continued the activities that had endeared him to the Jews of Paris, now at national and international levels. He organized relief efforts on behalf of Jews expelled from Russia, especially for those who now lived in France. He also actively supported the Alliance Israélite Universelle, a Paris-based international Jewish organization that promoted the ideals of Jewish self-sufficiency, especially through the establishment of French-language schools throughout the Middle East and in African countries bordering on the Mediterranean Sea.

A tribute to Kahn in the *New-York Daily Tribune* (1899) heralded his assiduous nature:

> He lives with his wife and family in a modest house in the Rue Saint-Georges, adjoining the sumptuous synagogue, the main entrance to which is on the Rue de la Victoire. He is a hard worker. As early as 6 o'clock in the morning he is at his desk in his library. He is small in stature and of slight, wiry build. His eyes are dark and penetrating, and they sparkle behind his spectacles. Besides his sacerdotal occupations, M. Zadoc Kahn devotes much time to numerous charitable works relating to hospitals, schools and mutual aid societies. He also takes an active share in the administration of the vast charitable funds bequeathed by Baroness Hirsch, by Mme. Furtado-Heine and by various members of the Rothschild family.[29]

Kahn was unwavering in his support of Alfred Dreyfus, at whose wedding he officiated shortly after becoming chief rabbi of France. He testified on Dreyfus's behalf at the court-martial proceedings, and, against the suggestions of many of his advisers, he repeatedly and publicly denounced what he saw as unfair coverage in the general press. "Judaism has no reason to be ashamed of either its past or its present," he declared in his characteristically forthright manner, "and this should be stated frankly and courageously."[30]

Kahn also found the time and energy to organize and participate in two other major activities: the multivolume *Jewish Encyclopedia* and a new French-language version of the Hebrew Bible—concomitant with a children's edition, *Bible de la jeunesse* (The Bible for children).[31]

La Bible du rabbinat français (The Bible of the French rabbinate) was first published in 1899. Subsequent editions appeared through 1906.[32]

As France's chief rabbi, Kahn persuaded other French rabbis to participate in this project. He supervised their work in addition to translating some books, such as Psalms and Job, himself. Kahn and his collaborators sought to present a straightforward translation of the Hebrew in a style that would be accessible to most members of the Jewish community. Moreover, the editions they produced were within an affordable price range for their target audience.

Individuals who had felt intimated by the style and lengthy, if erudite, annotations of Cahen's magnum opus welcomed this new, more popular approach to a French-language edition of the Hebrew Bible. Its sponsorship and supervision by the well-regarded chief rabbi added to its appeal and sales.

In its obituary of Kahn, the *New York Times* (of January 7, 1906) had this to say:

> Scarcely five years ago [Chief Rabbi Zadoc Kahn] assumed the supervision of "A Complete Translation of the Bible from the Original Text." Of this monumental labor he was not only the inspiration, but he did more of the work than anyone else. His translations of "The Psalms" and the "The Book of David" are excellent pieces of work, remarkable for their clearness and faithfulness to the text. And his version of "The Book of Job" brings home to the reader as never before the sombre eloquence of that masterpiece.

Italian

Jewish translations of the Bible into Italian date back to the medieval period. Subsequent versions came out a bit later, the second half of the sixteenth and the early seventeenth centuries—despite some criticism that such versions might cause the young (especially girls) to gravitate from sacred to secular Italian literature.[33]

Samuel David Luzzatto's *Ḥamishah ḥumshe Torah: 'im ha-hafṭarot 'im tirgum Italḳi* (The Five Books of the Torah with the *Haftarot* in Italian Translation)

The most famous Italian-language Bibles for Jews were the work of Samuel David Luzzatto (1800–65), also known as Shadal.[34]

Luzzatto was exposed to learning at a very early age. Leaders in both traditional Jewish and secular learning guided his education. His father, a well-known talmudist who made his living as a furniture maker, was one of his earliest teachers in subjects relating to traditional Judaism.[35] Luzzatto's secular studies soon encompassed classical and modern languages as well as science.

Like many other translators featured in this chapter, Luzzatto was something of a prodigy. At age eleven he began to write a Hebrew grammar in the Italian language and to compose exegetical notes on the Pentateuch. That same year, 1811/12, he translated into Hebrew *The Life of Aesop*, an anonymous work written in Greek around the second century CE. Even earlier, he had resolved to write a commentary on the book of Job to replace other studies, which he found deficient. Within the next three years, he embarked on a serious study of Aramaic, determined that the vowels and accents of the Masoretic Text were posttalmudic, and dated the *Zohar* (the key text of the Jewish mystical tradition) to a fairly late date because of its handling of these vowels and accents. These were no small achievements for a young man who had not yet turned fourteen![36]

Luzzatto went on to produce scholarly works as well as poems in excellent Hebrew. Between 1816 and 1817 he emerged as a biblical critic by suggesting textual changes at Ecclesiastes 10:1 and Habakkuk 2:16.[37] In 1829 he was appointed as a professor at the newly established Collegio Rabbinico in Padua, the world's first modern rabbinical seminary.[38] At this post he wrote a number of articles and books and maintained a substantial correspondence with almost all of the other leading Jewish scholars of his day.[39]

Well versed in all aspects of philosophy, from the ancient Greeks to his contemporaries, Luzzatto came to distrust those thinkers who deviated from his view of the truth. He censured even Maimonides for being a follower of Aristotle. Abraham Ibn Ezra and Spinoza were the targets of even more severe criticism. He much preferred Rashi to all others.[40]

For Luzzatto, the teachings of biblical and talmudic Judaism encompassed the truth. But these teachings, he asserted, were not immune to critical study; rather, application of scientific methods only enhanced their value, by allowing their innate truth to come to the fore. Thus he believed it was necessary to possess knowledge of ancient languages, including Syriac, Samaritan, and Aramaic, for the full explication of biblical and other early Jewish texts. He became a leading member of the Wissenschaft des Judentums movement, which sought to analyze all aspects of Jewish literature and culture through the use of critical, scientific methods in keeping with those developed for the study of other scholarly fields.[41]

In the mid-nineteenth century, he began to publish Italian translations of various biblical books. His Italian translation of Job appeared in 1853. From 1855 to 1867 he worked on an Italian translation of the book of Isaiah, along with a Hebrew commentary. During a portion of that period, from 1858 to 1860, he published his Italian translation of the Pentateuch and the *haftarot*. These were followed, after his death, by publication of his commentaries on the Pentateuch (in 1871) and on Jeremiah, Ezekiel, Proverbs, and Job (in 1876).[42]

His strong and sometimes seemingly contradictory opinions course through these works. Take, for example, his views on authorship and interpretation of the Hebrew Bible. Although Luzzatto was not a fundamentalist, he firmly believed that Moses was the author of the Torah (though he did not insist that all of the Psalms were written by David himself).[43] He did not take the first chapters of Genesis literally, but nonetheless insisted that they not be treated as mere allegory but rather as model lessons from which readers could derive essential moral and ethical values.[44]

Sometimes, Luzzatto's extensive analysis of portions of the Hebrew Bible led to what might be termed radical conclusions—as was the case with his argument that the author of Ecclesiastes was not King Solomon but rather a later author named Kohelet. Other times, Luzzatto came down on the side of tradition, such as when he argued for a single author for the entire book of Isaiah against what was fast becoming the scholarly orthodoxy of two Isaiahs: the first responsible for chapters 1–39 and the second for the remainder of the book. Here he felt strongly that denying authorship of the whole book to the eighth-century BCE prophet was tantamount to denying to Isaiah the full scope of divinely inspired prophecy.[45]

He also held that it was essential to maintain a firm belief in revelation and to treat the Torah text as sacred. Nonetheless, on occasion he did not follow the traditional wording as reflected in Masoretic notations and in the Talmud. In these instances, he was often guided by the *Targums*, with which he was acquainted from an early age.

All of this is in keeping with what distinguished Jewish scholar Israel Abrahams speaks of as two of

> the ten principles by which [Luzzatto] was guided [as] clearly adumbrated in the introduction to his commentary on the Book of Isaiah. . . . 9. In rabbinic interpretations . . . the vowels and the accents do not always indicate the actual meaning ascribed by the ancients to the verses in question. They often deliberately deviate, for their own reasons, from the true sense of the passages. . . . [and] 10. Although Holy Writ was treated at all times with the utmost veneration, it was inevitable that some variant readings, of which only one can be correct, should have crept in here and there.[46]

Differences of opinion on such matters led to instances of harsh exchanges between Luzzatto and some of his correspondents.[47] Characteristically, he accused them of going too far down the road of rationalism; they, in turn, saw him as only half-hearted in his acceptance of the scientific methods he professed to espouse.

A sampling of his commentary reveals the expansive ways in which he expressed his exegetical insights. For example, at Genesis 1:27 ("And God created man in His image [*tzelem*], in the image [*tzelem*] of God He created him; male and female He created them") he argued that *tzelem* does not signify the form of the body, as others held, but rather the likeness of something. Thus, the expression *tzelem Elohim* meant that humans resembled God because they possessed all of God's attributes, whereas other animals had only a single godly quality (e.g., the hard work of the ant or the chastity of the dove).[48] At Exodus 15:2, part of the Song at the Sea,

> The LORD is my strength and might
> He is become my deliverance
> This is my God and I will enshrine Him
> The God of my father, and I will exalt Him,

Luzzatto discoursed at some length on the uses and possible origins of parallelism in biblical poetry.[49]

Like other scholars of his day, Luzzatto expended considerable energy on illuminating nuanced differences in terms that were largely synonymous. Thus, while both *t-w-r* and *r-g-l* were verbs meaning "to spy," Luzzatto elucidated how the former had a positive connotation in the Bible (as in Ezek. 20:6, "I [God] swore to them to take them out of the land of Egypt into a land flowing with milk and honey, a land which I had sought out [translating the root *t-w-r*] for them, the fairest of all lands"), while the latter was consistently used in a pejorative sense (see, for example, the multiple uses of the root *r-g-l* in Gen. 42, with reference to Joseph's brother, which NJPS renders as "spy"). He noted, too, that while Hebrew *yare'* meant "to fear," its precise shade of meaning changed in accordance with the preposition or sign of the accusative that followed it.[50]

Just as Luzzatto had proposed emendations in the biblical text at Habakkuk 2:16 and Ecclesiastes 10:1 while still in his teens, later he saw need for textual emendation in other places outside of the Torah, such as at Isaiah 10:25, 11:15, and 30:6. He did not believe that such errors had entered inadvertently into the Torah, which to him was transmitted more diligently than other portions of the Hebrew Bible.

Given his conservative, but not fundamentalist, understanding of the biblical text, Luzzatto proposed emendations only after considered deliberation. He insisted that the received text should be altered only when it was absolutely essential to the proper understanding of the text and only after a full consideration of cognate languages and all other possible alternatives.[51]

Ultimately, Luzzatto's approach to the Bible exemplified a middle way that sought to synthesize the old (traditional) and the new (scientific). He hoped that in future times people would say, "Shadal made criticism compatible with belief; it alone satisfied the 'needs of the generation.'"[52]

Hungarian

Before the mid-nineteenth century, Hungarian Jews without knowledge of Hebrew had to use Yiddish or German versions or Bible translations produced under Protestant or Catholic auspices. That would change in the 1840s, when Mór Bloch produced a Jewish version of the Bible, *Mózes öt könyve magyarra fordította és jegyzetekkel fölvilágította* ([Mór Bloch] translated and annotated the Pentateuch), in Hungarian.

Mór Bloch/Ballagi's *Mózes öt könyve magyarra fordította és jegyzetekkel fölvilágította* ([Mór Bloch] Translated and Annotated the Pentateuch)

Mór Bloch (1815–91) was born in the Hungarian village of Inócz, in the county of Zemplén. He received his earliest instruction in Bible and Talmud from his father, a tenant farmer. Other childhood memories were not so positive: His father was imprisoned for a year for debt, and on occasion his mother had to search for wild berries in the forest to feed the family. So it was that at an early age Bloch learned to take care of himself, even when this entailed living off charity.[53]

An ambitious student, he was studying at two yeshivas by the time he was sixteen. He then supported himself as a tutor, while simultaneously gaining his first acquaintance with Greek and Latin. He also taught himself Hungarian.[54]

In his early twenties, he attended lectures at the University of Pest and also wrote newspaper articles championing the then pressing cause of Hungarian nationalism as distinct from German culture (a process that came to be known as "Magyarization").[55]

In the fall of 1839, in the midst of this intellectual and historical ferment, Bloch left Hungary for Paris, where he pursued a degree in engineering—an opportunity still denied to him, as a Jew, in his homeland. Meanwhile, in Hungary, support was growing for the emancipation of the Jews; the issue would be brought before the Diet, the Hungarian Parliament, the following year. In Paris, Bloch wrote a pamphlet, "On the Jews," which gave prominence to achievements by Jews that he viewed as beneficial to society (in this case, especially Hungarian society) at large. Shortly thereafter, at the urging of influential individuals, he returned to Hungary to devote himself to the Magyarization of the Jews.[56]

Bloch quickly gained recognition and acceptance as the foremost Jewish intellectual champion for the cause of Hungarian Jewry. From this platform, Bloch called on his fellow Jews to embrace the Magyar (that is, Hungarian) language as an essential element in their own emancipation.

To further this goal, he proposed and carried out a wide variety of educational projects. Among the first of these was *Mózes öt könyve magyarra fordította és jegyzetekkel fölvilágította*, his translation of the Pentateuch into Hungarian with commentary and philological notes, published in segments from 1840 to 1841.[57] He was then only twenty-five years old.

As the first Jewish translation of the Pentateuch (or any other portion of the Hebrew Bible) into Hungarian, Bloch's work attracted the attention of a number of individuals within the Jewish community and beyond. Along with many of his other initiatives, this version of the Torah, to which he later added Joshua, aimed to promote a strong sense of Hungarian identity among those in his target audience. As is clear from the commentary that accompanied his Bible translation, Bloch also promoted (and, in his estimation, exemplified) the compatibility between Jewish and Hungarian conceptions of the self and community.

On September 5, 1840, after Genesis appeared, Bloch was appointed a corresponding member of the Hungarian Academy of Science—a singular honor that recognized his patriotic and scientific endeavors.[58] He was the first Jew to have an official connection with the academy; full membership followed in 1858.[59]

Over the next four years, Bloch proceeded to produce other translated and original works: a prayer book, a translation of the biblical book of Joshua with commentary, a pedagogical text on teaching the Hungarian language to kindergarten students, a Magyar grammar, and a German-Hungarian dictionary.[60]

This extraordinary literary output did not exhaust Bloch's energies. During this same period he issued a public appeal to establish a Hungarian Jewish teachers' seminary. Such a seminary, he believed, would ensure a viable parochial educational system whereby Jewish students would continue to receive instruction in the Jewish religion and its moral teachings. Some influential members of the community supported his endeavor, but in general he faced indifference.[61]

It was apparently in response to this rejection that Bloch left Hungary for Germany to study theology. In 1843, while in Germany, he converted to Lutheranism.

Four years later he changed his name to Moritz Ballagi.

He remained a Protestant throughout the rest of his life. Ultimately he had a distinguished career as a Protestant theologian and champion of the Hungarian language and culture. His grammars, lexicons, and readers were influential in achieving the Magyarization of Hungary. Within this context, much of his work remains highly valued to this day.[62]

It is not clear what motivated Bloch/Ballagi to convert to Christianity. Some of his critics claimed that they had already discerned hints of distinctively Christian biblical interpretation in his translation and commentary on the Pentateuch. Others held that Bloch saw conversion as a means to achieve greater prominence and power than would have been possible had he remained a practicing Jew.[63]

We can only speculate on the possible course of his prodigious career had his ideas for Jewish parochial schools met with a more favorable response. Personally I think he would have continued his work on Bible translation, bequeathing to Hungarian Jewry a complete version of the Bible. It is also probable that he would have put all of the institutions associated with Hungarian Jews on surer and more profound foundations.

Still, Bloch/Ballagi did not entirely abandon ties to his Jewish past. He continued to use Yiddish in his diary for many years after his conversion. In later life, he published books on the Hebrew language and was known for his generosity toward promising Jewish students. He was also well thought of by Ignác Goldziher, a leading Hungarian Jewish intellectual of the late nineteenth and early twentieth centuries. Bloch/Ballagi reacted with bitterness, we are told, when he saw his own son become an antisemite.[64]

It would take another half century after the publication of Bloch's Pentateuch before the Jewish Hungarian Literary Society published a complete Bible translation in Hungarian, in four volumes (1898–1907). In addition to incorporating translations of biblical books Bloch did not work on, this version featured new Hungarian renderings of the Pentateuch and Joshua, to which Bloch had indeed devoted much work many decades earlier.

It is likely that Bloch's abandonment of Judaism in favor of Christianity had something to do with the replacement of his version by new renderings. At the same time, this new generation of translators did bring to fruition the vision that had initially motivated Bloch.

Russian

Throughout the nineteenth century, by far the largest number of Jews lived in Russia, especially in the western Polish and Lithuanian territories that Russia had acquired at the end of the previous century. Millions of Jews were subject to Russian law, which, especially in their case, was restrictive and punitive.

While Jews and Judaism in these times and locales did not generally fare well, to say the least, for brief periods vibrant Jewish society co-existed with repressive conditions.[65] A sliver of that vibrancy can be seen in Jewish translations of the Bible into Russian.

Similar to patterns we have seen elsewhere, in Russia Jewish Bible translation began with the enterprise of a single individual—Leon Mandelstamm—and only reached fruition years later, as a result of collective, collaborative endeavors.

Leon Mandelstamm's Russian Translation of the Pentateuch (1872)

Leon (Aryeh Löb) Mandelstamm (1809–89) was born in present-day Lithuania. His father, a merchant, was very much influenced by the progressive views associated with the Enlightenment in Germany, which he frequently visited during his business travels. He brought back home liberal German ideas and many German-language books. Under the tutelage of his father and older brothers, Mandelstamm became thoroughly conversant with traditional Judaism and with secular learning.

Not surprisingly, Mandelstamm's breadth of knowledge and support for progressive causes were not well received within the mostly traditional Jewish communities of Lithuania. Ultimately, he found an intellectual home at the University of Saint Petersburg, from which he received the equivalent of a bachelor's degree in philosophy at age thirty-five. He was the first Jew in Russia to obtain this degree.[66]

For a little more than a decade after his graduation, Mandelstamm headed a rabbinical commission that the Russian government had charged with establishing a uniform system of education for Russian Jewry. Meanwhile, he was writing, editing, and publishing books for use in the schools; establishing new institutions, including rabbinical schools; and corresponding with important Haskalah (Jewish Enlightenment) figures and poets, some of whom he was able to hire as teachers.[67] Among his projects during this period were texts accompanied by German translation, including selections from the Mishnah, an anthology of Maimonides' writing, and the Bible, supplemented by the *Biur* of Moses Mendelssohn and his collaborators.[68] This latter text ran to twenty-four volumes when it was published in 1851. Jews themselves had provided most of the financial support for these endeavors through a candle tax; it was Mandelstamm's responsibility to disperse these funds.

In 1857 Mandelstamm's opponents forced him to retire from this position. Some of them accused him of misappropriating money from the candle-tax fund.[69] He then tried his hand at a number of financial enterprises, generally without any great success.

He was far more successful in his literary pursuits, the majority of which he undertook in Berlin. It was there, for example, that he prepared his Russian translation of the Pentateuch, the first edition of which appeared in 1862.

Initially, copies of this version were not allowed in Russia because of a general prohibition against Bible editions that were not approved by the Russian Orthodox Church. But in 1872, through the intervention of the Society for the Promotion of Enlightenment among the Jews of Russian (OPE), Mandelstamm finally received permission to import and reprint his Bible translation in Russia, so long as it was accompanied by the Hebrew text. Bound in the same volume as this second edition of the Pentateuch in Russian was Mandelstamm's rendering of Psalms. In this form, Mandelstamm's Russian rendering circulated among Jews.[70]

Members of OPE, and more generally Jewish supporters of the Enlightenment, were enthusiastic about Mandelstamm's efforts to translate the Bible from Hebrew into Russian. For them, it was important for Jews to enter into society at large. To do so, acquaintance with, if not fluency in, the language of the dominant culture was necessary. This same impetus propelled other translators before and after Mandelstamm, such as Mendelssohn and Margolis.

But support by like-minded thinkers was not enough to ensure the fiscal viability of this project. Sales lagged, likely as a result of Mandelstamm's style, which resulted in an awkward Russian much influenced by the Hebrew source text. Foreseeing this criticism, Mandelstamm termed his version a "preliminary work" that would be serviceable "until a future translation of the Bible could be undertaken [for Jews] in a more elegant Russian language."[71]

Near the end of his life, Mandelstamm returned to Saint Petersburg, where he spent his last years in poverty and without any public acclaim. Only after his death and burial in a pauper's grave did the Jewish community belatedly recognize his achievements: He then received a proper burial in the Jewish cemetery of Saint Petersburg.

Interestingly, his extensive library was taken to the United States, where it was purchased by the New York Public Library. To this day, the library recognizes Mandelstamm's collection as the nucleus of its extensive holdings in Jewish studies.[72]

Judah Leib Gordon and Colleagues' 1875 Russian Translation of the Pentateuch

In almost immediate response to the criticism surrounding Mandelstamm's translation, Judah Leib (or Leon) Gordon (1830–92), a leading Hebrew poet of the Jewish Enlightenment,[73] embarked with colleagues on a subsequent Bible translation into Russian. Their goal was to provide a Jewish version in what Mandelstamm had called "a more elegant Russian language." They would largely succeed.

Gordon and his colleagues were well placed to produce such a version. Like Mandelstamm, Gordon was born into a prosperous household. His education, entrusted to the leading Jewish scholars in his hometown of Vilnius, Lithuania, also resulted in prodigious academic achievement at an early age, although in his case solely within the realm of traditional Jewish texts.[74] When his family's financial situation took a turn for the worse, Gordon embarked on a self-designed course of independent studies. In this way, he deepened his knowledge of traditional Jewish texts and expanded his intellectual horizons through exposure to secular literature and foreign languages. He also enjoyed close contacts with leading Jewish Enlightenment figures.

Like Mandelstamm, Gordon then pursued a career in Jewish education. He served as a school teacher in several towns—but, like Mandelstamm, was not content with being a classroom teacher alone. He began writing poetry in different styles, some in a Hebrew style that has been justly described as classical and pure. In this sense, he became a leader in the modern revival of Hebrew language and culture.

He was also praised as a gifted writer of prose. His often satirical works took aim at those he condemned as fanatics within the Jewish community as well as those who attacked Jews and Judaism from the outside. He typically placed his compositions within a Jewish historical context, covering periods from the biblical to his own day.[75]

In 1872, after about twenty years in Jewish education, Gordon was invited to Saint Petersburg to serve as secretary of OPE, the very organization that was then supporting Mandelstamm's efforts. There he continued his literary productivity and also became active in communal affairs.

During this period, the traditional wing of the Saint Petersburg Jewish community and the proponents of the Haskalah were habitually clashing, deepening intracommunal rifts. The newest dispute concerned the appointment of a rabbi. Such appointments generally involved individuals such as Gordon, who, as secretary of OPE, was recognized as a leading supporter of Haskalah.

On this occasion, Gordon was a main target of the traditionalists. They accused him, as a leader of reform, of political crimes, including participation in a failed attempt to assassinate Tsar Alexander II. After investigation by governmental and communal authorities, Gordon was vindicated. For the rest of his life he would enjoy the esteem not only of his fellow Jews (especially those who shared his enthusiasm for the Enlightenment) but also of the Russian government.[76]

It was under the aegis of OPE that Gordon, in collaboration with Jonah Gerstein and Lev Levanda, produced a new translation of the Pentateuch into Russian, which first appeared in 1875.[77]

During the process, conflicts arose between Gordon and his two equally strong-willed collaborators, both of whom considered themselves better prepared than Gordon when it came to niceties of the Russian language. After all, Gerstein and Levanda had collaborated on what became the standard Russian textbook for Jewish schoolchildren; additionally, Levanda was a very popular writer of Russian-language novels.[78] Ultimately, Levanda was forced out.[79] The completed version would probably have read quite differently had Levanda remained.

In addition to matters of style, the 1875 translation may be said to have represented an advance over Mandelstamm's earlier version in another important area: It followed Jewish exegetical traditions more rigorously and fully than the 1872 edition.[80] This was not a problem for the Russian Orthodox priests who oversaw all publications relating to the Bible, for the 1875 translation was marketed exclusively to Jews.

The 1875 translation sold fairly well among adherents of the Jewish Enlightenment, who composed most of its target audience. It would also serve as a basis for Russian Jewry's next foray into Russian-language Bible translating: the 1901–2 version prepared by a commission under the leadership of Yehoshua Shteinberg, a distinguished Hebraist and biblical scholar.[81]

Final Thoughts

This chapter features a remarkably rich cast of about a dozen characters—or translators—with a somewhat larger number of their Bible versions (many translators having published more than one edition of their translation or having prepared separate translations of different portions of the Hebrew Bible). They were all men of their time and place. Since circumstances of chronology and geography vary to a greater or lesser degree, each of these individuals stands out as unique. And yet they—as with other Jewish translators—share some characteristics that are worth considering here.

First is the remarkably high level of education each of these translators attained, formally through admission to universities and other institutions of higher learning, and less formally through contact with erudite fathers and other tutors. Where we know the details, this education came to include both traditional Jewish topics and approaches as well as methods and material we associate with the Enlightenment. In other words, these were high achievers from the get-go, whose Bible versions reflected thoughtful interaction with multiple traditions and trends.

Second, almost all of these men were deeply involved in their respective communities—Jewish and typically also non-Jewish. It follows then that Bible translating was an element—sometimes the most important aspect, more often one of several significant activities—that identified these individuals as leading Jews and Jewish leaders. Usually they were engaged in the world of education: primary schools through universities. Teachers, administrators, authors of textbooks and syllabi—they performed these tasks and many others in support of their belief that education, often thought of as some sort of balance between religious and secular subjects, was vital to what we speak of today as Jewish continuity.

Finally, then, we come to the recognition that no single activity of these multifaceted men can be understood in isolation. One or more versions of their Bibles were part and parcel of their preparing Jews, as individuals and communities, for greater participation in a world that was slowly, if unevenly, opening up to them. Propelling these significant achievements was a shared vision of disseminating Jewish traditions in the language of the larger society of which they were a part.

6

English-Language Versions

During the 1992–93 academic year, I was teaching at Oxford as a Skirball Fellow of the Oxford Centre for Postgraduate Hebrew Studies. Among the benefits was the opportunity to spend hours exploring the vast holdings at the Bodleian Library and other repositories. There, I become deeply acquainted with Anglo-Jewish Bible translations—that is, translations of the Bible into English by British Jews. I proceeded to investigate all these translations—from the latter part of the eighteenth century until the beginning of the twentieth century—tracking down details about the translators and the circumstances in which they worked.[1] It was a delight to delve deeply into the translations' cultural history and relationship to earlier and contemporary developments within biblical studies.

One day in the spring of 1993, if I remember correctly, I was in the library working through a folder containing miscellaneous items connected with British Jewry. One pamphlet was dated to the end of 1776. In the middle of the winter of that year, with the American Revolutionary War going badly from the British point of view, King George III appointed December 13 (equivalent to 3 Tevet 5537) as a fast day. This fast, along with activities held at churches and synagogues, was intended to solicit divine support for the British cause. Displaying their patriotism, London's Synagogue of the Portuguese and Spanish Jews held a special service in which the congregation's minister, Moses Cohen d'Azevedo, offered prayers and a sermon, all incorporating texts "from the original Hebrew and Spanish into English" (this quotation is taken from the pamphlet itself). These texts included biblical material. A careful examination of the wording of all the Hebrew Bible passages in English showed that it was identical to the King James Version (KJV).

Another pamphlet I discovered was printed in conjunction with an event held on Friday, March 26, 1790, in which the Great Jews' Synagogue was dedicated (or, rather, rededicated) at Saint James Duke's Place in London. Contained within "A Song and Praise to be Performed" on that occasion were the following psalms: 91, 30, 24, 84, 122, 132, and 100.[2] The English text of these psalms, prepared by Jewish translator and poet David Levi, was a new rendering of these biblical compositions, although it was clearly recognizable as a revision of KJV. Since distinctive English versions of the Bible were appearing by and for Jews precisely at this time, and since David Levi is identified with several of these versions, the Bodleian's preservation of these two publications is both heuristic and serendipitous.[3]

Prior to the Late Eighteenth Century

The first edition of KJV appeared in 1611. On the basis of the above-mentioned 1776 pamphlet, it appears that for well over a century and a half, when British Jews needed an English text of the Hebrew Bible, they made use of KJV. That said, we may need to reduce the time frame for such reliance, given that Jews had been expelled from England in the thirteenth century, and were not officially re-admitted until the mid-1600s.[4]

Nonetheless, a basic question remains: Did that first generation of British Jews and their descendants make exclusive use of KJV when it became expedient for them to consult Scripture in English? One of the very few scholars to have looked at this topic is Raphael Loewe. His observations lead to an affirmative "yes":

> There can be little doubt that, as Menasseh b. Israel's Spanish Pentateuch remorsely slipped into the penumbra of third-generation sentimentalism, English sephardim (most of whom will have needed a crib for Hebrew) will have been relying on the A.V. [or KJV]. Amongst Ashkenazim, the printed Yiddish translation had been used almost exclusively by women; and as, during the second half of the eighteenth century, poor Jewish immigrants from north-eastern Europe climbed through two or three generations into the Anglo-Jewish *bourgeoisie*, residual attitudes and a different educational philosophy will, to some extent, have delayed (but could not prevent) their resort to a Bible in English, after real competence in Hebrew had been lost. The point that is here being made is that English-speaking Jewry distinguishes itself from the Jewries of other countries, by its acceptance, apparently without significant protest or misgivings, of the national vernacular Bible of its Christian environment; it produced nothing comparable to Mendelssohn's German translation until the American Jewish version of the early twentieth century.[5]

There is scant documentary or literary evidence to back up Loewe's reconstruction, but I have no doubt that he is absolutely correct in his main assertion: When English Jews of this period (whether of recent or more established domicile in England) sought out an English-language version of the Bible, they relied on KJV. From researching the aforementioned documents as well as other primary documentation for this period, I have been able to isolate the timeframe when British Jews began, ever so tentatively, to move away from what I might call "the KJV-only tradition."

Christian Hebraism and the King James Version

Before turning to late eighteenth-century developments, let's cast an eye backward to the early seventeenth century, when KJV was first produced.

Harry M. Orlinsky, editor of The Jewish Publication Society's current version (NJPS), once remarked that all translations of the Hebrew Bible are basically Jewish—except one, which he chose not to reveal. Since few Jews were lawfully resident in England in 1611, when the first edition of KJV was published, and no Jews were on any of the six KJV translation "companies" (what today would be called committees or teams),[6] we might conjecture that perhaps this is the translation Orlinsky had in mind. But Orlinsky, an astute historian of Bible translations, surely did not have KJV in mind, as the evidence that follows amply demonstrates.

Although it is true that no Jews served as KJV translators—all, in fact, were Protestant Christians—many members of the Old Testament KJV teams were nonetheless deeply steeped in both the Hebrew language and the exegetical traditions of Judaism. In the words of one specialist, "Those gifted in Hebrew among the [KJV] translators are almost too many to number."[7] These Christian Hebraists, as scholars refer to them, embraced Jewish textual interpretations so enthusiastically that they led the KJV teams charged with preparing the Old Testament translation to adopt Jewish readings already incorporated into earlier English-language versions and to seek out others on their own.

As for sources of these readings, the Jewish exegete and grammarian David Kimchi (also known as Radak; 1160–1235) was most influential. As one example, an analysis of the first fifteen chapters of the book of Isaiah in KJV reveals a high number of English renderings that reflect Kimchi's interpretations. While, in most cases, KJV shares these interpretations with earlier English versions, especially the Geneva Bible, in at least a dozen instances (e.g., "the chaines" in Isa. 3:19, "and their honourable men are famished" in 5:13, "they shall lay their hands upon Edom and Moab" in 11:14, and "the golden city" in 14:4) KJV's dependence on Kimchi is unique.[8] Of course, traditional Christian theological considerations could on occasion prove more powerful than Kimchi.[9]

Of the Christian Hebraist translators, among the most notable were John Rainolds and Miles Smith. Both were members of the First Oxford Company, charged with rendering the Hebrew text from Isaiah through Malachi, under the direction of the company head, John Harding, Regius Professor of Hebrew at Oxford. At his death in 1607 (midway through the translation process), Rainolds bequeathed to Corpus Christi College, Oxford, a number of Bibles, among them an edition of *Miqra'ot Gedolot* (lit. "Great Scriptures," often called the Rabbinic Bible) first brought out in 1517 by the prolific Bible publisher Daniel Bomberg. The quantity and quality of these Bibles, which had been in Rainolds's personal library until his death, demonstrate the depth of his commitment to Christian Hebraism.

Many print editions of the Hebrew Bible had preceded the year 1500. The first of these, dated to 1477, was an edition of the Psalms accompanied by Kimchi's commentary. It had probably been printed in Bologna, where the first Pentateuch appeared in 1482. Subsequently, during the 1490s, members of the Soncino family (who derived their name from the northern Italian town where they had settled), prominent publishers from the 1480s through the mid-sixteenth century, issued the first complete Hebrew Bibles at various sites in northern Italy. The Soncinos were especially noted for their easily readable and aesthetically appealing fonts, including Hebrew fonts that they pioneered.

Of even greater historical significance were the Rabbinic Bibles, which included not only the Hebrew text, but also Targumic versions of the Torah, Prophets, and Psalms, as well as commentaries by Rashi, Kimchi, Ibn Ezra, and other authorities. As noted above, Daniel Bomberg published the two earliest Rabbinic Bibles, the first in 1517–18, and the second, with many errors corrected, in 1525. Christian scholars, including the KJV translators and those responsible for earlier English-language versions, made extensive use of these Rabbinic Bibles, along with the earlier publications by Soncino, in either the original forms of these Bibles or in later editions.[10]

Rainolds's bequests to his fellow scholars—which also included the works of Maimonides, Nachmanides, Joseph ben Gorion, Joseph Karo, and David Kimchi, among others[11]—reveal how highly these Christian Hebraists valued the scholarship of Jewish biblical commentators.

Rainolds was no recent convert to the study and appreciation of Hebrew. In a letter dated July 4, 1577, he spoke approvingly of Hebrew study: "I thank God [that I] continued a student in it. Wherefore the Word of God, and that, if it may be, out of the very wel-spring, not out of the brook of translations (if I may so tearme them) must be diligently read."[12]

Miles Smith, who at the time of the translation was a canon, or priest, at Hereford, joined Rainolds at Corpus Christi to work on the Prophets. His surviving books, housed at the Hereford Cathedral Library, reveal that many of his tools as a biblical translator were Hebrew texts: David Kimchi's *Sefer Michlol*, comprising a Hebrew grammar and dictionary printed in Venice by Daniel Bomberg (1525 and 1529, respectively); a second Hebrew dictionary, printed in Basel (1599); Elia Levita's *Lexicon Chaldaicum*, printed by Paul Fagius (1560); and Old Testament Hebrew texts printed by Bomberg and Robert Estienne with accompanying rabbinic commentaries, including those of Ibn Ezra, Rashi, and Kimchi on the twelve Minor Prophets (published throughout the first half of the sixteenth century).[13]

Christian Hebraists tended to esteem the works of Rashi and Kimchi in particular. Rashi was especially appreciated for his efforts to discern and highlight the plain meaning of the text. Kimchi's attraction was largely due to his lexical, linguistic, and grammatical astuteness. So valuable a resource was Kimchi that David Daiches, a distinguished Scottish scholar and literary critic, spoke of him as "the one Jewish commentator who was universally used by Christian scholars at this time."[14]

Kimchi's approach to the biblical text crucially influenced the Christian Hebraist Edward Lively, Regius Professor of Hebrew at Cambridge and head of the First Cambridge Company, which was charged with preparing the translations of the first book of Chronicles through the Song of Solomon. Other KJV translators, acknowledging Kimchi's influence on Lively, likewise frequently drew from the works of this Jewish commentator, as Daiches observes: "For points of grammar and vocabulary [Lively] refers frequently to David Kimchi's *Liber radi-*

cum. Kimchi himself he refers to as 'doctissimus Hebraeus'. . . . Lively's procedure in discovering the exact shade of meaning of Hebrew phrases and idioms is worth noting, for it was probably the method adopted by the other [KJV] translators also. He would cite as many passages as he could where the same phrase occurred and, by careful examination and comparison, draw a conclusion."[15]

As we shall see in greater detail, Hebrew studies were rediscovered in England during the sixteenth century. A powerful impetus for this rediscovery came from humanistic and Protestant circles on the Continent, and particularly such key figures as Johann Reuchlin, Santes Pagninus, and Sebastian Münster. Following the example of these Continental figures, learned Englishmen adopted the study of Hebrew philology, which the first Protestants had regarded as part of the science of theology, thus laying durable foundations for the growth of Hebrew studies in Great Britain.[16]

Knowing Hebrew enabled these individuals to read the Bible in the original and to appreciate the exegetical comments of postbiblical Jewish scholars. This made the contribution of medieval rabbis all the more valuable in solving textual difficulties. Further, in their efforts to maintain a distinct theological position from that of Roman Catholics, who made exclusive use of the Latin text of the Vulgate, Protestants enlisted Hebrew as a tool in doctrinal debates with Catholic apologists. As it turns out, on more than one occasion Protestants adduced medieval Jewish commentaries to support their interpretation.

The first recognized teacher of Hebrew in Tudor England was Robert Wakefield, who initially taught at Cambridge (in the 1520s) and then at Oxford (beginning in 1530). By the mid-1540s the establishment of Regius Chairs put Hebrew teaching on a sound financial basis at both universities.[17]

By 1600 at least a few schools were providing their senior pupils with the necessary groundwork for further study in the Hebrew language. Two of the most prominent were Merchant Taylors' School and Westminster School. It was at Merchant Taylors' School that bishop and scholar Lancelot Andrewes, who led the first Westminster Company, responsible for the first twelve books of the Old Testament (Genesis through 2 Kings), became proficient in Latin, Greek, and Hebrew. Access to Hebrew books accordingly became easier. On the basis of inventories and catalogs, we can judge that, by the end of the sixteenth century, Hebrew Bibles, rabbinic commentaries, and related grammars and dictionaries were all on the market.[18]

Christian Hebraism and Sixteenth-Century Translators

A survey of English Bible translators of the sixteenth century, starting with William Tyndale, provides the necessary background to appreciate the subsequent achievements of KJV translators in the early 1600s. In 1516 the great humanist scholar Erasmus issued a clear statement in favor of vernacular translations of the Bible and called for individuals who were willing to undertake this task.[19] In England, William Tyndale first responded to Erasmus's plea, applying himself to producing an English version of much of the Bible from 1526 to 1534. Tyndale's version would become the basis of later official versions, including KJV.

Although there is no question about Tyndale's literary ability, some scholars have questioned his skills as a translator. Was his Hebrew sufficiently well developed for him to have translated directly from the Masoretic Text? Or did he rely almost entirely on the Vulgate and Luther's German Bible for his rendering of parts of the Old Testament? Does he, or does he not, deserve the title, "the father of English Hebraists"?

Yes, says historian G. Lloyd Jones.

If so, from whom did Tyndale learn Hebrew? Jones admits that a definitive answer is not easy to formulate: "The answers to such questions are hard to find."[20]

Tyndale may have learned some elements of Hebrew at Cambridge after 1515. It is more likely, however, that he did so in Germany. Almost all scholars agree that he had some exposure to Hebrew studies while in Germany. Furthermore, it is "tempting" to think that at Worms, where his New Testament translation was published in 1526 and where he stayed for almost two years, Tyndale came into contact with Jews, and as such had firsthand experience of Jewish exegetical traditions.[21]

Yet there is still a question as to Tyndale's Hebrew proficiency. Clearly, he did rely on previous translators, especially Jerome and Luther. This, however, in and of itself does not speak against his own expertise in Hebrew, since competent-to-accomplished translators often had recourse to earlier versions. Nor should examples of such reliance be allowed to obscure the "fact" that Tyndale was capable of tackling the original text himself.[22] In conclusion, Jones avers: "That [Tyndale] worked from a Hebrew original admits of no doubt, and the fact that he made liberal use of all the aids available to him in translations, grammars and dictionaries, does not detract in any way from his greatness as a biblical scholar."[23]

As it happened, subsequent creators of English-language Bible versions evinced quite a range of Hebrew knowledge. Miles Coverdale (1488–1569), an ecclesiastical reformer who compiled an English-language version published in 1535, knew no Hebrew and had only slight knowledge of Greek. He himself admitted that he was not capable of translating the Bible from the original languages.[24] By contrast, clergyman John Rogers (1500–55), who also produced an English-language version of the Bible (written under the name of "Thomas Matthew"), was an accomplished linguist who had at least some familiarity with Greek, Aramaic, and Hebrew. This remains the case regardless of the fact that "Rogers was essentially an editor," says KJV scholar Gareth Lloyd Jones. "His 'translation' contained little that was original."[25]

Coverdale subsequently produced another version, *The Great Bible*, in 1539. His Hebrew knowledge had not improved by this time, but in this latter work he made use of Sebastian Münster's Hebrew-Latin version, which acknowledged traditional Jewish interpretations. Through this and other means, many distinctively Jewish readings entered into the tradition of the English Bible.

And so, although we cannot credit Coverdale or Rogers with the same depth of interest in Hebrew as Tyndale had demonstrated, it is precisely because they wished to produce the best possible English translations that they came to recognize the importance of the Hebrew language and the value of Rabbinic exegesis. Even though they themselves did not read the works of the Rabbis, they chose to follow scholars who did, thus ensuring the inclusion of Jewish renderings in the text of the English Bible.[26]

When the Roman Catholic monarch Mary assumed the throne of England in 1553, many Protestants left England. A small group eventually settled in Geneva, where they founded an English church in 1555. Study and translation of the Bible were then significant activities in Geneva, and so the English Protestants there decided to produce a new version for themselves.

One of the translators, Anthony Gilby, who had previously written commentaries on Micah and Malachi, was known for his Hebrew learning. At Christ's College in Cambridge, Gilby had acquired "an exact knowledge of the Latin, Greek, and Hebrew languages."[27] Subsequently, his knowledge of Rabbinic exegesis was almost certainly gained through scholarly interactions in the German city of Münster.[28] Indeed, already in his commentary on Micah, he had exhibited considerable ability as a Hebraist, making explicit references to the Hebrew text and discussing the interpretation of individual Hebrew words and phrases.

Another translator, Thomas Sampson, was proficient in linguistics and a close friend of Thomas Harding, then the Regius Professor of Hebrew at Oxford. In all probability this association contributed to Sampson's knowledge of the Hebrew language.

While researchers cannot assuredly identify any of the other Geneva Bible translators as Hebraists, we can "confidently assert that they worked directly from the Hebrew text."[29] This can be seen from statements in the preface to the translation as well as in the translation itself, where on occasion literal renderings of the Hebrew were printed in italics in the margins, so as to explain or justify a new translation in the text itself.

Moreover, in Geneva the translators had ready access to Jewish commentaries—both in Hebrew and through many more recent Latin translations produced by Christians, especially those of Münster, Leo Jud, and Pagninus. "Since all three consciously drew on Jewish exegesis in their search for the plain meaning of the text," wrote Lloyd Jones, "it is hardly surprising that echoes of the Hebraic tradition abound in the Geneva Bible."[30] In the end, he concluded: "From this brief examination of the background against which the Geneva Bible was produced, the conclusion is justified that points of Jewish exegesis found their way if only indirectly, into the version. . . . In addition to [the Christian] mediators of Jewish scholarship . . . the exiles were afforded help and encouragement from John Calvin who, whatever his views on rabbinic exegesis, was no mean Hebraist."[31]

The popularity of the Geneva Bible prompted the commissioning, in England, of a new version—the Bishops' Bible—which would be published in 1568. There is some evidence of Hebrew learning among those chosen for this task. For example, William Alley, an Anglican priest who later became the Bishop of Exeter, was a contemporary of Anthony Gilby at Cambridge. Alley was knowledgeable in Hebrew and known to appreciate Jewish exegetes. In an earlier work, *The Poor Man's Library* (1565), he referred those readers who might need help in answering textual and even doctrinal questions to medieval rabbis and noted Christian Hebraists (especially Nicholas of Lyra, Petrus Galatinus, Münster, and Reuchlin). Of the Hebraists, Alley held Nicholas of Lyra in particularly high esteem, often relying on him for the comments of Jewish exegetes. Still, Alley did not hesitate to challenge all of these authorities when he believed they were insufficiently attentive to doctrinal or linguistic issues.

For the most part, then, Alley appears to have made use of Jewish sources through the work of intermediaries. At the same time, he may have had firsthand (albeit limited) recourse to Rabbinic writings. So, on several occasions he appears to be quoting directly from Jewish sources, including both Rashi and Kimchi.[32]

We cannot speak with certainty regarding the Hebrew expertise of other Bishops' Bible translators. Evidence exists that they were in fact praised by their contemporaries for such expertise, but these Hebraists left no published evidence of their Hebrew abilities. While the libraries of some of these individuals did in fact contain significant volumes related to Jewish studies (as would also be true of many KJV translators), some of these volumes show little indication of having been used very much (either by being thumbed through or annotated). At the least, these individuals evinced some sympathy to Jewish exegetical traditions through the inclusion of these volumes in their personal collections.[33]

Matthew Parker (archbishop of Canterbury from 1559 until his death in 1575), who initiated the project that led to the Bishops' Bible, is listed as the translator for Genesis and Exodus. Although there is nothing concrete to suggest that he was a Hebraist, he was at Cambridge during the 1520s, when several budding Hebraists were also in attendance (per above). Parker's huge personal library, which he bequeathed to Corpus Christi College at Cambridge, contained many works indicative of their owner's interest in Hebrew. His volumes by Reuchlin, Giovanni Pico, Pagninus, and Paul Fagius, as well as his substantial collection of Old Testament commentaries, all featured numerous references to the Hebrew text. A Hebrew manuscript of the Psalter, now at the Bodleian Library in Oxford, had also once belonged to Parker. Moreover, he was a generous patron of other scholars whose work addressed the Hebrew language and Rabbinic exegesis.[34]

From this accumulation of evidence, we see that, right up until the decades just preceding KJV, those involved in the preparation of English-language versions of the Old Testament were generally expected to display an authentic knowledge of and appreciation for the text of the Hebrew Bible itself and the extensive writings of major Jewish biblical exegetes. Some of these British scholars were able to access this Hebrew-language material directly, and even to delve deeply into its finer linguistic or theological points. Others needed to work through Christian intermediaries who wrote in Latin.

In both cases, these translators were seeking "to produce the definitive vernacular version of the Old Testament."[35] From a linguistic as well as a doctrinal and political perspective, such a version was impossible to create without bringing to bear knowledge of biblical Hebrew and postbiblical Jewish exegesis. Contact with actual Jews (which did occasionally occur on the Continent) was not a corresponding necessity.

Beyond these specifics is the larger question of KJV style. Here, we can easily demonstrate that much of what we call "biblical English" is quite literally a reflection of the Hebrew original. Indeed, the KJV translators themselves, exhibiting a humility many of their later supporters lacked, acknowledged their appreciation for and reliance on the Septuagint, the earliest of all Bible translations, which had been prepared by and for Jews beginning in the third century BCE.[36] In fact, scholars now recognize (from David Daiches's careful study) that all English-language Bible translators drew deeply from the Septuagint, directly or indirectly.

Anglo-Jewish Versions in the Eighteenth and Nineteenth Centuries

As the Jewish community grew more rooted in English soil, it sought to cast off at least some of the trappings that identified its members as immigrants. For example, the two pamphlets from the Bodleian mentioned earlier signal that the preparation of an English version of the Hebrew Bible was not an isolated event. English-language sermons and English-Hebrew prayer books were being produced almost simultaneously—and sometimes under the same auspices.[37]

Larger political and social events during the eighteenth and nineteenth centuries would also have their effect on Anglo-Jewish translators and their respective translations. In 1753, Parliament passed the Jewish Naturalization Bill (often simply referred to as "the Jew Bill"), which would have provided the means through which foreign-born Jews could acquire the privileges of native Jews. But popular agitation against this bill led to its almost immediate rescission. In the early decades of the 1800s Jews mounted increasingly effective campaigns to achieve official equality. Along with their allies, they were rewarded in 1833 with the passage of an emancipation bill in the House of Commons, only to see their hopes thwarted by the bill's defeat in the House of Lords.

Outside of Parliament, Jews were received more favorably. In 1833, the same year the emancipation bill failed, the first Jew was admitted to the bar. Two years later, a Jew was appointed as sheriff, another first in English history. In 1837, Queen Victoria knighted the influential banker, philanthropist, and Jewish communal leader Moses Montefiore. In 1841, the financier Isaac Lyon Goldsmid was made a baronet—the first Jew to receive a hereditary title.[38] In 1855, Sir David Salomons took office as the first Jewish lord mayor of London.

Finally, after this series of actions that were advancing the status of British Jews (or at least a few of them), Parliament began to respond positively. In 1858 Parliament changed the rules regulating membership in the House of Commons: For the first time, members could take office without swearing an oath as to their adherence to Christianity. As a result, that year, Parliament officially recognized its first Jewish member: Lionel de Rothschild.[39] He had actually been elected to his seat more than a decade earlier, but it took until July 26, 1858, for Parliament to formally accept him. In 1885, Nathan Mayer Rothschild became the first Jew to ascend to the House of Lords. By 1890, almost all other legal impediments to full participation in civic life had been removed for British Jews.

Concurrently, the Jewish community took a number of significant steps to strengthen its cohesion and leadership. In 1841, for example, the first Anglo-Jewish periodical, *The Jewish Chronicle,* began publication. In 1855, Jews' College was founded in London as a theological seminary; in the early 1880s it became affiliated with University College London. The Jewish Board of Guardians began offering welfare services to the community's poor in 1859. In 1863, leaders of the Ashkenazic and Sephardic communities joined forces to provide greater stature to the Board of Deputies of British Jews, the main representative body for the community at large.

At the same time, the production of a Jewish Bible of any sort in English was at least in part a response to outside forces. For example, the British and Foreign Bible Society was founded in 1804, and the American Bible Society a few years later in 1816. A primary purpose of such societies was to make Bibles available to the largest number of people at the smallest cost. Such inexpensive Bibles were frequently used by missionaries, including those trying to convert Jews.[40] Therefore, a number of Jews felt the need to produce (if not mass-produce) texts of their own to combat the growing number of "Christian" Bibles.[41] In short, developments culminating in distinctive English-language Bibles for Jews likely resulted from forces both inside and outside the Jewish community.

Anglo-Jewish Versions of the Late Eighteenth Century

Stylistically, the first Anglo-Jewish Bibles consisted of KJV and the Hebrew text on facing pages, with notes drawn from Jewish sources, typically Rashi, at the bottom of the page. Yet the titles of such works did not serve to immediately identify them as Jewish versions. Here, for example, is part of the title of David Levi's *Genesis* of 1787: *The First Book of Moses, called Genesis, in the Hebrew, with English Translation on the Opposite Page. With Notes, Explanatory, Exegetical, Critical, and Grammatical. . . .* Levi's work did, however, include a title page in Hebrew, and the work opened from right to left—sure indicators of an intended Jewish audience.

Strikingly, Levi and other early Anglo-Jewish Bible translators were not always on the best of terms with the British rabbinical establishment, which, at least at this point, might have looked askance at such attempts to Judaize what was clearly a Christian text (that is, KJV).[42] Levi may have had such thoughts in mind when he subtly enhanced his role from notes corrector to text translator in subsequent editions of his work.[43]

It was left to Isaac Delgado to produce the first freestanding work that differed at all from KJV. We can detect his goals from a partial citation of the characteristically lengthy title of his work: *A New English Translation of the Pentateuch: Being a Thorough Correction of the Present Translation, Wherever it deviates from the genuine sense of the Hebrew Expressions, or where it renders obscure the Meaning of the Text; or, lastly, when it occasions a seeming Contradiction*. . . . In spite of the seemingly clear import of the title, this work was not in fact a continuous text; rather, Delgado reproduced only the KJV verses for which he offered a new translation or a new interpretation.

A few examples from his preface are indicative of his modus operandi. At Exodus 32:29 Delgado insisted that the KJV wording, "For Moses had said," was insufficient to alert readers to the fact that this verse belonged sequentially before and not after the preceding verse. He offered two slightly longer renderings to correct the deficiency he detected: "Moreover, Moses had said" and "Moses had also said." Elsewhere, by the transposition of two letters in a Hebrew word, Delgado changed part of the KJV rendering of Psalm 76:4, "thou art more glorious and excellent than the mountains of prey," to "more terrible and excellent."

It is uncertain whether Delgado's "thorough corrections," taken individually or cumulatively, constituted an advance in Bible translation. In any case, his edition, with its emendations and their rationale, is characteristic of the initial stages not only of English Jewish Bible translating but also of English Jewish Bible marketing: His volume was dedicated to the Lord Bishop of Salisbury, and contained an appropriately impressive list of fairly prominent non-Jewish subscribers.[44]

Jewish Translations in England during the First Half of the Nineteenth Century

We jump the decades, as it were, to arrive at Solomon Bennett, whose 1834 pamphlet, *Specimen of a New Version of the Hebrew Bible*, was prominently dedicated to "His Royal Highness the Duke of Sussex." Courting support from royalty, and if possible from the Anglican hierarchy, points to a desire for acceptance, financial aid, and, I suppose, social or cultural support.

Among Bennett's textual innovations were two from the Servant Song contained in Isaiah 53. At verse 9, KJV reads, "And he made his grave with the wicked, and with the rich in his death; because he had done no violence, neither *was any* deceit in his mouth." Bennett's text here is, "And he delivered himself to the grave like wicked men; but suffered death on account of his riches; though he committed no violence, nor was there deceit in his mouth." At verse 12, the KJV rendering is, "Therefore will I divide him *a portion* with the great, and he shall divide the spoil with the strong; because he hath poured out his soul unto death: and he was numbered with the transgressors; and he bare the sin of many, and made intercession for the transgressors." Bennett's version of verse 12 is as follows: "Therefore will I reward him publicly; and he shall divide the spoil with the mighty; because he has exposed his soul unto death; he was numbered amongst transgressors; though he bare the sins of many others, and made intercession for transgressors."

For the most part, Bennett's English-language text is the same as KJV or easily identifiable as a revision of it. This may be indicative of Bennett's desire to stay in the good graces of the wealthy and influential Anglicans who supported him. But, as a Jew, Bennett also must have wanted to present interpretive renderings of these verses that ran counter to the Christian appropriation of them as a prophecy of Jesus's death and burial. So, in verse 9, Bennett rendered "he [that is the servant] suffered death on account of his riches" (rather than KJV's "with the rich in his death"), and in verse 12, "I [God] will reward him [the servant] publicly," rather than KJV's "I will divide him *a portion* with the great." In both instances Bennett's rendering lessened the likelihood of a Christological interpretation of these admittedly difficult words of the prophet Isaiah. It is highly likely that Bennett fashioned his text carefully, weighing the effects of such wording on the Jewish audience he sought to attract. Balancing the perceived desires of his sponsors and the perceived needs of his audience in this way could not have been easy.

Bennett's effort was followed five years later, in 1839, by Selig Newman's succinctly titled *Emendations of the Authorised Version of the Old Testament.* Identifying himself as author of the "Abridged Hebrew Grammar" and the "Complete Hebrew and English Lexicon," Newman judiciously omitted the fact that at least once before he had been involved in a heated dispute over the Christological interpretation of certain Old Testament passages—a dispute so vociferous and potentially violent, according to the *Sunday Times,* that women needed to be escorted away![45] In Newman's *Emendations,* I detect the same passion seething somewhere just below the surface. As an example, consider his revision and supporting analysis at Exodus 11:2, 12:35, and 36 (as earlier in Exodus 3):

> [There are many passages where KJV] translators were either decidedly wrong, or where the meaning in the original is dubious, they have not given the happiest rendering. [Such cases] may prove dangerous to the infidel, by strengthening him in his unbelief, as well as to the believer, by raising doubts in his mind, of the authenticity of a book, which apparently contains so many incongruities. For example: "One shall borrow of his, or her neighbour": but the meaning of *sh'l* in the original is not borrow, but ask: I.e. "One shall ask or demand." This is perfectly in accord with justice . . . whilst the permission or order to borrow without intending to restore, being a licence to defraud, could not have emanated from the fountain of justice.[46]

Almost one hundred years later, J. H. Hertz, then chief rabbi of the British Empire, wrote:

> [KJV] translates, "every woman shall borrow of her neighbour." This translation is thoroughly mischievous and misleading. If there was any borrowing, it was on the part of the Egyptians, who had been taking the labour of the Israelites without recompense. [Chapter 3] vv. 21 and 22 lend a poetic and unforgettable

> touch of beauty to the going out of Egypt; and yet these verses, as few others, have been misunderstood and been looked upon as a "blot" on the moral teaching of Scripture. . . . In modern times, enemies of the Bible vie with one another in finding terms strong enough in which to condemn the "deceit" practised on the Egyptians.[47]

From Newman's perspective, and he was not alone, the stakes were equally high at Judges 11:31. There, Jephthah's vow was almost always rendered as something like, "Whatever comes out of the door of my house to meet me on my safe return from the Ammonites shall be the LORD's and shall be offered by me as a burnt offering." Since it was Jephthah's own daughter who came out to meet him, Newman softened the text through the introduction of a nonfatal alternative: "Whatsoever cometh forth of the doors of my house to meet me . . . shall surely be the Lord's, or I will offer it up for a burnt offering." Newman's rendering, with "or" instead of "and," allowed for the possibility that Jephthah could have offered up a "normal" burnt offering of thanksgiving rather than sacrificing his daughter to keep a vow. The "and" interpretation, by contrast, could have been interpreted as confirming the view of hostile readers that the Israelites were cold-hearted and bloodthirsty.

What, then, motivated Jewish translators like Newman? They seem to have been especially concerned about removing from their English versions (since they could not change the Hebrew text!) any possible inconsistencies, to say nothing of outright contradictions. With equal or even greater vehemence, they sought to extirpate any expression that would suggest character flaws on the part of biblical personages. Even the hint that an Israelite would have acted improperly and with anything less than complete probity was enough to impel many translators to seek out even the most obscure linguistic or syntactic parallel to avoid such infelicities—especially when such actions had divine sanction behind them.

In the view of these same translators, considerably more than the sanctity of the text was at stake. Rather, the safety—perhaps even the survival—of their fellow Jews was in jeopardy. After all, British Jews lived in a society where they still labored under many social and legal impediments. In the hands of the Jews' enemies, a shifty Jacob of the Bible could easily become a shiftless Jacob from London's East End. Similarly, Israelites in the Bible who pretended to borrow from Egyptians with no intention of repaying their debts could easily become unscrupulous modern moneylenders.

The biblical text also needed to be defended against the onslaughts of those who directed their hatred at "the Book" rather than at "the people of the Book." In Newman's time, as well as in our own, such individuals regularly plucked passages out of their context in order to pit one biblical verse against another. Only very carefully worded renderings, as Newman sought to provide, could stymie such misguided efforts.[48]

In 1841, just two years after Newman's work, David Aaron de Sola (1796–1860) produced *Genesis,* the first entire biblical book in "an independent [English-language] Jewish translation."[49] De Sola had come from a celebrated family; many distinguished intellectuals and medical doctors were among his ancestors. His family had settled in Amsterdam after the 1492 expulsion. There, de Sola was born and received an outstanding secular and religious education, which led to his obtaining a rabbinical diploma. In 1818 he came to London to serve as one of the rabbis at the Bevis Marks Synagogue, a leading Spanish and Portuguese institution. He would go on to marry a daughter of the chief rabbi (or *haham*) of this congregation.

The flavor, as it were, of de Sola's version of Genesis, which he hoped would be the first of many other books of the Bible, can be detected in his rendering of the beginning of Genesis (Gen. 1:1–3), which he translated in this way: "In the beginning God created the heaven and the earth. But the earth was without form and a confused mass; darkness was on the surface of the deep, and the spirit of God hovering on the surface of the waters. God said: 'Let light be'; and light was."

We may profitably compare this with KJV: "In the beginning God created the heaven and the earth. And the earth was without form, and void; and darkness was upon the face of the deep. And the Spirit of God moved upon the face of the waters. And God said, Let there be light: and there was light."

De Sola retained much of KJV throughout, but the differences are telling. For KJV's rather colorless "void," de Sola introduces the far more evocative "confused mass." He dispenses with the literal rendering, "face of the deep," in favor of the more accessible "surface of the deep." The activity of the spirit (Spirit in KJV) is much more expressively reproduced as well, with "hovering" in place of KJV's rather general "moved." And, finally, de Sola's translation of God's formulaic language at the end of verse 3 (and elsewhere in this chapter) — "'Let light be'; and light was" — is a finely fashioned reflection of the poetic substructure that underlies the Hebrew here. All in all, de Sola had made effective use of his training in the English language, his synagogue experience, and his immersion in Jewish tradition to produce memorable and effective readings.

De Sola's English-language version of Genesis proved to be a major achievement, on its own terms and in serving as the basis for subsequent renderings. He was most famous, however, for his prayer book, *Translation of the Forms of Prayer According to the Custom of the Spanish and Portuguese Jews*. Its first edition in 1836 preceded his Bible translation; the second edition in 1852 followed it. Furthermore, his pioneering efforts in the English language were not limited to written form. In March 1831, he had preached the first English-language sermon at the Bevis Marks Synagogue. The institution's Board of Directors had encouraged him to do so.

In sum, de Sola's Genesis was as significant for its translator as it was for the translation itself. Moreover, the professional and personal status de Sola achieved is indicative of the fact that Bible translations and translators among English-speaking Jews were now moving from the periphery to the center of the community's establishment. Further examples of this follow in our discussion of other nineteenth-century Anglo-Jewish versions.

Jewish Translations in England during the Second Half of the Nineteenth Century

As much as they were concerned with combating inimical individuals and movements outside of their religion, succeeding Jewish translators were also intent upon finding a place for their works at the highest levels within the Jewish community. For example, the last edition of *The Way of Faith*, David Asher's English-language Bible version that appeared in 1848, includes this endorsement on its title page: "Specifically sanctioned by the Rev. Dr. Adler, Chief Rabbi of the United Congregations of the British Empire."

Asher, a native of Dresden, Germany, had come to London at the invitation of a wealthy relative. While in Great Britain, he learned English and filled various positions at several synagogues. Asher relied on this experience in producing his English-language version, which, as he freely acknowledged, was based on an earlier rendering into German by Büdinger.

Asher also served as a tutor to the chief rabbi. Most likely this is how his *Way of Faith* came to the attention of Rev. Dr. Adler. A similar notice appears in *Jewish School and Family Bible*, Abraham Benisch's Pentateuch of the next decade: "Newly Translated. Under the Supervision of the Rev. the Chief Rabbi." Expounding on this, Benisch's preface reads: "The proof sheets were submitted to the Rev. the Chief Rabbi, whose suggestions were implicitly complied with in all those particulars bearing on religious subjects." Along these lines, the *Jewish Family Bible* by Michael Friedlander, issued decades later in 1881, is also "printed with the sanction of the Rev. Dr. Adler, the Chief Rabbi."

It is commonly asserted that Jews never produced an "authorized" version of the Bible. Surely this is correct, if by "authorized" we adopt the connotation of the Church of England: authorized for use in churches (or, in the present case, in synagogues). Unlike the Anglican "authorized" Bibles, the Jewish "sanctioned" Bibles were centered on use at home and in schools. So Asher's text was "intended for the use of Jewish Schools and Families." Importantly, no Jewish version was intended to usurp the central place of the Hebrew text in synagogue worship.

Close inspection of the figures behind these English-language versions offers further indications that they were in fact adopted (or, more cynically, coopted) by the Jewish establishment. Translator Marcus Kalisch served for several years as secretary to the chief rabbi, after which he held posts as tutor and literary adviser to the Rothschild family (it doesn't get much more establishment than that). Hermann Gollancz, the first Jew to obtain the LitD degree from the University of London and a professorship at University College London, served as rabbi at several prominent London synagogues. For his part, *Jewish Family Bible* translator Michael Friedlander had as his son-in-law the renowned scholar Moses Gaster, who also served as the Sephardic chief rabbi of London.[50]

Notably, the pattern of Jewish versions during the latter half of the nineteenth century is not nearly as clear as their enhanced pedigree. In the always astute judgment of Joseph H. Hertz, who was chief rabbi from 1913 to 1946, the "revisions" of Gollancz (1880) and Friedlander (1881), for example, "were practically limited to the correction of Christological passages."[51]

That said, Friedlander's *Jewish Family Bible* is the only nineteenth-century Anglo-Jewish version still in use (albeit in a somewhat revised form) in the twenty-first century. It formed the "basis" for *The Jerusalem Bible*, published and marketed by Koren Publishers. As stated in the introduction to this version, "the 'Jewish Family Bible of M. Friedlander' . . . was selected . . . as a basis for this edition. That version had two important merits [which the present version preserves]: it was faithful to the *Masora* or received Hebrew text, and it retained as much as Jewish sentiment permitted of the unsurpassed language and rhythm of the 'Authorized Version' of 1611."[52]

On the other hand, the versions produced by Marcus Kalisch (beginning with his Exodus volume of 1855) and Abraham Elzas (who produced editions of Proverbs, Job, and several of the Minor Prophets during the first half of the 1870s) tended to separate themselves from the paradigm established by the KJV translators. The distinction is pronounced in Kalisch, as, for example, in his rendering of Genesis 1:2: "The earth was emptiness and dreariness" (in contrast to KJV's "the earth was without form and void)." Elzas, for his part, rendered Proverbs 31:30–31 with much of the KJV retained: "Favour is deceitful, and beauty is vain; A woman that feareth the Lord she will be praised. Give ye unto her the fruit of her hands, And let her deeds praise her in the gates!" Here KJV reads: "Favour *is* deceitful, and beauty *is* vain: *but* a woman *that* feareth the LORD, she shall be praised. Give her of the fruit of her hands; and let her own works praise her in the gates."

But there were limitations on the quantity and extent of such differences from KJV, imposed not by the translators but by their respective Jewish communities. In this context, the successive editions of Abraham Benisch's work are instructive. In part, he was concerned, as were Jewish translators before and after him, that distinctive Jewish understandings of the text were being lost in versions prepared by non-Jews. He cited, as one example, Leviticus 23:40, where KJV's "boughs of goodly trees, branches of palm trees, and the boughs of thick trees and willows of the brook" failed to do justice to the Jewish experience of Sukkot, as Benisch understood it. Also, he noted, KJV's rendering of Leviticus 23:15, "And ye shall count unto you from the morrow after the Sabbath," did not accord with Rabbinic calculations for determining the time between Passover and Shavuot.[53]

Above and beyond these particular considerations, Benisch included this statement in a later (1854) edition of his Pentateuch, titled *Jewish School and Family Bible*:

> The Anglo-Jewish community, in common with all other religious denominations whose vernacular is the English tongue, are so wedded to the diction of the authorised version that every

> departure from its phraseology, however well-founded, seems to grate upon their ears. For this reason we have in this version restored the renderings of the Anglican translation in all those cases where it can be done without doing violence to the principle of fidelity. This is a sacrifice which we regret, but which appeared to us absolutely necessary, if we did not wish unconsciously to themselves to bias against this Jewish translation the conservative feelings of many co-religionists in whose eyes, from long association, the Anglican Version, despite its manifest unfitness for Jewish families and schools, is invested with a kind of semi-sacredness.[54]

Given the reticence and restraint generally characteristic of prefaces or introductions to Bible translations, this is quite an admission. The Anglo-Jewish community had spoken. Any full-scale project to produce an English-language Bible for Jews outside of the KJV model would have to come from American, not British Jews.

As we see from the discussions and analyses that follow, that is exactly what happened in the United States, although not right away.

Isaac Leeser's Bible (1853)

The continuing connection between the Protestant King James Version and Jewish translations into English is nowhere better or more fully documented than in *The Holy Scriptures According to the Masoretic Text*, published in 1917 by The Jewish Publication Society of America (JPS). (Henceforth, I will refer to this version as OJPS, the Old Jewish Publication Society edition, in contrast to NJPS, The New Jewish Publication Society edition, which would later follow.)

OJPS was the culmination of more than a decade of efforts to replace an earlier American Bible translation by Isaac Leeser (1806–68). Leeser, a well-known, energetic rabbi and communal leader in nineteenth-century America, had written a Torah translation, *The Law of God*, published in 1845. His rendering of the entire Hebrew Bible, titled

The Twenty-Four Books of the Holy Scriptures, would follow a decade later in 1853.

As early as 1828, four years after his arrival in the United States from Germany, Leeser had experimented with English translation of isolated biblical passages that he included in his first publications. Sometimes he followed KJV; elsewhere he produced his own wording to correct what he saw as errors made by the KJV translators. Later, he recalled that even then, when he was barely twenty, he gave serious thought to translating the entire Hebrew Bible into English, primarily for the benefit of American Jews.[55]

Leeser was the sole translator and editor for virtually all of his English-language version. This prolonged his project, especially since he simultaneously held major rabbinic and publishing posts, but it was also editorially advantageous: Leeser could pursue his goals and vision without having to compromise with co-editors and other members of an editorial committee.

As an Orthodox Jew, Leeser took the Bible and Rabbinic exegesis seriously. But he was also a man, we might say an American, of his times, who sought to teach and exemplify the achievement of a "dynamic symbiosis of contemporary culture and Jewish tradition."[56] Determining that the authors of the Hebrew Bible had used plain language, he endeavored to emulate this stylistic feature in his English-language version. Although this led him to adopt a literal, or formal equivalence, approach to rendering the Hebrew, on occasion he introduced Rabbinic interpretations into his version and made efforts (as had the Rabbis) to harmonize what otherwise might be taken as conflicting biblical passages. With this approach, Leeser combined "contemporary culture" (through plain language) and "Jewish tradition" (through reliance on Rabbinic exegetical practice).

While Leeser certainly made good on his promise to consult the Hebrew text directly, he did make extensive use of KJV. He was also indebted to the German-language versions of Zunz, Mendelssohn, and Philippson. The latter can be viewed as something of a surprise, since Philippson conspicuously relied on the critical scholarship that

Leeser, with equal care, studiously avoided. In the process, Leeser and Philippson, hardly kindred theological spirits, frequently corresponded and publicly offered positive appraisals of each other's works.[57]

In fashioning his commentary, as well as the translation itself, Leeser had two other goals in mind. He saw the language of his English version as a guide for recent German-Jewish immigrants. His notes, which regularly featured distinctive readings from Jewish Bibles in German, would have been an added feature attracting the readership of these recent arrivals. Moreover, throughout his commentary, Leeser sought to soften, if not eliminate, any passages or images that would make contemporary Jews, as heirs to the ancient Israelites, objectionable to the majority of mid-nineteenth-century Americans, who were Christian.

Here are a few examples of the distinctive features inherent in Leeser's version.

Exodus 21:6: "And he [i.e., the servant] shall serve him [i.e., the master] till the Jubilee." In effect, here Leeser overrode the Hebrew, which has the adverb "forever," so as to avoid the possibility of contradiction between this Exodus passage and the pronouncement found in Leviticus 25:10: "[In the Jubilee year] ye shall return, every man, unto his family." Jewish exegetes had of course seen this difference and variously explained it. Leeser's readers, on the other hand, would have been completely unaware of this difficulty.

Ezekiel 20:25: Leeser rendered this as, "And also I let them follow statutes that were not good," in comparison to KJV's, "Wherefore I gave them also statutes that were not good." The KJV wording accurately reflected the Hebrew, which here (as sometimes elsewhere) presented a theological difficulty: in this case a picture of God giving the people bad laws. Leeser's wording followed the interpretation offered by the renowned exegete Rashi; thus his version had an impeccable Jewish pedigree. But once again he kept his readers ignorant of a difficulty that those knowledgeable in Hebrew (or with access to other versions) would encounter.

Leeser was well known throughout the Jewish communities of the United States. He enjoyed widespread, if not unanimous, respect and admiration. His version garnered praise from both learned Christian theologians and most rabbis. At first a few Reform leaders raised critical voices because of Leeser's use of traditional Jewish interpretive traditions, but very quickly Reform Jews, as individuals and as organizations, became among Leeser's most ardent supporters.[58] They reasoned that the easy access Leeser provided for English-speaking Jews who no longer had more than rudimentary knowledge of Hebrew (if that) outweighed sporadic theological or stylistic infelicities.

So it was that, because of this acclaim as well as Leeser's efforts to render the text as close to the Hebrew as possible, his commentary that was well suited for German immigrants, and the publication of subsequent editions that more families could afford, Leeser's version found its way into most American Jewish homes as the standard Bible. Ultimately, however, the very stylistic and theological features that spoke to mid-nineteenth century American Jews would not prove equally attractive for later generations.

The Holy Scriptures According to the Masoretic Text, or the Old Jewish Publication Society Version (1917)

By the final decade of the nineteenth century, a number of leading Jewish religious and communal leaders judged that Leeser's work (both text and notes) was no longer serviceable. In the view of The Jewish Publication Society of America (JPS), among others, Leeser's version was too parochial to suffice as *the* English-language Bible for a growing, upwardly mobile Jewish community that aspired to wider acceptance and respectability.

In 1892, JPS (founded in 1888) embarked on a plan to produce a new biblical version as its replacement. In its leaders' estimation, no such translation could be the result of a single individual working alone: A version for American Jews should reflect the major theological and denominational audiences within this community. As such, a number of scholars would be enlisted.

The model they designed was a kind of hybrid. One person, in this case the capable Marcus Jastrow, a prominent Polish-born scholar, would serve as editor-in-chief and chairman of an editorial committee, which would assign biblical books to translators, one translator for each book. Once the translator had completed his task (only males were asked to participate), he was to submit his manuscript to the editorial committee, which would then revise the submission and later harmonize all of the manuscripts.

This process was even more cumbersome to carry out than it is to explain. After ten years (at untold cost in time and money), only one book, Kaufmann Kohler's rendering of the Psalms, appeared in print. So it was that by 1908, JPS, joining together on this project with the Central Conference of American Rabbis (CCAR, the professional organization of Reform clergy), determined that only a major structural overhaul would salvage their shared goal: a new Jewish version of the Hebrew Bible.

The new plan called for a strong board of editors with a single editor-in-chief. This person would have sole responsibility for preparing preliminary drafts of the new version, which would then undergo a series of revisions by the board at regularly scheduled meetings. The abilities and dedication of the editor-in-chief would be crucial to the successful completion of this process in a reasonable timeframe. The emphasis on timeframe was meant to remedy the almost infinitely open-ended and ill-producing process of the previous decade, which had accomplished very little. Meanwhile, each member of the board of editors needed to exhibit an equally deep sense of commitment to constructive collaboration with the editor-in-chief and all the other board members—even if their previous interactions had been marked by acrimony.

Selected as editor-in-chief was Dr. Max L. Margolis, then the leading Jewish scholar of the Bible in the United States. Having emigrated from Lithuania, Margolis had completed his PhD at Columbia

University and taught at Hebrew Union College (HUC) in Cincinnati twice, with employment at the University of California, Berkeley, in between his two HUC stints. During the previous phases of preparation for the Bible translation project Margolis and his wife, Evelyn, were in Europe, where Margolis was conducting advanced academic research at German universities.

Six other men were chosen for the committee. JPS appointed Solomon Schechter, Cyrus Adler, and Joseph Jacobs; the CCAR representatives were Kaufmann Kohler, David Philipson, and Samuel Schulman. In these selections attention to the Jewish academic world was matched by an equally concerted effort to bridge the spectrum of Jewish observance as much as possible. Two of the six individuals were associated with HUC (Reform), two with the Jewish Theological Seminary in New York City (Conservative), and two with the recently founded Dropsie College of Philadelphia (which was unaffiliated with any of the denominations).

At its inception there were no guarantees that this ambitious project would succeed. While several of these individuals were accomplished scholars, none of them came close to matching Margolis's preeminence in biblical studies. Others had made their mark not as scholars but as institutional leaders. Furthermore, they would have to put aside countless personal and professional disagreements through the years of extensive correspondence and lengthy sessions needed to complete the new Bible.

For his part, although Margolis was unrivaled in his scholarship, he carried with him an extensive amount of what we might today call "baggage." This was especially true in connection with Kohler and Philipson, with whom he had worked and frequently butted heads at HUC. Margolis's ardent defense of Zionism (Kohler and Philipson, who were leading opponents of Zionism, might well have preferred to characterize Margolis's defense as "strident") was a major reason for his second, and final, departure from Cincinnati.

The committee went about its work exactly as the project's JPS and CCAR leaders had envisioned. Prior to the committee's first meeting, in December 1908, Margolis had completed his first draft of the Torah. By early fall 1909 (that is, in just about a year), he was finished with his first draft of the rest of the Hebrew Bible. His text then became the basis for committee discussion, via correspondence and in person.

The committee as a whole met sixteen times, each time over a ten-day period, from 1908 to 1915. Every extended session was taken up with a verse-by-verse, sometimes word-by-word, analysis of Margolis's draft, in canonical order from Genesis 1 to 2 Chronicles 36:23. A seventeenth, and final, meeting was held in autumn 1915 to sort through and adjudicate the three hundred or so problems that until then had eluded a satisfactory solution. The number three hundred may seem huge and formidable, but in retrospect it was a reassuringly small percentage of potentially problematic passages.

Indeed, during that last meeting all the problematic passages were resolved. It is a credit to Margolis, and all the other editors on the board, that the group made it through the entire process with tempers in check and reputations intact.

The year 1916 was taken up with debating and determining what we now speak of as the extratextual components of the version: the color of the cover; the wording of the title, subtitle, and all other front and reference material; the number and nature of notes; the text font; the margins of the printed pages, and so on. Although these and a veritable mountain of other details are largely relegated to the small type in discussions of translations, they loom large when it comes to the overall impression a volume makes on its intended audience and beyond.

Overall, KJV served as something of a model for determining how this new Jewish translation would look as a book. In this way, JPS hoped that its new version, properly bound and fitted in many editions with a place to record family milestones (births, bar mitzvahs, weddings, etc.), would take the same prominent place on the library shelf in middle- and upper-class Jewish homes that KJV occupied in Protestant abodes. Robust sales figures and positive reviews attest to JPS's success in achieving these and related goals.[59]

Among the goals JPS realized was the relative speed with which the new volume was produced. Taking all factors into account, JPS moved with discipline and dispatch from formulation to publication in just under a decade.

One additional factor was of great importance in keeping this project on the fast track: OJPS was not actually a fresh translation, but rather a revision.

On the basis of the correspondence that circulated among the translators and sponsors, we learn that, from its inception, OJPS was viewed as a revision of the 1885 Revised Version, a mostly British project that was itself the first authorized revision of KJV. Editor-in-chief Max Margolis had enthusiastically endorsed this procedure. As an immigrant from Eastern Europe, he strongly urged his fellow immigrants not to learn their English from what they read in the daily paper, and certainly not from what they heard on the street. The best writers in English, Margolis extolled, had based themselves on KJV—and JPS should follow their lead.[60]

That's exactly what the OJPS editors did. Working from a large-print edition of the Revised Version, Margolis pasted each of its pages, from Genesis 1 through 2 Chronicles, on a larger sheet of white paper. (Having located some of these sheets myself, I can confirm the contemporary accounts that describe this.) On the margins Margolis entered his corrections and those suggested by other committee members. In quite a few instances, OJPS ended up reproducing the precise wording of the earlier English-language version it was revising. This is true in narrative passages—for example at Genesis 11:5, where they both read, "And the LORD came down to see the city and the tower, which the children of men builded"; as well as in legal sections—such as at Exodus 21:15, "And he that smiteth his father, or his mother, shall be surely put to death"; and Deuteronomy 24:16, "The fathers shall not be put to death for the children, neither shall the children be put to death for the fathers; every man shall be put to death for his own sin." Outside of the Torah, this is seen, for instance, in Jeremiah 31:29–30 (and Ezekiel 18:14): "In those days they shall say no more,

The fathers have eaten a sour grape, and the children's teeth are set on edge. But every one shall die for his own iniquity: every man that eateth the sour grape, his teeth shall be set on edge."

When Margolis did introduce new (that is, non-KJV) wording into the JPS version, he—aided by his wife, Evelyn—ensured that it fit seamlessly into the linguistic context the KJV translators had constructed.

Occasionally as well, the Protestant exegesis of KJV ran counter to the theological predilections of the JPS translators. Sometimes only a small change was needed, one that most readers might not even notice. For example, at Genesis 1:1–2, KJV read, "In the beginning God created the heavens and the earth. . . . And the Spirit of God moved upon the face of the waters"; OJPS subsequently offered, "In the beginning God created the heaven and the earth. . . . And the spirit of God hovered over the face of the waters." For theological purposes, the major difference was the substitution of "spirit" (with a small "s") in OJPS for KJV's "Spirit"—where the capital "S" was intended to capture the distinctly Christian concept of the trinity: the Father, the Son, and the Holy Spirit. The capitalization also conformed to Christian practice.

In other passages the change was sure to be noticed. Consider Isaiah 7:14. Whereas KJV, in agreement with traditional Christian exegesis, reads, "Behold, a virgin shall conceive, and bear a son, and shall call his name Immanuel," OJPS has this rendering: "Behold, the young woman shall conceive, and bear a son, and shall call his name Immanuel." The OJPS wording, "the young woman," is a better contextual rendering of this expression within the prophecies of Isaiah himself, and foreclosed any facile connection between this figure and the Virgin Mary.

In still other passages, the JPS translators were the first (in my view) to hit upon exactly the right way to say something in English. My favorite example of this is at Proverbs 31:10: "a woman of valour." By comparison, KJV provides "a virtuous woman," and the 1985 NJPS translation is "a capable wife." In my opinion, no rendering before (or since) is an improvement over "a woman of valour" in doing justice both to the original Hebrew text and to a target audience of English speakers.[61]

The actual printing of OJPS presented a last opportunity to make corrections—or, alas, to inadvertently introduce new mistakes. The original and subsequent printings of KJV, beginning three hundred years before the first appearance of OJPS, were even more susceptible to error. For KJV, British scholar Alister McGrath astutely observed:

> The early printings of the King James Bible included many errors. Many of these arose from weaknesses in the book production processes of the period. Proofing was often a haphazard business.... Contemporary sources suggest that a "reading-boy" would then read the proof copy aloud to the compositor, who would check it against the original copy. Errors could arise in all kinds of ways.... A further factor contributing to the large number of errors in English Bibles was the constant pressure to reduce their production costs.[62]

Probably the best-known printing error in OJPS occurred in its first edition. To its credit, JPS immediately accepted responsibility and recalled all copies of the Bible in order to redress the matter. A number of prominent American Jewish leaders received the following letter in late January 1917:

> Dear Sir, Owing to an error in one of the folios in the several advance copies of the New Translation of the Bible, which we gave to our guests at the dinner held in New York on January 22, 1917, we are asking you to kindly return to us the copy which you received and we shall in turn send you a perfect one. Please be good enough to forward it to us as soon as you possibly can.[63]

In his autobiography, *I Have Considered the Days,* the then JPS president Cyrus Adler recalled the details of this incident:

> On Monday evening, January 22, 1917, the Publication Society celebrated the completion of the new Jewish translation of the Bible by giving a dinner at the Hotel Astor in New York. It was a very interesting and noteworthy occasion, but a strange thing happened. While we were seated at the table, Rabbi Charles I. Hoffman, of Newark, discovered two misplaced lines in the first chapter of the Book of Isaiah. Of course there was consternation among us, and since every person present had been given a copy of the Bible as a souvenir at the dinner, we asked them all to return them and finally had the plates corrected. It seems that a printer's boy had dropped a page of type and covered up the fact. He had the whole page reset, and the errors occurred in this way. But it was very strange that Rabbi Hoffman, with his eagle eye, and possibly because his middle name is Isaiah, should have discovered this error in a few minutes.[64]

The JPS TANAKH, or New Jewish Publication Society Version (1985)

About half a century later, as early as 1953, JPS leaders began to explore the society's options for a new English-language version of the Bible that would have wide (if not unanimous) appeal to a growing and changing North American Jewish population.

Taking a cue from the existing market for Bible translations, which Protestants dominated, JPS had two major options. The first was to update the KJV-sounding (and looking) OJPS. This was the approach taken by those responsible for the New King James Version, New American Standard Bible, and the Revised Standard Version. Although these translations differed from each other in many respects, all three were nonetheless dependent on KJV for their overall approach to rendering Hebrew into English. And they were all also selling well.

The second option entailed the abandonment of the KJV model in favor of a contemporary English-language style version that would be at home among other exemplars of mid-twentieth-century middlebrow literature. In particular, the American Bible Society was promoting this approach in its popular *Good News Bible*.

Fairly early in this process of exploration, JPS selected Canadian-born biblical scholar Harry M. Orlinsky (1908–92) to head up this project. In many ways, Orlinsky was the obvious choice. A far-ranging scholar, communicating in an array of popular as well as more specialized venues, he was uniquely able to galvanize scholarly as well as general audiences through an erudition leavened with humor and autobiographical anecdotes. Christian scholars as well as Jewish colleagues held him in high regard. And, to top it off, he had worked on the committee that had produced the Old Testament part of the Revised Standard Version, then in wide use in pulpits, classrooms, and study groups. In fact, Orlinsky had been the first Jewish member of a committee for what was essentially a Christian (at this point, Protestant) version.

Given Orlinsky's vast experience, he could have gone with either of the options outlined above, or devised a third one of his own! Ultimately, he came down squarely on the side of the modern-speech paradigm being championed by the American Bible Society. As JPS leaders, guided by Orlinsky, engaged in debate about the nature of the forthcoming translation, they began to conceive of it as a decisive break with KJV—which was exactly in line with Orlinsky's evolving approach to Bible translation.[65]

During this period, Orlinsky was becoming the primary proponent of functional equivalence translation within the Jewish world. He favored a functional, or freer, approach to translation, over against the formal, or more literal, text developed by the KJV translators. Allying himself with Protestant scholars associated with the American Bible Society, most notably Eugene A. Nida and Robert Bratcher, Orlinsky asked: What did the original biblical authors intend to say to their audience, and how can a new Bible version convey that meaning to today's audience?

Up until then, very few Jewish Bible versions had made use of functional equivalence—Saadiah Gaon was Orlinsky's closest model in this regard. Earlier English-language versions for Jews, including OJPS, had been designed to take the reader to the text—in other words, to emphasize the distance and foreignness that separated the original Hebrew Bible from modern audiences. This new Bible text aimed to take the (original biblical) text to the reader.

To make the original text intelligible for all who could not read the biblical Hebrew, Orlinsky believed the translator needed to carefully gauge the style of English that would be most accessible and comfortable for the target audience. The ensuing translation needed to look and read like almost any other piece of contemporaneous English-language literature for that same audience.

The committee Orlinsky assembled to produce the new JPS version of the Torah consisted of two academic heavyweights in addition to himself—H. L. Ginsberg of the Jewish Theological Seminary and Ephraim Speiser of the University of Pennsylvania—and three well-respected rabbis, one from each of the major branches of American Judaism: Max Arzt (Conservative), Bernard J. Bamberger (Reform), and Harry Freedman (Orthodox). The committee secretary was JPS editor Solomon Grayzel.

The actual process of constructing the new edition would turn out to be quite different than that of JPS's earlier effort. On the committee responsible for the older JPS version of 1917, everyone had recognized editor-in-chief Max Margolis as the only major scholar in their midst. Those committee members tended to defer to Margolis on exegetical and philological matters, even when they disagreed on current controversies such as Zionism. By contrast, this new committee had three towering figures, each of whom (it must be admitted) was something of a prima donna. Those close to the committee reported that debates among Orlinsky, Ginsberg, and Speiser often turned into shouting matches, admittedly learned ones. Nonetheless, with Grayzel as timekeeper and referee, deliberations stayed on track for the most part, and the committee accomplished its collective goal in a reasonably timely manner.

It published the first edition of the JPS Torah in September 1962. A second, revised edition, published five years later, incorporated changes suggested by the translators, often following up on reviewers' comments.[66]

The following examples, comparing the JPS Torah (NJPS) to OJPS, highlight characteristic features that resulted from the NJPS approach to translation. (Readers are also encouraged to contrast these examples with the corresponding KJV renderings, as most of the selected passages also appeared in the previous OJPS discussion comparing KJV and OJPS.)

Genesis 1:1–2—OJPS: "In the beginning God created the heaven and the earth . . . And the spirit of God hovered over the face of the waters." NJPS: "When God began to create heaven and earth. . . . And a wind from God sweeping over the water." With "In the beginning God created," OJPS replicates the traditional English-language rendering of the grammatically difficult wording of Genesis's (and the Bible's) beginning. As such, OJPS understands the first verse of Genesis as a complete sentence with a full stop. For NJPS, verse 1 ("When God began to create . . .") is the start of a sentence completed by verse 3 ("God said, 'Let there be light'; and there was light"), with verse 2 ("—the earth being unformed and void, with darkness over the surface of the deep and a wind from God sweeping over the water—") essentially serving as a parenthetical statement, as indicated through the use of participles and a pair of dashes. The NJPS wording, however, is in accord with the interpretation offered by the influential Jewish exegete Rashi. Moreover, it precludes the understanding, which became dominant in Christianity, that God created the universe "out of nothing" (in Latin, *ex nihilo*). In their extended notes, the JPS translators adduce one further piece of evidence in support of their choice of wording: other ancient Near Eastern creation accounts (especially the Mesopotamian "Enuma Elisha" myth) clearly began with "When."

NJPS differs from OJPS here in other ways as well. It renders the Hebrew term *ruach* as "wind," rather than as a form of "spirit" (both renderings are legitimate and contextually appropriate; "wind" precludes any facile identification of this divine activity with the "Spirit" of Christian theology). Particularly characteristic of the functional equivalence translation Orlinsky promoted, NJPS succeeds in simplifying the literal "face of the water" with the more modern-sounding "the water."

Genesis 11:5—OJPS: "And the Lord came down to see the city and the tower, which the children of men builded." NJPS: "The Lord came down to look at the city and tower that man had built." Almost all post–World War II English-language Bible versions updated archaic verb forms, such as substituting "had built" for "builded" in this passage. More noteworthy is the use of the generic "man" (but not yet a term like "mortals," which is seen in the roughly contemporary New Revised Standard Version, or NRSV) for the literal but perhaps misleading "children of men." In like manner, NJPS consistently replaced the earlier rendering, "children of Israel," with "Israelites."

Exodus 21:15—OJPS: "And he that smiteth his father, or his mother, shall be surely put to death." NJPS: "He who strikes his father or his mother shall be put to death." The NJPS phrase, "He who strikes," sounds far more natural to today's readers than "he that smiteth" (OJPS and KJV). By contrast, many other modern translations changed the masculine pronouns "he" and "his." The NRSV formulation (in which Orlinsky also played a role), "Whoever strikes father or mother, . . . ," accomplished this by a combination of rephrasing and omission. The male-gendered rendering, however, is a precise reflection of the Hebrew wording. Although Orlinsky's sympathies in such passages lay with NRSV's gender-neutral approach, the NJPS Torah tended to resist innovation in these instances.[67]

Deuteronomy 24:16—OJPS: "The fathers shall not be put to death for the children, neither shall the children be put to death for the fathers; every man shall be put to death for his own sin." NJPS: "Parents should not be put to death for children, nor children be put to death for parents: a person shall be put to death only for his own crime." In this case, NJPS showed considerable, although not consistent, sensitivity to gendered language. The NJPS translators reckoned that "fathers" (as in OJPS and KJV), although a literal translation of the Hebrew, did not reflect the more inclusive meaning of the term, and hence substituted "parents." In like manner, they rendered "every man" more accurately as "a person." However, NJPS still used "his" before "own crime." By contrast, NRSV managed to eliminate all vestiges of male-oriented language by rendering the text as "only for their own crimes may persons be put to death." Although this approach is more consistent, it would have involved a greater degree of restructuring the Hebrew than the NJPS Torah translators found desirable.

Outside of the Torah, JPS translators followed a similar procedure at Jeremiah 31:29–30 (so also Ezek. 18:14): OJPS: "In those days they shall say no more: The fathers have eaten sour grapes, and the children's teeth are set on edge. But every one shall die for his own iniquity; every man that eateth the sour grapes, his teeth shall be set on edge"; NJPS: "In those days they shall no longer say: The parents have eaten sour grapes, and the children's teeth are set on edge. But all shall die for their own sins; the teeth of everyone who eats sour grapes shall be set on edge."[68]

The JPS version of the Prophets (Nevi'im), with the same translation committee as for the Torah, first appeared in 1978.[69] For the Writings (Kethuvim), a new committee was appointed: Moshe Greenberg (University of Pennsylvania, then Hebrew University), Jonas Greenfield (Hebrew University), and Nahum Sarna (Brandeis University), all relatively young scholars, constituted the academic component; the rabbis were Saul Leeman (Conservative), Martin S. Rozenberg (Reform), and David Shapiro (Orthodox). Chaim Potok, then JPS editor, was secretary of this committee. Their version was first published in 1982.[70]

At last, in 1985, the JPS TANAKH—incorporating the latest editions of all three portions of the Hebrew Bible—made its first appearance.[71] In addition to the text of the translation itself, the notes appearing at the bottom of each page were also very important to how readers experienced the TANAKH. Numerous footnotes consisted primarily of: (1) notations where the translation committees acknowledged they didn't understand a Hebrew word or passage;[72] (2) possible renderings (other than the one in the text); (3) familiar English renderings that the NJPS editors excluded in the text; (4) cross-references to other biblical passages that could aid in comprehension; and (5) important ancient variants. In effect, these footnotes gave readers insight into how the translators worked, especially highlighting their own uncertainties.

Significantly, the editors of most functional translations such as NJPS have tended to gloss over textual and related difficulties in their efforts to give readers a clear, typically unambiguous sense of the Hebrew. Not NJPS. The JPS TANAKH consciously fashioned these footnotes to accord with the traditional Jewish attention to every detail of the Hebrew text. If a detail was not in the translation itself, then readers could count on its appearing in the notes.

From its inception, NJPS was—and continues to be—very influential and well received in non-Orthodox (and even some Orthodox) Jewish circles. Among the many prominent examples of publications that use the JPS TANAKH as the basis for their own commentary and further reflection are *The JPS Torah Commentary*,[73] *Haftorah Commentary*, and subsequent commentaries on the five *megillot* and other biblical books; David L. Lieber, Jules Harlow, et al., *ETZ HAYIM: Torah and Commentary*, still widely used in Conservative synagogues; W. Gunter Plaut, *The Torah: A Modern Commentary*, used in Reform congregations; and Adele Berlin and Marc Brettler, *The Jewish Study Bible*, an indispensable resource for scholars, study groups, and interested individuals. NJPS has also come to be the standard version for Jewish communal activities and for study in Conservative, Reform, and Reconstructionist synagogues.

That said, not all Jews and Christians prefer NJPS over OJPS. To some, even though it prides itself on functional equivalence, NJPS "just doesn't ring true as a rendering of the Hebrew text." Perhaps they share in the judgment of OJPS editor-in-chief Margolis, who once commented: "[The KJV] has an inimitable style and rhythm; the coloring of the original is not obliterated. . . . What imparts to the English Bible its beauty, aye, its simplicity, comes from the [Hebrew] original."[74]

In 1999 JPS published the *JPS Hebrew-English Tanakh*, its first Hebrew-English diglot edition.[75] To my mind, this filled a significant lacuna in JPS Bible versions up until that time. Whenever possible, I believe, the translated text and the Hebrew should appear next to each other—in facing pages or parallel columns. This serves as one more reminder that the version, as culturally and theologically significant as it is, is nonetheless always, or nearly always, subservient to the Hebrew text it is rendering.

The Contemporary Torah: A Gender-Sensitive Adaptation of the JPS Translation or Contemporary JPS (2006)

Seven years later, in 2006, JPS introduced *The Contemporary Torah: A Gender-Sensitive Adaptation of the JPS Translation*, also known as CJPS (Contemporary JPS).

In the decades following the publication of the JPS TANAKH, scholars, rabbis, and members of religious communities for whom the Bible is important all came to recognize that traditional renderings of MT could be misleading. In keeping with this insight, CJPS strove for gender-neutral language when referring to God, as well as a thorough re-analysis of what the Hebrew text was saying (and was not saying) about gender with respect to humans. Along with several consulting editors, revising editor David E. S. Stein "selected language that judiciously portrays ancient gender roles in order to reflect a more nuanced understanding of the biblical world and its original audience."[76] In a sense, then, *The Contemporary Torah* was designed to bring the modern reader to a fuller appreciation of ancient language (with special emphasis on language related to gender) than is possible with many other Bible versions.

Consider these characteristic readings.

Genesis 11:5—CJPS: "YHWH came down to look at the city and tower that humanity had built." This is an intentional revision of the NJPS wording, "The LORD came down to look at the city and tower that man had built," with the goal of conveying to modern readers that the builders consisted not only of males (a likely inference from NJPS's "man") but females as well. Both are included in the term "humanity," which also contrasts fallible and frail humans with a strong and stable God.

Exodus 16:16 (see also Exod. 16:28–30)—CJPS: "This is what the Eternal has commanded: gather as much of it as each of you requires to eat, an *omer* a person for as many of you as there are; you shall each fetch for those in your tent." Here NJPS reads, "This is what the LORD has commanded: Gather as much of it as each of you requires to eat, an omer to a person for as many of you as there are; each of you shall fetch for those in his tent." KJV has this: "This *is* the thing which the LORD hath commanded, Gather of it every man according to his eating, an omer for every man, *according to* the number of your persons; take ye every man for *them* which *are* in his tents." With its "every man" and "his," KJV is a literal rendering of MT. But, as the NJPS translators understood it, this rendering would likely give modern audiences a misleadingly narrow picture of the recipients of this command, limiting it to males only. Going to considerable lengths to avoid what they understood as a misconception arising from an admittedly literal rendering, the NJPS translators changed almost all of the third singular masculine references to the second person, "you" (which in English is gender-neutral). It was left to the CJPS editors to complete the task with the use of "your tent" instead of "his tent" at the end of the verse.[77]

Deuteronomy 24:16—CJPS: "Parents should not be put to death for children, nor children put to death for parents: one should be put to death only for one's own crime." NJPS: "Parents shall not be put to death for children, nor children be put to death for parents: a person shall be put to death only for his own crime." KJV: "The fathers shall not be put to death for the children, neither shall the children be put to death for the fathers: every man shall be put to death for his own sin." Here, once again, KJV is literal, NJPS removes almost all of the gender-specific language, and CJPS completes the task. As at Exodus 16:16 (just above), the renderings of NJPS and CJPS constitute deliberate efforts by their respective translators to restore to English-language versions what they understand to be the intended scope of the original Hebrew text. From a broader perspective, these examples also demonstrate that a literal rendering is not always the best or closest to the original.

ArtScroll *Tanach*

In addition to NJPS and its *Contemporary Torah* adaptation, today's English-speaking Jews have several other Bible options from which to choose.

More traditional than the JPS—and primarily marketed among Orthodox segments of the Jewish community—is the ArtScroll *Tanach*, first published in 1996 by Mesorah Publications of Brooklyn, New York.[78] Especially for the Torah, its translators often incorporated into their version classic interpretations of the influential medieval exegete Rashi. For individual books of Hebrew Scripture, the publishers have also prepared different editions, some more fully annotated than others.

Here are some characteristic readings from ArtScroll's rendering of the Torah.

Genesis 2:2: "By the seventh day God completed His work which He had done, and He abstained on the seventh day." Given the fact that ArtScroll renders the preposition differently at the beginning of this verse—"by [the seventh day]"—and at its end—"on [the seventh day]"—careful readers of this English-language version might think that the underlying Hebrew must also be different. This is not in fact the case. MT includes identical prepositional phrases in both places, and both are generally translated the same, "on the seventh day." This, however, creates an exegetical difficulty. Everywhere else in the Hebrew Bible, Creation is described as a six-day event; on the seventh, as at the end of this verse, God rests (or, as ArtScroll would have it, "abstains"). ArtScroll's rendering at the verse's beginning is according to much Rabbinic exegesis. At the same time, it obscures the problem inherent in the original wording, thereby separating its readers from what I would call an authentic biblical difficulty.

Exodus 12:15: "For a seven-day period shall you eat matzos, but on the previous day you shall nullify the leaven from your homes." Note ArtScroll's use of "on the previous day," whereas MT literally says, "on the first day." In other biblical passages, the leaven is said to be "nullified" before the Passover began. ArtScroll's rendering here, in accordance with the understanding of many rabbinical exegetes, has the "advantage" of aligning this passage with the others in terms of when the nullification takes place. But, as at Genesis 2:2 (above), this practice also masks a difficulty, perhaps even a contradiction, in MT.

Exodus 20:7: "You shall not take the Name of HASHEM, your God, in vain, for HASHEM will not absolve anyone who takes His Name in vain." Here, as frequently elsewhere, the Tetragrammaton (YHVH)—which in most English-language versions is represented by the title "the Lord"—is replaced by an expression that literally means "the Name," reflecting the ineffability of the personal name of the deity.

Exodus 22:24: "When you lend money to My people . . . do not lay interest upon him." Notably, the conjunction rendered here as "when" is the common Hebrew term *im*, which in the vast majority of instances is translated literally as "if." The use of "when" here, paralleled in two other places in the Torah, is in accordance with the tradition (see, for example, Rashi) that in Judaism charity is not a matter of "if," but "when."

Leviticus 23:11: "He shall wave the Omer before HASHEM to gain favor for you; on the morrow of the rest day the Kohen shall wave it." This verse describes the Jewish ceremony of counting an offering called the Omer (literally meaning "sheaf") on the fifty days from Passover to Shavuot. Whereas the biblical Hebrew text simply states that the counting of the Omer starts the day after "the Shabbat," Rabbinic Judaism understood "Shabbat" here not in its usual sense, but as "the day of rest"—that is, the first day of Passover. This interpretation standardizes when the counting of the Omer begins (it's the day after the first day, whereas Shabbat could occur on a different day of Passover each year). Today, all Jews follow this interpretation, except the Karaites, who do not acknowledge the authority or authenticity of

Rabbinic interpretation or interpreters. And so, as is true elsewhere in this TANAKH, the text follows Rabbinic interpretation rather than a more literal rendering of the biblical text itself.

The Living Torah

Another version intended primarily for Orthodox and other traditional Jews, *The Living Torah*, was first published in 1981.[79] Its translator, Rabbi Aryeh Kaplan (1934–83), was a physicist before serving as a rabbi at several American synagogues. He wrote voluminously on a wide variety of topics, from physics to biblical studies to mysticism.

In his writings, Kaplan always sought clarity of expression and thought for an audience that typically included individuals who were turning (or returning) to traditional Judaism. His later works emphasized mystical or spiritual elements in Jewish thought, which he himself incorporated into his daily life. He also introduced these elements into the text and the notes of *The Living Torah*. After his death, his followers continued his work with *The Living Nach*, three additional volumes covering the Prophets and the Writings.[80]

Characteristic readings include the following.

Leviticus 17:14: "Tell the Israelites not to eat any blood, since the life-force of all flesh is in its blood. Whoever eats it shall be cut off [spiritually]." Note that this version explicitly introduces a spiritual element into the biblical text that is, at best, implicit in the literal Hebrew. This is also true at Deuteronomy 12:23, which *The Living Torah* renders as, "Be extremely careful not to eat the blood, since the blood is associated with the spiritual nature [elsewhere, "the life"], and when you eat flesh, you shall not ingest the spiritual nature [elsewhere, "the life"] along with it." Similarly, Leviticus 19:14 is rendered, "Do not place a stumbling block before the [morally] blind." Through the use of brackets, both "spiritually" (at Lev. 17:14) and "morally" (at Lev. 19:14) are identified as exegetical additions by the translator. This, however, is not the case at Deuteronomy 12:23.

Leviticus 18:7: "Do not commit a sexual offense against your father or mother. If a woman is your mother, you must not commit incest with her." In biblical Hebrew there is no specific word for "incest." The more general term is usually rendered as "sexual offense" (as in the first part of this verse, for example). Kaplan's commitment to explicitness in the service of clarity led him to modify the literal text.

Leviticus 19:29: "Do not defile your daughter with premarital sex." Here as well, Kaplan rendered a fairly general Hebrew term (which in English translation would typically appear as "degrade" or "debase,") with a specific one: "defile . . . with premarital sex." In a sense, he may have been responding to those who, with some justification, made statements such as, "There is no specific prohibition against premarital sex in the Old Testament." While that is true in MT and other English-language versions, Jewish and non-Jewish alike, the explicit prohibition does appear in *The Living Torah*.

One final example of Kaplan's modification, in this case amplification, of the biblical text to erase any possible doubt in his readers' minds is found in his rendering of one of the Ten Commandments: "Remember the Sabbath to keep it holy. You can work during the six weekdays and do all of your tasks. But Saturday [literally, "the seventh day"] is the Sabbath to God your Lord" (Exod. 20:8–10). While I acknowledge the value of Kaplan's motivation here, the modern-sounding designation "Saturday" strikes me as odd in the context of an ancient text.

The Schocken Bible

Adopting an approach reminiscent of Martin Buber and Franz Rosenzweig's (for an analysis of their work, see chapter 4), Everett Fox, the Glick Professor of Judaic and Biblical Studies at Clark University, spent many years on what would become volume 1 of *The Schocken Bible: The Five Books of Moses*.

He had first encountered Buber and Rosenzweig's work as a student at Brandeis University. As they sought to engage the German reader with a text that stretched the German language to—and, on occasion, beyond—the breaking point, so Fox endeavored to draw the contemporary English reader into the world of antiquity through a modern-language version that incorporated distinctive aspects of the ancient Hebrew text otherwise absent in other renderings.

When his *The Five Books of Moses* was published in 1995, it attracted considerable interest (as have his later renderings of portions of the Prophets).[81] His approach has been useful in classroom settings and for Bible study groups, wherever teachers or preachers seek to maximize the process of taking the reader to the text that is a hallmark of formal equivalence. Additionally, his work has resonated with a sizable number of conservative Christians, who see it as a laudable effort to provide invaluable links with the "Bible" as Jesus read and heard it.

Here are some characteristic readings. We begin with passages from the early chapters of Genesis that illustrate well the look and sound of Fox's renderings.

Genesis 1:1–2: "At the beginning of God's creating of the heavens and the earth, when the earth was wild and waste, darkness rushed over the face of Ocean, rushing-spirit of God hovering over the face of the waters." Similarly, Fox rendered Genesis 1:8 as, "God called the dome: Heaven / There was setting, there was dawning: second day"; and Genesis 17:5 as, "No longer shall your name be called Avram, rather shall your name be Avraham, for I will make you Av Hamon Goyyim / Father of a throng of Nations!"

We follow with in-depth analyses of renderings elsewhere in Fox's version.

Genesis 25:30–31: "Esav said to Yaakov: Pray give me a gulp of the red-stuff, that red-stuff, for I am so weary! Therefore they called his name: Edom/Red-One. Yaakov said: Sell me your firstborn-right here-and-now." Similarly rendered is Genesis 27:36: "He [Esav] said: Is that why his name was called Yaakov/Heel-Sneak? For he has now sneaked against me twice"; and Genesis 30:24: "She [Rahel] became pregnant and bore a son. She said: God has removed/asaf my reproach! So she called his name: Yosef, saying: May YHWH add/yosef another son to me!" Here and elsewhere, Fox presented the biblical names in their Hebrew form, thereby allowing English readers to hear more clearly what the ancient listener would have heard and to enjoy something of the wordplay hitherto accessible only to Hebrew speakers.

Notably, he also chose to present these wordplays within the text itself, unlike other Bible versions, which tend to relegate attention to wordplays to their accompanying notes. In addition, he characteristically used dashes to indicate that what takes more than one "word" to say in English required only one word in Hebrew.

Genesis 43:3: "The man [Yosef] warned, yes, warned us, saying: You shall not see my face unless your brother is with you." The original Hebrew text used the same root (in this instance, "warn") twice in proximity to strengthen the force of the verb. Some English translations ignore this construction (among them NJPS: "The man warned us. . . ."). Those that don't overlook it typically paraphrase (so NRSV: "The man solemnly warned us. . . ."). By contrast, in this passage and elsewhere, Fox represented this verbal repetition as literally as possible.

Genesis 45:12–13: "Here, your eyes see, as well as my brother Binyimin's eyes, that it is my mouth that speaks to you. So tell my father of all the weight I carry in Egypt, and of all that you have seen, and make haste, bring my father down here!" NJPS: "You can see for yourselves, and my brother Benjamin for himself, that it is indeed I who am speaking to you. And you must tell my father everything about my high station in Egypt and all that you have seen; and bring my father here with all speed." Gone in the NJPS translation are the concrete references to body parts ("eyes" and "mouth") that form part of MT and Fox's rendering of the Hebrew. Additionally, Fox's choice of "weight" retains the ambiguity of the corresponding Hebrew term with its nuances both of a heavy burden and of exalted status. JPS's "high station" catches only one of these nuanced meanings.

Exodus 12:42–43, 48: "It is a night of keeping-watch for YHWH. . . . YHWH said to Moshe and Aharon: This is the law of the Passover-meal. Any foreign son is not to eat of it. . . . But any foreskinned-man is not to eat of it." As in other passages cited in this section, Fox presented proper names—here Moshe and Aharon—in forms that carry over the form and sound of the Hebrew into the English. Moreover, Fox employed specially constructed compound nouns such as "keeping-watch" and "foreskinned-man" to draw the modern reader into the evocative resonance of the ancient text.

Exodus 13:2: "Hallow to me every firstborn, breacher of every womb among the Children of Israel, of man or of beast, it is mine." Here NJPS has: "Consecrate to Me every first-born; man and beast, the first issue of every womb among the Israelites is Mine." Although Fox's words, "hallow" and "breacher," are recognizable English, they have a somewhat archaic, perhaps also foreign tinge to them. By contrast, the NJPS renderings, while admittedly not framed in everyday contemporary language (for example, "consecrate" and "first issue"), lack the defining features of Fox's carefully wrought wording. For Fox, such wording serves the useful purpose of reminding readers that the passage they are approaching, albeit in translation, is separated from them by a vast expanse of time, geography, and culture. Additionally, to Fox, the grammar of this verse, convoluted in comparison with today's standard English, works well as another indication that his readers are encountering a translation of a text that arose in very different circumstances than our own.

The Steinsaltz Humash: Humash Translation and Commentary

Adin Steinsaltz's English-language edition of Talmud Bavli was a constitutive element in opening up study of this material to an audience that went beyond traditional circles. Overall, his efforts along these lines have been judged successful and fruitful.

Recently Steinsaltz oversaw the production of a *Humash* (that is, Torah) translation and commentary. As has often been the case with Jewish versions, it is the commentary that has attracted the most attention. This was Steinsaltz's responsibility.

The translation itself, prepared by the rabbi's colleagues, is based on the commentary. It appears in boldface within the commentary, in brief segments rather than continuous text. Beyond that it is fashioned to stay as close as possible to the wording and structure of the original Hebrew. Its diction and vocabulary are said to exemplify modern American English.

Here are a few examples.

Genesis 6:11–12: "The earth was corrupted before God, and the earth was filled with villainy. God saw the earth and behold, it was corrupted, as all flesh corrupted its path upon the earth." This version invites readers to consider the all-consuming nature of human destructiveness.

Genesis 37:3–4: "Israel loved Joseph more than all his sons, because he was a son of his old age. His brothers saw that their father loved him more than all his brothers. And they hated him, and could not speak peaceably to him." Simple, direct language in both the Hebrew and English serves to highlight the raw emotions Joseph's brothers exhibited.

Exodus 15:2–3: "The Lord is my strength and my song. . . . The Lord is a warrior. The Lord is His name." Rendering these verses in this way is by no means the only option. But its directness and concreteness effectively convey the effect of the Hebrew.

Friedman's *Commentary on the Torah with a New English Translation*

Two other individual efforts also merit our careful attention. The first is Richard Elliott Friedman's *Commentary on the Torah with a New English Translation*, published in 2001.

Formerly a distinguished professor at the University of California, San Diego, Friedman is now Davis Professor of Jewish Studies at the University of Georgia. He is probably best known for his popular account of the Documentary Hypothesis, *Who Wrote the Bible?*, a Book-of-the-Month Club selection in 1987.

Believing that "translation is an art, not a science," as he explains in his "Notes on the Translation," Friedman endeavored to "produce a translation that is consistent in the English it employs." He continues:

> The Hebrew conjunction begins almost every verse. It usually means "and," but it has a wider range of meanings as well. . . . I usually leave it as "and" in English, but I do use . . . other terms in cases in which the context directs us to take it differently. . . . The name of God: I write it the same as it appears in the original, with the four consonants showing, thus: YHWH. . . . The gender of God: . . . I have . . . conveyed the masculine Hebrew conception [of the original] in translation as well. . . . Etymologies of names: Often a story is told that explains the origin of a name of a person or place. . . . As most translators have done in the past, I have left the text itself alone, accepting the fact that this is one of the inherent limitations of translation, and I have explained some of the etymologies in the comments. . . . The text: The translations follows . . . the Masoretic Text.[82]

Fellow scholars warmly received Friedman's work. Notably, they praised both his commentary and his translation. Frequently singled out was his ability to present traditional exegesis and critical scholarship clearly and evenhandedly.

However, beyond the academy and into the pews, as it were, this book has not had the influence of his earlier (e.g., *Who Wrote the Bible?*) or later (notably, *The Exodus*) publications, which formed the basis of numerous study groups and adult education classes. Given the high literary and intellectual quality of his *Commentary*, there is reason to hope that it will find a place of greater prominence within Jewish communities in the future.

These readings are characteristic of Friedman's version.

Genesis 1:1: "In the beginning of God's creating the skies and the earth." As Friedman observes (and we have noted elsewhere in this chapter), the precise meaning of the first phrase of the first chapter of the first book of the Hebrew Bible is contested. In part, his rendering arose out of his desire to highlight the parallel he perceived between Genesis 1:1 and Genesis 2:4, which can be understood in this way: "In the day of YHWH God's making earth and the skies." For Friedman, as for most other critical scholars, Genesis 1:1 is not only the beginning of the Bible but also the beginning of the P (Priestly) account of Creation. According to this viewpoint, Genesis 2:4 starts the second account of Creation, attributed to J (the Yahwist).

Genesis 2:18, 20: "And YHWH God said, 'It's not good for the human to be by himself. I'll make for him a strength corresponding to him.'" With this wording, Friedman achieved two related objectives. First, he made use of the gender-neutral term "human" where traditional translations have "man." Second, through the phrase "a strength corresponding to him," he made clear that females are the equals of males in all ways—and that this was built into Creation in these two biblical verses as well as others.

We may profitably compare Friedman here with NJPS: "The LORD God said, 'It is not good for man to be alone; I will make a fitting helper for him.'" In English, although not in biblical Hebrew, the term "helper" implies a subservient role. It is just such a hierarchical structure—male over female—that Friedman was seeking to dispel.

Genesis 11:5: "And the Lord came down to see the city and the tower that the human creatures had built." Where Friedman has "human creatures" (see also Gen. 2:18, 20, just above), NJPS uses "man," and OJPS, along with KJV, reads "children of men." Beyond his determination to provide gender inclusivity, Friedman's decision to include the word "creatures" appropriately highlights the infinite chasm that—especially on such an occasion—separates all-too-fallible humans from the infallible deity.

Leviticus 23:11: "And he shall elevate the sheaf before the Lord to be acceptable for you, from the morrow of the Sabbath the priest shall elevate it." In accordance with contemporary scholarship, Friedman spoke of "elevating" the sheaf rather than "waving" it (the term found in KJV and other earlier English-language versions). His literal translation, or rather transliteration, of the Hebrew word "Shabbat" leaves open the possibility that in this context the word is equivalent to "feast day"—that is, the first day of Passover, as interpreted by the Rabbis.

Alter's *The Hebrew Bible: A Translation with Commentary*

Robert Alter, a noted writer and literary critic who taught for many years at University of California at Berkeley, is among those who have sought to produce a contemporary Bible version aiming to offer "an appropriate modern English equivalent to ancient Hebrew style." Alter explained the rationale for his approach this way:

> The right direction, I think, was hit on by the King James Version, following the great model of Tyndale a century before it. There is no good reason to render biblical Hebrew as contemporary English, either lexically or syntactically. This is not to suggest that the Bible should be represented as fussily old-fashioned English, but a limited degree of archaizing coloration is entirely appropriate. . . . An adequate English version should [also] be able to indicate the small but significant modulations in diction in the biblical language—something the stylistically uniform King James Version, however, entirely fails to do.[83]

Like Friedman, Alter also chose to include the word "commentary" in his title, thereby reflecting a practice widely observed in earlier Jewish versions. As we have seen, commentary is at least as important as translation in Bible editions prepared by/for Jews. Earlier notable translators/commentators such as Saadiah Gaon, Moses Mendelssohn, Samuel David Luzzatto, and Samson Raphael Hirsch also used titles or subtitles to signal the high value they placed on the interpretative/exegetical portions of their work.[84]

Alter's *The Five Books of Moses: A Translation with Commentary* appeared in 2004. Alter followed up with his renderings of additional biblical texts with commentary, all of them following the same approach as his edition of the Torah. He ultimately covered all of Jewish scripture in *The Hebrew Bible: A Translation with Commentary*, published in 2018.

Alter's versions appear to have had their largest impact on fellow literary critics and others who find value in the Bible as literature (with the English-language version closely reflecting significant features in the Hebrew). One such reviewer commented that his *Hebrew Bible* "shows what it means to take the idea of the Bible as literature seriously."[85]

This is not to say that Alter is unfamiliar with the range of interpretive approaches to biblical interpretation, especially among traditional Jewish exegetes.[86] This is apparent in the extent and depth of his extensive sections of commentary.

I am sure that Alter understood these two elements—literature and exegesis—to be complementary. However, not all critics have seen it this way. In a prominent review of *The Five Books of Moses*, the novelist John Updike, while generous in his praise for Alter's translation, protested the "sheer amount of accompanying commentary" on almost every page of the translated text and, further, what he termed "the overload of elucidation [that Alter] imposed on the basic text."[87] In these statements, I believe Updike was being disingenuous at best, downright prejudiced at worse. As a Protestant, he was entitled to like his versions of the Bible commentary-free. But he had no literary or theological right to impose his strictures on Alter, who in this respect was carrying on a long-standing Jewish exegetical tradition.[88]

The following passages, all from Alter's version of Genesis, exemplify many of the distinctive characteristics of Alter's Bible.

Genesis 6:4 (last clause): "they are the heroes of yore, the men of renown." NJPS: "they were the heroes of old, the men of renown." As it happens, this passage, which immediately precedes the flood narrative, is virtually the same in Alter and NJPS. The NJPS translators did not provide any explanation for their rendering; probably they did not feel they needed to. In contrast, Alter offered an extended explanatory note here. For him, the Hebrew text at this point exemplifies a heightened, possibly archaizing style. Its wording in this style is either a citation from an older poetic composition or an illusion to the genre of epic literature. The form of the Hebrew word "they"—*h-m-h* rather than *h-m*—is for Alter a sure, if subtle, indicator of this. His use of "of yore" reflects his understanding of the archaic context out of which this clause was drawn. Given his commentary, I suppose that while the NJPS rendering, "of old," means pretty much the same thing as Alter's "of yore," it lacks the nuance Alter strove to achieve.

Genesis 22:17: "I will greatly bless you and multiply your seed, as the stars in the heavens and as the sand on the shore of the sea, and your seed shall take hold of its enemies' gate." NJPS: "I will bestow My blessing upon you and make your descendants as numerous as the stars of heaven and the sands on the seashore; and your descendants shall seize the gates of their foes." Alter chose the concrete English word "seed" as his rendering of the Hebrew, over against the extended term "descendants" found in NJPS or a similar option, "progeny," in other modern translations. Although "descendants" (or "progeny") is not technically incorrect here, in Alter's view these translations failed to do full justice to the Hebrew word, which focuses the readers' attention on the recent birth of Isaac as the (singular) "seed" that will ultimately produce numerous (plural) "descendants."

Genesis 24:16–20: "And the young woman was very comely to look at, a virgin, no man had known her. And she came down to the spring and filled her jug and came back up. And the servant ran toward her and said, 'Pray, let me sip a bit of water from your jug.' And she said, 'Drink, my lord,' and she hurried and lowered her jug onto her hand and let him drink. And she let him drink his fill and said, 'For your camels, too. I shall draw water until they drink their fill.' And she hurried and emptied her jug into the trough and she ran again to the well to draw water and drew water for all his camels." NJPS: "The maiden was very beautiful, a virgin whom no man had known. She went down to the spring, filled her jar, and came up. The servant ran toward her and said, 'Please, let me sip a little water from your jar.' 'Drink, my lord,' she said, and she quickly lowered her jar upon her hand and let him drink. When she had let him drink his fill, she said, 'I will also draw for your camels, until they finish drinking.' Quickly emptying her jar into the trough, she ran back to the well to draw, and she drew for all his camels."

Many features are worthy of comment here. Vocabulary wise, Alter chose the rare term "comely"; by contrast, NJPS has the everyday word "beautiful." Grammatically, at the end of verse 16, Alter employed a decidedly nonstandard construction, "a virgin, no man had known her" (awkward in English, nothing unusual in Hebrew), whereas NJPS, in conformity with contemporary English usage, reads "a virgin whom no man had known."

Even more noteworthy is another point that Alter himself singled out: the use of the conjunction "and." In Alter's text, this word appears sixteen times, exactly the same number of times as the corresponding term in Hebrew. NJPS, with four "ands," has only a fourth as many as Alter—and MT. For Alter, the frequency of the Hebrew conjunction is essential for establishing the rhythm of this story: It drives the narrative forward. As he sees—and hears—it, the repetition of the conjunction is as vital in an English-language version as it was in the Hebrew original.

Genesis 37:23: "And Reuben said to them [his brothers]: 'Shed no blood! Fling him [Joseph] into this pit in the wilderness and do not raise a hand against him [Joseph]'—that he [Reuben] might rescue him [Joseph] from their hands to bring him back to his father." NJPS: "And Reuben went on, "Shed no blood! Cast him into that pit out in the wilderness, but do not touch him yourselves"—intending to save him from them and restore him to his father." To Alter, it was important to retain the concrete reference to a body part—here "hand"—found twice in this Hebrew text. From his vantage point, the use of "hand" (in Hebrew and in English) highlights the paradox implicit in Reuben's argument—since flinging Joseph into a pit did necessitate their "hand"ling of him—and points to their taking his garment and dipping it in blood in the next scene.

For Those Wanting to Read the Versions Themselves

The presentation of translations in this section follows the same order as the prior discussion of English-language versions.

***The Koren Jerusalem Bible*:** Michael Friedlander's *Jewish Family Bible* formed the "basis" for Koren Publisher's *Jerusalem Bible*, formally titled, *The Koren Jerusalem Bible*. The latest hard-copy edition appeared in 2008 and is readily available.

***The Twenty-Four Books of the Holy Scriptures*:** In 2018, Isaac Leeser's *The Twenty-Four Books of the Holy Scriptures* appeared in the Forgotten Books Classic Reprint Series, published in both hardcover and paperback editions.

***The Holy Scriptures According to the Masoretic Text*, or OJPS:** First published in 1917, OJPS has appeared in many formats: hard copy (among others, English-only in one volume, a two-volume Hebrew-English edition, a quarto-sized pulpit Bible, and even a large-size illustrated version that was sold door-to-door), paperback, electronic, and online. Many of these are still available. In addition, JPS issued a reprint edition in 2018.

The JPS TANAKH, or NJPS: For the NJPS, two publication dates are especially significant: 1985 and 1999. The year 1985 saw the first appearance of the entire JPS TANAKH. It incorporated revisions of earlier versions of all three portions of the Hebrew Bible (Torah, Prophets, and Writings). In 1999, JPS produced its first Hebrew-English diglot edition, the *JPS Hebrew-English Tanakh*. Both of these books are still available in their original hardcover format as well as in leather-bound and presentation formats. They also appear in pocket and student editions, as paperbacks, and through electronic media, such as the fee-based software platforms Logos and Accordance. The JPS Torah appears in its own volume; selected, individual books of the Bible have been published with illustrations. An audio version, read by Theodore Bikel, among others, is also available. Full listings of the JPS TANAKH editions as well as a JPS Tanakh Customer Guide to Choosing Your Bible can be found at The Jewish Publication Society website https://jps.org/resources/tanakh-customer-guide/.

***The Contemporary Torah: A Gender-Sensitive Adaptation of the JPS Translation,* or CJPS:** In 2006, JPS introduced *The Contemporary Torah: A Gender-Sensitive Adaptation of the JPS Translation,* also known as CJPS (Contemporary JPS), edited by David E. S. Stein, who had been involved in a number of other JPS projects. Covering solely the Five Books of Moses, it is available in hardcover and as an ebook.

ArtScroll *Tanach*: ArtScroll first published its *Tanach* in 1996. It is sometimes referred to as the Stone Edition, after the name of the family that provided major financial support for this undertaking. In common with many other volumes produced by Mesorah, *Tanach* is readily available in editions that display high-value production features. A student-sized edition can be found in hard copy or paperback. All formats include both the Hebrew text and an English-language rendering.

***The Living Torah* and *The Living Nach*:** Aryeh Kaplan's *The Living Torah* first appeared in the early 1980s. This was followed in the 1990s by three volumes of *The Living Nach,* featuring translations of the Former Prophets, Latter Prophets, and Writings, prepared by disciples of Kaplan who made use of their teacher's approach to text and commentary. All four volumes are available in hardcover.

***The Schocken Bible,* volumes 1 and 2:** Two books constitute the first volumes of Everett Fox's *Schocken Bible: The Five Books of Moses: A New Translation with Introductions, Commentary, and Notes* (vol. 1, 1995); and *The Early Prophets: Joshua, Judges, Samuel, and Kings* (vol. 2, 2014). These are his definitive renderings of this biblical material, since they incorporate earlier versions. Volume 1 is available in hardcover and paperback. It is also included in fee-based software platforms like Logos and Accordance. At this writing, hardcover is the only format for volume 2. Both volumes can also be read as ebooks.

The Steinsaltz Humash is available in an elegantly printed and formatted edition at korenpub.com and other online vendors. It contains a number of features that make it accessible to the general reader as well as the scholar.

***Commentary on the Torah with a New English Translation*:** Richard Elliott Friedman's *Commentary on the Torah with a New English Translation* is available in hardcover, paperback, and as an ebook. It was first published in 2001.

***The Hebrew Bible: A Translation with Commentary*:** Between 2000 and 2014, Robert Alter brought out five volumes, each containing a portion of the English-language rendering of the Hebrew Bible on which he was working. In 2018, he published his final installment in three volumes, titled *The Hebrew Bible: A Translation with Commentary*, and covering the entire canon of Jewish Scripture. Hard-copy and paperback editions of all five of the partial translations can also be found. Alter's complete English-language version is available only in hard copy at this writing.

Final Thoughts

For many Jewish translations into English, the King James Version has remained the explicit point of reference—as something to be retained and emulated or as something to be corrected or rejected. Even in versions that lack specific reference to KJV, we can still detect the translators' awareness of "biblical [that is, KJV] English" among members of their intended audience. In no other language or culture does a single non-Jewish version exert such influence over Jewish translations.[89]

This point is brought home explicitly at least three times in this chapter. In explaining why British Jews waited almost a century and a half after their reentry into their country to prepare their own revision, to say nothing of their own version, of the Hebrew Bible, British scholar Raphael Loewe had observed: "English-speaking Jewry distinguishes itself from the Jewries of other Protestant countries, by its acceptance . . . of the national vernacular Bible of its Christian environment [KJV]." Then, in the mid-1800s, while responding to criticism of earlier editions of his Jewish Bible, the translator Abraham Benisch commented: "The Anglo-Jewish community . . . [is] so wedded to the diction of the authorized version (KJV) that every departure from its phraseology, however well-founded, seems to grate upon their ears."

Loewe seemed to express no view, positive or negative, about the early Anglo-Jewish dependence on KJV. Benisch, on the other hand, seemed to be venting his own frustrations with reader rejection of some of his innovative turns of phrase. By contrast, the third example, from Max Margolis, also a practicing translator (but this time in the United States rather than in Great Britain), was positive to the point of rapturous in his praise of KJV and its influence upon the world of Jewish Bible translation. He reasoned: "[The KJV] has an inimitable style and rhythm; the coloring of the original is not obliterated.... What imparts to the English Bible its beauty, aye, its simplicity, comes from the [Hebrew] original."

Perhaps here too Margolis got it right. Jewish translators (as well as all others, we would suppose) of the Hebrew Bible need a knowledge of the Hebrew language, in all of its aspects, to satisfactorily accomplish their goal.

But there is more. As we have shown throughout this book, Jewish translators displayed a greater degree of linguistic knowledge—deeper, and also more intimate—than others. And this was true whether a given translator was practicing a more literal (formal equivalence) or a freer (functional equivalence) approach to his task.

When it came to English-language versions, then, KJV translators were uniquely well versed both in the source language (Hebrew, as understood and interpreted by generations of Jewish exegetes) and the target language (English, as produced and polished by generations of playwrights and poets). This makes especially good sense when we recall the huge role Christian humanists played in creating the KJV. Christian humanists were Protestants! But that really didn't matter for the earliest Anglo-Jewish and American-Jewish Bible translators.

Until it did. By the middle of the twentieth century, new stylistic and theological impulses asserted themselves. Or, rather, the NJPS lead translator Harry M. Orlinsky asserted them within the Jewish world. The KJV mold had become, well... moldy, outdated, stale. A new translation was needed, something that would appeal more directly to the literary and perhaps also theological sensitivities of a modern audience. Hence the appeal to, and of, the freer style of functional equivalence, as exemplified in NJPS.

But there is an irony here. If KJV, in spite of the wide erudition of its translators, is ultimately a Protestant product, so is functional equivalence, at least as a theoretical construct on which to build a Bible version.

Still, in its own way, such irony is built into most of the history and practice of Bible translation. Even when Jews and Christians did not get along on a personal level (or even acknowledge the existence of the other group), the results of Jewish and Christian exegetes were in conversation (if I can use that term) with each other. Acknowledged or unacknowledged, this mixture of perspectives has enhanced, rather than diminished, the translators and the versions they produce.

7

Non-Jewish Translations with Jewish Features

In this chapter we add several non-Jewish translations with Jewish features.[1] None of them are, broadly speaking, well known. Their inclusion here is intended to broaden the scope of our analysis, to delineate where we can appropriately fix the border between Jewish versions and all others.

We will first examine Yiddish-language translations, especially of the New Testament, prepared by Christian Bible societies and widely distributed by groups seeking to convert Jews to Christianity. Most of these translators were themselves Jewish converts to Christianity, a change in status that did not go unmentioned in Bible societies' internal documents and public pronouncements.

Next, we'll focus on "Jewish Bibles" prepared by members of a group that adheres to Messianic Judaism. Those responsible for these Bibles contend that they are uniquely well placed to highlight aspects of Jesus's life and teaching that are overlooked or underrepresented in most other New Testaments.

We will conclude with the life and accomplishments of a single individual who twice translated the Bible into Chinese. Born and reared in mid-nineteenth-century Eastern European Judaism, he acknowledged and drew from his upbringing even after he converted to Christianity and served the Episcopal Church in China.

Yiddish Translations of the Bible

Intent on providing Christian missionaries with another tool in their proselytizing arsenal, the British and Foreign Bible Society (BFBS, or the Bible Society) produced Yiddish translations of both Testaments within fifteen years of its founding in 1804. These efforts continued for more than one hundred years.

Yiddish Translations of the New Testament

The first Yiddish New Testament BFBS produced was published in 1821 primarily for the London Jews' Society. Although this may sound like a Jewish communal organization, it was in actuality the common shorthand for the London Society for Promoting Christianity among the Jews, one of the major groups seeking to convert British and immigrant Jews. The translator of this version, Benjamin Nehemiah Solomon, was "a convert from Judaism, who [had come] over to England from Poland."[2]

A half a century later, another converted Jew, Paul Isaac Hershon, spent six years revising Solomon's version to appeal to the increasing number of Eastern European Jews who were making Western Europe their home or sojourning there as a way station en route to North America.[3] His new translation, in the Galician or Polish dialect of Yiddish, then spoken by large numbers of Eastern European Jews, would be frequently reprinted, especially in its revised form.

In 1901, three individuals, including a J. Rabinowitz (probably Joseph Rabinowitz), issued a Bible Society–sponsored revision of Hershon's translation designed to combine "the three main forms of Yiddish—Bessarabian, Lithuanian, and Galician." Then, from 1909 to 1919, yet another major revision took place, supervised by, among others, the Reverend Samuel Hinds Wilkinson (the BFBS editorial superintendent) and the London Jews' Society's Reverend Aaron Bernstein. Bernstein, too, was a converted Jew.

Repeated revision and high-powered representation (as, for example, from the editorial superintendent) are two indicators of how prominently the Yiddish New Testament figured in BFBS's multifaceted activities during this period. By 1917, according to the BFBS's own accounting, somewhat more than 700,000 copies of the Yiddish New Testament had been published.[4] And, as several of the translators' or revisers' names make clear, converted Jews who spoke Yiddish were indispensable to the production of these Yiddish New Testaments.

Other BFBS Translations

The earliest BFBS Old Testament that was at all related to Yiddish dates to 1858. This was a diglot (or bilingual) edition: "the Hebrew text [appeared] side by side with Luther's German version slightly modified and transliterated into Hebrew characters."[5] The relationship of this to Yiddish is twofold: First, much of Yiddish is drawn from German; second, Yiddish is also written using Hebrew characters.

A full BFBS Yiddish Old Testament appeared in 1898, followed by revised versions.[6] And in a subsequent decade, BFBS reported with delight: "The Old Testament in Yiddish, Revised Union Version, has at last been published."[7] This was the most complete Yiddish edition of the Old Testament BFBS had published to date.

Characteristics and Goals of Bible Society Translations

By December 1900, as BFBS translators worked on the 1901 Yiddish New Testament, they and others associated with the Bible Society became concerned about the designation of its language. Although we have been speaking of these volumes as "Yiddish" versions, BFBS had not yet settled on a single name for this language. A variety of designations were considered and discarded—among them Judeo-Polish, Jargon, Hebrew-German, Mamalushon, Lishon, Ashkenazy, B'laz (meaning a "foreign tongue"), Rashi German, and Women's German—before BFBS finally adopted the term "Judeo-German (Yiddish)" in its contemporary catalogs.

Decisive support for use of the term "Yiddish" had come from British Jews themselves: "A day or two ago," a staffer in the BFBS Editorial/Translation Department wrote in early 1901, "I was shown a note from the chief Rabbi of London, Dr. Adler in which he promised to write in 'Yiddish' something to be printed."[8] The BFBS staffer did not elaborate on the context in which Adler wrote this note, but Adler's use of this term seems to have been instrumental in BFBS's decision to adopt the term henceforth.

A. S. Geden, who played a major role in several Yiddish translations of the Bible, emphasized the scholarly or academic side of BFBS's efforts in this regard:

> To a large extent, therefore the Committee of revision had to feel its way, and to endeavor in each instance to ascertain the prevailing usage—with the ultimate hope of producing a version which might be generally accepted by all Yiddish-speaking Jews, might help to unify the varieties of dialect, and might furnish a standard both of orthography and of grammar. Time and experience alone can show how far those who have been engaged on this task have achieved success.[9]

At the same time, for BFBS such scientific endeavors were not an end unto themselves—or at least not the only end in mind:

> For the evangelization and enlightenment of the Jews generally throughout the world, Yiddish is the only available medium; and consequently there is no work more important than that of supplying them with the Scriptures in a form which they will appreciate and may be led to study. . . . They have a strong claim . . . on Christian sympathy, and there is an urgent need that the truth of the Gospel should be presented and brought home to them in a form they can appreciate and understand.[10]

In the establishment of a new committee to revise the 1901 Yiddish New Testament, this mixture of scientific and evangelical motives became apparent. Just a few years later, in 1907, for example, attention would be called to the "great missionary" value of "a complete translation of the Bible into Yiddish."[11] There was no question about the need for some "Hebrew Christian brethren," but now the translation committee itself had to be "presided over by a Christian-born Theologian with a University Degree." According to the organization's minutes, the three earlier revisers had been "unscholarly, strangers to philology, and not students of grammar in any language." Thus the new committee would have both proselytizing and philologizing on its plate.

It would take nearly three decades—until 1928—for the definitive BFBS version of the Old Testament in Yiddish to finally appear. The minutes for that year record many words of praise and at least one "warm eulogy" for this new version.[12]

Jewish Reactions, as Reported Primarily by Bible Societies

Not surprisingly, BFBS reports and publications generally presented a positive picture of missionary activities aimed at Jews. Frequently, the presence of a BFBS Bible in a language Jews could read—Yiddish or Hebrew—was cited as a factor in this success.

The Amsterdam agent of the London Society for Promoting Christianity among the Jews, for example, reported "a deepening of interest among the emigrant Jews who pass through Rotterdam . . . the majority are more decidedly bent on knowing as much as possible about Christ."[13] The BFBS minutes recounted that "Jewish emigrants from Russia and Romania on their way to America are regularly visited on board in Rotterdam, and have the Gospel preached to them in Yiddish with the sanction of the authorities. They sometimes fight for a N.T. in Yiddish."[14]

BFBS publications also mention a southern Russian movement springing up among the Jews—"We cannot doubt that this movement, with the outspoken recognition . . . of Jesus Christ as the promised Messiah of the Jews, is 'of God, and cannot be overthrown'"—and highlight the case of an insurance agent, who also taught Jewish children. Having gotten caught up in this movement, he "respectfully request[ed] a Hebrew Old Testament and also a New Testament in Hebrew, with the German and Polish translation." With these and other tools, he assured BFBS, "I will unveil the new hidden light gradually to my scholars, and may the Eternal One in Heaven be with the Society and its supporters."[15] Elsewhere, the Bible Society tells of an indigent Jew, to whom a missionary had lent a New Testament to read, grasping it and saying, "That Book, sir—that Book has brought peace to my troubled soul." Another Jew was said to have reported, in the presence of a rabbi, "I have read the New Testament and there is not a more interesting Book."[16] Still another vignette pictures a Rabbi Weiss, who converted to Christianity and was now being prepared for baptism. The rabbi had offered to translate the Old Testament for the society, but BFBS did not look upon his offer favorably.[17]

Among the challenges the Bible societies faced was isolating the dialect or form of Yiddish that would have the widest appeal to Jews. One private American Bible Society communication assured their BFBS counterparts that "it is not the desire of the A.B.S. to bring out a Yiddish translation to take the place of any versions existing at present, but to see if there is an American Yiddish which needs to be considered in what may become the standard Yiddish N.T. later on."[18] The following remarks about a member of the International Missionary Council in 1933 elaborated upon the issue:

> During his travels in Europe and America he has received many complaints about the Yiddish Bible. Says that there is a classic Yiddish. The League of Nations publishes pamphlets in it, and he asks whether it is not possible to provide a good translation of the Bible for the 8,000,000 Jews who use Yiddish as their language. Points out that a new interest among Jews in our Lord makes it the more desirable that the Scriptures should be acceptable to them as regards literary form.[19]

In response, the BFBS editorial superintendent replied: "Great difficulty has always been caused by the fluctuating character of Yiddish.

None of the versions in which the Bible Society has been concerned for the last thirty years seems to have given complete satisfaction."[20] This is a far more somber assessment than those from earlier decades.

It is difficult to gauge the overall "success" of the Bible societies' experience with Yiddish Bibles, especially New Testaments. Undoubtedly a certain number of Jews would have been attracted to Christianity on the basis of Bible texts in a language they themselves could read. As an example, the Protestant Bible translator Joseph Schereschewsky's conversion from Judaism is generally attributed to his contact as a teenager with one of these Bibles (on this, see the last section of this chapter).

At the same time, the widespread availability of these Bibles in the hands of missionaries most likely contributed to the development of English-language Bibles by Jews themselves (on this development, see chapter 6).

The *Complete Jewish Bible*: Messianic Judaism

Let us imagine that you are invited to attend a bar or bat mitzvah ceremony. You decide that an English-language edition of the Bible would be an appropriate gift. However (we are imagining), you do not know which version to purchase. Like others in similar circumstances, you go to Amazon.com and search for "Jewish Bible." The first search result may be the *Complete Jewish Bible*, translated by David H. Stern.[21] What, you might ask, could be a better choice?

If you read the full description of the volume, at least two aspects might well stand out. First, this "complete" Jewish Bible includes the New Testament as well as the Old Testament/Hebrew Bible, even though the New Testament is not part of the Jewish Bible in any of the generally recognized denominations within Judaism. Second, the book's publisher is Messianic Jewish Resources International.[22] The vast majority of Jews—and Christians, for that matter—do not recognize Messianic Judaism as a valid manifestation of Judaism.[23]

Characteristic Features of the "Jewish New Testament"

In my experience, academic scholars of the Bible tend to consider works like Stern's as too tendentious to merit sustained analysis. Yet, from my perspective, denying Stern's messianic beliefs as Jewish is not the same as denying any value to his translations.

Let us, for example, compare his *Jewish New Testament: A Translation of the New Testament That Expresses Its Jewishness* (1989) with the *Restored New Testament: A New Translation with Commentary, Including the Gnostic Gospels Thomas, Mary, and Judas* (2009), created by the well-known literary figure and translator Willis Barnstone.[24]

Notably, both Barnstone and Stern set out to produce a New Testament that highlights the Jewishness of Jesus and his closest associates, as well as the many links between the Old Testament and the Good News (Gospel) being propagated. By contrast, other translations of the New Testament, which severed the connections between Jesus and his fellow Jews, had allowed for antisemitic readings and interpretations, especially of the Gospels. In what follows we look at one of the ways—namely, personal names—in which Barnstone and Stern sought to "restore" (to use Barnstone's terminology) Jesus to the first-century CE Jewish community in which he was active.

Although these two modern translators differ as to details, in this regard their goals closely align. For example, both Stern and Barnstone name two of the Gospels using Semitic forms—Mattityahu and Yochanan (Stern) and Mattityahu and Yohanan (Barnstone)—in place of the usual Matthew and John in almost all other English-language New Testament versions. The names Matthew and John are formed from the Greek, which was fine for the Gospels' audience of Greek speakers but obscured the fact that both men were Aramaic-speaking Jews—just like almost all the other figures in the New Testament, including Jesus.[25]

As for Jesus, the main character of the New Testament, and his family, Stern's edition identifies them as Jewish precisely as Barnstone does—through the use of proper names closely reflecting their first-century BCE and CE environments. Jesus is Yeshua, his mother is Miryam, and his father is Yosef. Stern also identifies Yaakov (similar to Barnstone's Ya'akov) as one of Jesus's brothers and one of the apostles.[26]

This is not to say that the experience of reading Stern's "Jewish" New Testament and Barnstone's "restored" text is exactly the same. For his part, Barnstone sought to present transliterations of both Semitic-rooted names and those from the Greek world. So, while Stern leaves the originally Greek names Mark and Luke untouched (that is, in the same Anglicized form found in other English-language New Testaments), for Barnstone and his readers, these Gospel writers are Markos and Loukas, just as they would have been known in the first century CE. In addition, Barnstone's more literary rendering honors the often poetical qualities of the Greek text that are largely absent from the mostly pedestrian versions of modern times. Stern displays no such aspirations.

Still, Stern and Barnstone are, as it were, united in their efforts to bring to the fore the essential Jewishness of Jesus and his environment. In fact, the subtitle of Stern's work is *A Translation of the New Testament That Expresses Its Jewishness*. And as Stern observes in his introduction, the New Testament is in fact a very Jewish book.[27] Much of what is in the New Testament, he asserts (and I affirm), can be comprehended only within its Jewish context.[28]

For his part, Barnstone firmly supports the view that many earlier translators of the New Testament, all of them Christians, were themselves antisemites who intentionally sought to distance Jesus—and ultimately Christians—from their Jewish roots. Stern does not attribute such intentional activities to earlier translators; rather, he holds that they rather uncritically and passively produced anti-Jewish versions from having absorbed substantial elements of antisemitic theology.[29]

Further, Stern writes, the *Jewish New Testament* brings out the New Testament's Jewishness in overlapping ways. One example (beyond the transliteration of proper names already cited) concerns the figure usually known as "John the Baptist." At Mark 1:4 Stern introduces us to Jochanan the Immerser; in Barnstone, we meet Johanan the Dipper. Both translators jettisoned the use of "Baptist" because of the common association in English of baptism with Christians. Whatever John/Jochanan/Johanan was doing with individuals who came to him on the banks of the Jordan River, he was doing as a believing and practicing Jew of his era.[30]

Similarly, throughout almost all English-language versions of the New Testament, each of the twelve men who formed Jesus's inner circle is referred to as an "apostle." Uniquely, Stern hit upon "emissary" as his term of choice. Even though the word "apostle" has a number of possible referents, for almost all English-speakers who are thinking of the New Testament, this word refers to Jesus's closes associates, who are then typically assumed to be (already) Christian—when in fact they, like Jesus, were Jewish. Precisely because Stern's choice of terminology is so unexpected here, I sense he is inviting readers to reconsider any facile and erroneous equation between Jesus's followers and Christians.

That said, Stern takes one further step to achieve his aims of a Jewish New Testament. His version also draws on "Jewish English," which he defines as "Hebrew and Yiddish expressions which English-speaking Jews incorporate into everyday speech."[31] These include *tsuris* (instead of "troubles") and do *tzedakah* (instead of "give to charity") along with *nudnik* (instead of "keep bothering") and *shmoose* (instead of "greet") in Luke (18:4–5 and 10:4, respectively); as well as *bubbe-meises* (instead of "old wives' tales") in 1 Timothy 4:7. "I used [these expressions] in order to add a little 'ethnic spice' to my version," he explains in a letter, "since one of my stated purposes was to demonstrate to Jews, Christians, and everyone else that the New Testament is a Jewish book."[32] Acknowledging in the work itself that some readers may find these renderings anachronistic, he appeals to their tolerance.

I consider myself among the most tolerant of readers and researchers. However, I have no sympathy for Stern's practice here: Simply put, to place Yiddish expressions in Jesus's mouth is not just anachronistic; it is bizarre.[33]

A "Jewish" Bishop and Bible Translator

Joseph Schereschewsky (1831–1906), a born Jew turned Episcopal leader and Bible translator, created two other Bible versions. Both were in Chinese.[34]

From Eastern Europe through the United States to the Far East of Asia

Schereschewsky was born in 1831 into a Jewish family in the town of Taurage, or Tavrig, in Russian Lithuania, near the Prussian border. Orphaned as a small child, he was raised by his half-brother's family, who ensured that he, like other young Jewish boys, received an education at a *heder* (traditional Jewish elementary school). Either on his own volition or at his family's urging, Schereschewsky left home at age fifteen for the Ukrainian city of Zhitomir. There he immersed himself in both traditional Jewish and secular studies at a newly established, state-sponsored rabbinical seminary. In this institution Jewish teachers oversaw the study of Judaism and non-Jews regularly taught secular subjects.

In this way Schereschewsky came into contact with the same currents of Jewish Enlightenment that decisively influenced many of the translators featured in chapter 6. So, for example, here Schereschewsky would study the Bible in Moses Mendelssohn's German translation and come to know Hebrew as a living language. In Zhitomir, Schereschewsky also had his first extended contact with non-Jews, both inside and outside the seminary, and came across a copy of the New Testament in Yiddish (or, possibly, in Hebrew), most likely distributed by the London Jews' Society. Five years later, though, Schereschewsky left for Breslau without completing the curriculum in either rabbinical or pedagogical studies. We don't know why.

He entered the University of Breslau, which had recently begun to admit Jewish students. The city was also an especially active center for Protestant missionary societies, which often included at least one Jewish convert in their midst.

From there, he continued to move from place to place. Taking up residence in New York City, he worked among Christian missionaries to the Jews and formally converted to Christianity as a Baptist in the company of others who had been born Jewish. Studying henceforth at the Western Theological Seminary in Allegheny, Pennsylvania, near Pittsburgh, he imbibed the enthusiasm for missionary activity in far-flung lands that was central to this Presbyterian seminary's identity. Returning to New York City, he enrolled at the Episcopal General Theological Seminary, and when his mentor at the seminary recommended him for a position in China, the newly ordained deacon (who nevertheless had not completed his coursework) set sail in mid-summer 1859.

In China and Japan

Schereschewsky traveled from New York to Shanghai on a boat equipped with sails. During his more than five months aboard ship, he concentrated on acquiring knowledge of the Chinese language. By all accounts, he was an extraordinarily quick and thorough student.

His language proficiency, rather than his pastoral skills, would characterize his years in China. Acknowledging that he wasn't adept at preaching sermons, founding traditional ecclesiastical institutions, or attracting converts, he poured his prodigious skills into preparing Chinese-language texts for use by converts or those in the process of converting to Christianity.

In 1864, while living in Peking, Schereschewsky became part of a committee, composed of other Protestant missionaries, tasked with producing a version of the Bible in the popular northern vernacular called Mandarin colloquial. Given his religious background and training (Schereschewsky never hid or denied his Jewish background, for which he was honored by almost all of his colleagues), he was given the entire Old Testament to work on.

He collaborated with Chinese copyists and scholars for a decade. In 1875, at long last, Schereschewsky's full translation of the Old Testament in the Chinese vernacular appeared. Contemporary reviewers of this work were favorable. In their opinion, Schereschewsky combined an unparalleled mastery of biblical Hebrew with near native sensitivity to the nuances of Mandarin colloquial.

In 1881, by which time Schereschewsky was serving as missionary bishop of Shanghai, a debilitating stroke incapacitated him physically for what would be the last twenty-five years of his life. Yet Schereschewsky's mental capacities and linguistic resolve remained unabated. Using only one finger, he typed out a significantly more annotated version of the 1875 translation that would appear in 1899. Three years later Schereschewsky published a version of the entire Bible in a simplified literary Chinese known as "easy wenli." Reviewers praised both translations. However, only the 1899 Mandarin colloquial version attracted a substantial audience as measured by sales figures (its initial printing of three thousand copies sold out fairly quickly).

Much of Schereschewsky's colloquial Mandarin text would be taken up in the Chinese Union Version that appeared in 1919 and is still in use today. In this respect, Schereschewsky has had a significant and long-lasting impact on the Bible in Chinese.

Behind Schereschewsky's Translations

Schereschewsky did not favor "slavishly literal" translations. "Idiom and clearness should not be sacrificed to literality," he wrote. "To translate literally Hebrew . . . into Chinese is often mistranslating." At the same time, he "believe[d] that the Hebrew text is to be preferred to any version, old as it may be,"[35] and insisted that his translations uphold the primacy of the Hebrew language in all its subtleties and nuances. This included maintaining the distinctive qualities of Hebrew poetry, especially parallelism, in the Chinese text.

In this way also, Schereschewsky's Jewish upbringing and education appear to have had a profound influence on his Chinese Bible translations. He was intent on imbuing the new translations with the qualities he esteemed in biblical Hebrew.

What is more, he turned to Jewish biblical exegesis when he felt it would be of value to serious readers of the biblical text.[36]

Jewish Influences in Schereschewsky's Translation and Commentary on the Old Testament

Schereschewsky's respect for biblical Hebrew is also evidenced by his use of Hebrew pronunciation rather than later forms that, by his time, had achieved near universal acceptability. In his Genesis, for example, "Eve" is transliterated as *Xiawa,* reflecting the Hebrew *Hava,* and "Gemorrah" is *Emala,* which is close to the Hebrew form for this place name.[37]

Furthermore, Schereschewsky relied heavily on the comments of the medieval Jewish exegete Rashi, and exhibited a wide and deep acquaintance with the entire midrashic literature associated with the Hebrew Bible.[38] Consider the following examples of this dependence.

Genesis 4:17–24 tells the story of Lamech, the only descendant of Cain for whom more than a passing notice is provided. Verses 23–24 constitute an enigmatic piece of poetry. As translated in OJPS, the second half of verse 23 reads: "For I have slain a man for wounding me / And a young man for bruising me." NJPS follows this wording except for substituting "lad" for "young man." The wording in Schereschewsky's Mandarin text falls within this understanding of the Hebrew, but the note that follows presents an extensively reworded rendering: "If I kill a warrior I harm myself, [if] I harm a youth I damage my [own] body."[39]

There is an unmistakable connection between this rendering and Rashi's interpretation:

> Lamech was blind and his son Tubal-cain would lead him. One day, Tubal-cain saw Cain and, mistaking him for an animal, he bade his father to shoot an arrow, which killed Cain. When Lamech realized he had killed Cain, he beat his hands together in grief, and accidentally killed his son. His wives were angered and refused to live with him. [With reference to Gen. 4:24] he tried to appease them: "If the punishment of Cain, an intentional murderer, was delayed until the seventh generation, surely my punishment will be deferred many times seven because I killed accidentally!"[40]

Genesis 47:21: During the famine in Egypt, OJPS tells us, "And as for the people, he [Joseph] removed them city by city, from one end of the border of Egypt even to the other end thereof." NJPS puts it this way: "And he [Joseph] removed the population town by town, from one end of Egypt's border to the other," noting that the meaning of the Hebrew in the first clause is uncertain. For its part, the ArtScroll *Tanach* text reads: "As for the nation, he [Joseph] resettled it by cities, from one end of Egypt's borders to the other." Within the immediate context, it is clear that "the people" or "the population" or "the nation" refers to the Egyptians.

Rashi, however, understood this passage quite differently. In his interpretation, the "people," "population," or "nation" referred not to the native Egyptians, but to the Hebrews, whom Joseph moved from their present location to various cities throughout the land of Egypt. Schereschewsky's rendering abides by this understanding. As he observed in a note, such an action was to allow for the virtual integration of the Hebrews into the urban centers of Egypt, thereby removing from Joseph's kin any stigma attached to their status as outsiders.[41]

Where appropriate, Schereschewsky used the notes to elucidate the meaning of Hebrew names he transliterated in the text. At Genesis 3:20 he made an explicit connection between *Hava* (Eve) and the Hebrew word meaning life.[42] An apt parallel appears in Everett Fox's approach to the passage in his *Schocken Bible*: "The human called his wife's name: Havva/Life-giver!"[43]

At Genesis 27:36 Schereschewsky noted that Jacob's name is related to the word for cheating.[44] Again, a comparison with Fox is instructive: "Is that why his name was called Yaakov/Heel-Sneak? For he has now sneaked against me twice."[45]

Perhaps it is self-evident to say that when Schereschewsky furnished alternate renderings or explanatory comments in his notes, he was intent upon instructing his readers and, in turn, the students or hearers of these readers. When we consider that almost all of Schereschewsky's readers were converts or in the process of converting to

Christianity, we can acknowledge one further point of importance. In this specific context, Schereschewsky made the conscious decision to transmit, as part of Christian Scripture, distinctive features of Jewish biblical transmission and exegesis.

Even though later generations of Chinese Christians might well have been unaware of these Jewish antecedents, this material did become part of their culture—due largely to the determined efforts of Jewish-born Joseph Schereschewsky.

Further Thoughts

In this chapter we first looked at Yiddish- and Hebrew-language Bibles, in particular New Testaments, that BFBS sponsored. Here, converted Jews played leading—we might say indispensable—roles, furnishing both linguistic and cultural expertise. Their participation in these activities led in two directions—one surely anticipated, the other decidedly not.

Although overall numbers are difficult to arrive at, it is certain that some Jews became Christians on the basis of their reading or hearing portions of the New Testament in languages they knew, Yiddish and Hebrew. This was expected. At the same time, the widespread appearance of "Christian" Bibles among immigrant Jews ultimately led members of the Anglo-Jewish community to support English-language versions of the Hebrew Bible that highlighted aspects of Sacred Writ perceived as vital to the immediate survival and ultimate growth of Judaism. It is pretty clear that this was not one of the goals of Bible societies or missionary groups.

We then turned our attention to so-called Jewish Bibles that abide by the distinctive beliefs shared by adherents of Messianic Judaism. As with the Christian Bible societies' Yiddish-language translations, these Messianic Bibles place greater emphasis on the New rather than the Old Testament. As part of the process, primary translator David Stern made use of linguistic and stylistic features to emphasize the often overlooked and essential Jewishness of Jesus's words and works.

Those who read Stern's translation cannot help but be impressed by the deeply Jewish contexts in which Jesus lived and taught. They can also easily trace the genealogical and ideological roots of Jesus from the Old to the New Testament. Setting aside Stern's idiosyncratic insistence on inserting Yiddish phrases into his otherwise well-thought-out version, he was only a bit less adept than writer-scholar Willis Barnstone at achieving this goal.

We concluded with the life and accomplishments of Joseph Schereschewsky, who converted to Christianity, moved to China to serve as a missionary, and, as the major part of that work, spent many decades translating the Bible into Chinese. As he acknowledged, and his colleagues readily accepted, Schereschewsky's substantive Jewish upbringing and education fully informed the way in which he rendered, and commented on, the Old Testament. This pertains both to substance, as, for example, his knowledgeable use of Rashi, and to style, through which he showed uncommon feeling for the intricacies and nuances of biblical Hebrew.

As with the earlier examples, Schereschewsky's efforts also moved in two directions. Working primarily in accordance with his own approach, he was in fact able to produce a widely read and referenced Chinese version, in colloquial Mandarin, that in essence (directly or indirectly) became *the* Bible for generations of Chinese who converted to Christianity. To the extent that these individuals studied the text—and I suspect that a large percentage of them did—they came into contact with Jewish exegesis and Jewish sensitivities.

On the other hand, Schereschewsky's singular devotion to translation, as laudable as it was, displaced the opportunities he might otherwise have had to express his Jewish perspective through sermons or incidental but popular writing. Admittedly, he was not, if I may use the term, a natural orator or essayist. But still, his singlemindedness deprived those in his and succeeding generations of these other means of exploring rich connections between Judaism and Christianity.

In all of these scenarios, the translators' Jewish heritage remained a salient feature of their self-identification and/or their designation by others. Many of the scholars involved with the Bible societies continued to be referred to as Jewish, even after they had formally converted to Christianity. The Old and New Testament texts produced by Messianic Jews are pointedly titled as parts of a "Jewish Bible," and the Jewish background of the primary translator appears in the foreground of information provided about the volume. In Schereschewsky's case, his Jewish upbringing and training remained such a well-known part of his identity that he was sometimes referred to as a Jewish bishop.

Let's be clear: None of these phenomena are Jewish Bible translations. But they (along with other exemplars like the Alba Bible and the King James Version) do seem to share some of the same headwaters. Here we might more expansively imagine Jewish Bible translations as a wide-ranging river (or torrent?), fed by many sources and branching off in numerous tributaries. Rendering this imagery into the quotidian language of actual versions and translators is the task of the following chapter, with which we conclude this volume.

Conclusion

In the previous chapters I have introduced a considerable number of Jewish Bible translators. They lived at different times and worked in different circumstances. Some worked alone, and others as members of a committee. Some sought to reproduce as many as possible of the distinctive features of the underlying Hebrew text. For others, the primary goal was to fulfill the expectations of an intended target audience seeking a version of the Bible that looked, read, and sounded as much as possible like any other piece of literature in their language. Some of these translators are well enough known to have been the subject of one or more full-length biographies. With respect to others, only their names are known, and sometimes not even that.

It Really Does Matter Which Version You Use

Many people, frequent Bible readers as well as occasional users, assert that when all is said and done, it really doesn't matter which version you use—they all say pretty much the same thing. Based on passages discussed in earlier portions of this book, we can see that this is in fact not the case. In support of this assertion, I review two issues, both obviously central to the Hebrew Bible: how humans understand God, and which humans are commanded by God (the gender question).

How Humans Understand God in the MT and *Tafsir*

As discussed in chapters 2 and 3, respectively, the anonymous translators of the *Targums* and Saadiah Gaon in his *Tafsir* consistently avoided a straightforward representation of any anthropomorphisms or anthropopathisms associated with God that they found in the Hebrew text they were rendering. Let us recall a few representative examples from Saadiah's Arabic version.

Exodus 9:3—MT: "Then the hand of the LORD will strike your livestock in the fields." Saadiah: "Behold God's affliction is striking. . . ."

Exodus 24:10—MT: "Under God's feet there was the likeness of a pavement of sapphire." Saadiah: "Beneath his Light . . ."

Genesis 6:6—MT: "And the LORD regretted that He had made man on earth, and His heart was saddened." Saadiah: "And he made pain enter their hearts."

Psalm 2:4—MT: "He who is enthroned in heaven laughs." Saadiah: "He Who dwells in heaven makes people laugh."

Genesis 11:5—MT: "The LORD came down to look at the city and tower that man had built." Saadiah: "And God caused something hidden to descend [or, brought down an instruction of intimidation] to see the city and the tower that the people built."

Deuteronomy 4:24—MT: "For the LORD your God is a consuming fire." Saadiah: "God's punishment is a consuming fire."

The deity as pictured in the traditional Hebrew text—and in almost all of its Jewish translations, from literal to free—is physically and emotionally dynamic, the very opposite of a static being. God moves as humans do, feels as humans do, changes direction as humans do. Admittedly, all of this is on a cosmic scale, far more expansive than the circumscribed stage upon which humans live. But we can relate to this God, connect with this God, perhaps even befriend this God.

Not so the deity of the *Targums* or the *Tafsir*. This God is formidable indeed—immutable, incorporeal, and in no discernable way like humans. We lack any personal connection with this God, whom we may fear and respect, but probably do not draw close to. If we imagine, as I do, that readers of the Bible in Aramaic or Arabic drew their emotional and intellectual appropriation of God from what was to them Sacred Writ, then theirs was an austere deity far different from that depicted in the *peshat* of the Hebrew original and the versions that derive more directly from it.

Which Humans Are Commanded by God in OJPS and CJPS

As for the gender issue, let us compare the 1917 JPS version (OJPS) with *The Contemporary Torah* (CJPS), which places great emphasis on its gender-related renderings.

Genesis 11:5—OJPS: "And the Lord came down to see the city and the tower, which the children of men builded." CJPS: "YHWH came down to look at the city and tower that humanity had built."

Exodus 16:16 (see also Exod. 16:28–30)—OJPS: "This is the thing which the LORD hath commanded, Gather of it every man according to his eating, an omer for every man, according to the number of your persons; take ye every man for them which are in his tents." CJPS: "This is what the Eternal has commanded: gather as much of it as each of you requires to eat, an *omer* a person for as many of you as there are; you shall each fetch for those in your tent."

Deuteronomy 24:16—OJPS: "The fathers shall not be put to death for the children, neither shall the children be put to death for the fathers; every man shall be put to death for his own sin." CJPS: "Parents should not be put to death for children, nor children put to death for parents: one should be put to death only for one's own crime."

As we see in these exemplars, which are representative of many others, there is a significant difference between the traditional Jewish (and non-Jewish) translations and the more gender-sensitive renderings that have arisen since the middle of the twentieth century. These latter renderings invite readers to consider that God's commands and God's concerns for humanity are rarely reserved for males only. Without seeking to justify or mitigate the patriarchy under which ancient Israel labored, the newer renderings open up vistas of inclusiveness that the original Hebrew did in fact allow for. Once again, these distinctions can be crucial for those who rely on a modern-language version for their understanding of what Scripture teaches.

Seven Shared Characteristics of Jewish Bible Translations

Without negating or neglecting these very real differences and others we could cite, I want to highlight other noteworthy features that join most, if not all, these Bible translations. Here are seven such characteristics that, as we have seen, abide across time and place, for over two millennia.

1. Jewish Bible translations have been uniformly rendered by individuals learned in the Bible. This is especially true in connection with the Hebrew Bible and its exegesis within Judaism, but often these translators (many of whom were intellectual child prodigies) have also been familiar with interpretive approaches associated with non-Jews as well. All the more so, this deep knowledge of Jewish biblical exegesis has been shared equally by those individuals or groups who consciously broke with the tradition. This erudition is apparent in the Jewish translators' often extensive notes and expanded introductions.

Such erudition has not always been brought to bear in translations of the Christian Bible. So it is that some of the best-selling Christian versions of the Bible were produced by individuals who lacked the knowledge and hence the ability to read either Testament in its original language. *The Living Bible,* which Kenneth Taylor developed out of existing English-language versions—a necessity for him, since he did not possess knowledge of biblical languages—is the best known of such offerings.[1]

This is not simply a matter of the quantity of citations drawn from Jewish sources. Less quantifiable but nonetheless discernible are the ways in which Jewish translators assemble and interact with earlier exegetes. The conversation that takes place has the ease and familiarity of those who see themselves as colleagues or, better, as collaborators in a process or project spanning well over two millennia.

2. Jewish Bible translations have typically been created by individuals who served as community leaders, and their community focus has helped to shape their translations. Notably, Jewish Bible translators have been educators and innovators in elementary and secondary schools as well as in higher education. They have involved themselves in everything from planning social and cultural events to organizing synagogue liturgy. In fact, only a few of these individuals are best known as Bible translators, and even for them, Bible translation seemed to flow out of the myriad other activities in which they engaged. And because they have seen themselves as part of the communities in which they lived, these Jewish translators (even those who worked alone) have typically shaped their versions with their specific intra-Jewish concerns in mind.

Some of them have emphasized traditional, Rabbinic interpretations rather than present their readers with exegesis that drew from other approaches, such as those of the Karaites, that they viewed as heterodox. Others have offered the results of interpretive studies that depended on critical approaches, instead of emphasizing the work of individuals within the Rabbinic exegetical tradition. Still others have provided a roughly equal sampling of both. But these translations have never been neutral, even if this were possible.

Nineteenth-century and early twentieth-century Jewish Bible versions in Germany richly illustrate these options. So, for example, Ludwig Philippson gave his readers substantial servings of the critical, nontraditional scholarship then being developed by Protestant researchers. At the opposite end, as it were, the neo-Orthodox translator Samson Raphael Hirsch never explicitly referred to any individuals outside of the admittedly broad Rabbinic exegetical traditions.

3. A considerable number of Jewish Bible translations—produced when Jews were seen and treated as outsiders—have served as a means of achieving greater integration into the larger (usually, Christian) world Jews inhabited. Integral to this process, many Jewish translators have paid special attention to the level of style, diction, grammar, and vocabulary in their target language. As we saw, for example, the first Jewish translation into German and the preeminent English-language version for most of the twentieth century were both assiduously prepared as tutors for "proper" German and English, respectively. These efforts were intended to ease the passage of Jews, as individuals and as communities, into society at large.

In Western and Central Europe, such versions were part of the practice encouraged by the Enlightenment. This was also the case in East Central and Eastern Europe, among Hungarian and Russian speakers, where the very act of translation was fraught with political meaning: Jewish Bible versions in the prevailing languages were seen as a means of self-defense as well as self-definition.

4. All works of Jewish Bible translation are circumscribed and unified by the canon of authoritative texts set roughly since the second century CE. The scope of what can appropriately be designated as a Jewish Bible translation is limited to the contents of the biblical canon the Rabbis formally accepted around the second century. For almost two millennia, documents beyond this canon have not been acknowledged as authoritative for Jews. Thus, a Jewish translation of Scripture renders only the Hebrew Bible in whole or in part—not the New Testament or the Apocrypha or any other ancient literature.

5. Jewish translations serve to remind the reader that they are just that—translations. Translations can be good, they can be better, they can be the best possible. But they have only rarely been fashioned to serve as the equivalent of, much less a replacement for, the original in the language of the original. In contrast, scriptural translation was an integral part of the formation and development of Christianity from its earliest stages.

Editions that place the Hebrew and its translation on facing pages or in adjacent columns make this point most immediately and effectively. Other versions eschew this practice, but nonetheless retain biblical book and parashah (a portion of the Torah, read weekly) titles in Hebrew. Very few translated Jewish Bibles do not include some Hebrew at the beginning of each book or weekly portion. Finally, volumes that open right-to-left alert even casual readers to the fact that their text was not originally in the vernacular.

Among twentieth- and twenty-first-century English-language versions, these practices are most apparent when translators, addressing themselves to traditional audiences, adopt a formal or more literal approach. But even freer, functional equivalence versions, aimed primarily at Conservative and Reform individuals and communities, display a sufficient number of these elements to appear distinctively and distinguishably Jewish.

6. Most Jewish Bible translations—traditional or not—have consciously and consistently stayed within the parameters the Masoretes established in the Middle Ages—what's known as the Masoretic Text (MT). The MT consists not only of the Hebrew consonants, but also the vowels, accents, and other markers the Masoretes introduced to guide interpretation at the level of word meaning and syntax. This has been the case even when a translator has determined that a given passage in the MT, honored and favored by tradition, is faulty, unclear, or incomplete.

So, too, very rarely has a Jewish translator promoted an alternate reading of the MT within the translated text itself. In some modern Jewish editions, translators have cited ancient variants, and sometimes even conjectures, in the notes—but not in the text.[2] This practice and principle hold true throughout the Hebrew Bible, especially so in connection with the Torah. The Five Books of Moses have always enjoyed a unique sanctity for Jews.

All of this provides remarkable consistency to Jewish renderings of the Hebrew Bible, since the text of that Hebrew has remained the same, for all intents and purposes, since at least the tenth century CE. The earliest extant Masoretic manuscripts—the Leningrad Codex and the Aleppo Codex—date from that time. By contrast, over the centuries there has been considerable variation in identifying the best Greek manuscripts on which to base New Testament translations.

7. Jewish Bible translations have typically relied heavily on traditional commentators. Among others, these have included Rashi, Moses Maimonides, Abraham Ibn Ezra, and David Kimchi. Individuals such as Saadiah Gaon and Samuel David Luzzatto, who appear in this volume primarily because of their work as translators, also form part of this tradition, which, far from being static, continues to expand. As a result—even though these exegetes may make occasional appearances in non-Jewish Bibles, and some Jewish Bibles cite non-Jewish commentators as well—by simply reading the annotations, it becomes immediately apparent when a reader is consulting a Jewish translation of the Bible.

With this list of commonalities, we could construct something of a checklist of criteria by which to determine the authenticity of a translation's Jewishness, although only rarely could I imagine that a procedure of this sort would yield valid or valuable results.[3] More succinctly, I would characterize a Jewish version of the Bible as one that a Jew or group of Jews has prepared, based on the Jewish biblical canon, drawing from the preceding centuries—if not millennia—of Jewish tradition for the benefit of the contemporary Jewish community.

In this sense, then, all Jewish versions of the Bible are revisions. There is no such thing as a brand-new Jewish translation of the Bible. Nor should we rejoice if the possibility for one existed. Every Jewish translation builds on the foundations established by previous translations, whether or not the new version accepts or largely rejects what has come before.

This is not, I would say, a task for the fainthearted or the poorly prepared. In this context, it is worth remembering the expression used in the Letter of Aristeas to describe the criteria necessary to be among the seventy-two translators. All of them needed to be "of exemplary lives, with the experience of the Law and ability to translate it." Modern readers may be reluctant to delve into the "private lives" of prospective translators, but we ought not to in any way diminish the need for a translator's in-depth knowledge of both the biblical text and its exegesis ("the experience of the Law"), and the language and culture of the audience targeted for the translation ("ability to translate it").

Future Jewish Bible Translations

In the sphere of English Bible translation in the future, I believe we are likely to see three types of versions, each of which has precedents in the past or present.

1. New translations for Orthodox Jews. Among today's Orthodox Jews, the priority or, better, the necessity of the Bible in Hebrew—for synagogue practice, for education, and as a guide for daily living—remains unabated. At the same time, no segment of the contemporary Jewish community, no matter how traditional, can overlook the fact that such facility can no longer be taken as a given. Some reliance at some time on an English-language version of the Bible is increasingly common.

As in the past and present so also in the future: In most, if not all, translations for Orthodox Jews the more literal, or formal equivalence, approach will continue to be favored, because this approach is deemed more suitable than freer techniques for rendering Sacred Writ. Yet because the term "literal," no less than the designation "free," is far from monolithic or uniform, we can expect additional versions (of the entire Hebrew Bible, the Torah, or other biblical sections) aimed at different segments of the Orthodox world. Reliance on particular exegetes or traditions of interpretation will be important here, in addition to the crucial role played by the appropriation of a given rabbinic authority. From a marketing perspective, we might term such editions "niche" products, but that will not diminish their appeal among followers of endorsement-bestowing rabbinic figures.

2. New individual translations, such as those of Alter, Friedman, and Fox. Although it may seem like an overstatement, I view these editions, and others by major Jewish scholars that are likely to follow in their successful wake, as something of a paradigm shift among Jewish translations: A significant percentage of new Jewish Bible translations are intentionally going beyond the scope of the Jewish community.

The fact that these academic leaders have been highly successful in attracting both Jewish and non-Jewish readers to their editions, which uniquely combine their distinctive translations and commentaries, demonstrates the widespread acceptance of Jewish scholars and Jewish scholarship in the broader world. As never before, the broadly realized presentation of Jewish perspectives, in particular through modern-language versions of the Hebrew Bible, is being well received commercially as well as critically. And this trend is not likely to abate.

3. The continued use of the 1985 NJPS version. For the foreseeable future, NJPS, which occupies a middle position on what I term the literal-free continuum, will continue to be the version of choice for those seeking an accessible, easy-to-understand vernacular translation. It should maintain its place within almost all nontraditional (that is, Conservative, Reform, and Reconstructionist) synagogues in North America. And it should remain the biblical text for public events within the larger Jewish community. NJPS has also shown itself to be adaptable for commentaries and revisions. Because the NJPS editors chose for the most part an English style and vocabulary that remain accessible without being faddish or clichéd, I don't see the production of another, entirely new functional equivalence version for Jews any time in the near future.

In the years and decades ahead we can expect that Jewish Bible translators, in English as well as in other languages, will remain true to their task of finding and perfecting distinctive ways to link their communities with the sacred texts of the Torah, the Prophets, and the Writings. In a world where Jews are largely free to pursue their goals and in which there seems to be an endless array of media outlets, it would not be surprising if new formats appear well beyond our imagination. But no matter what the technology, we can expect that every authentically Jewish version of the Bible will remain an imaginative revision of all the efforts that preceded it.

Notes

Introduction

1. Bobrick, *Wide as the Waters*; McGrath, *In the Beginning*; Nicolson, *God's Secretaries*.
2. Carpenter, *Imperial Bibles, Domestic Bodies*.
3. Nida and Taber, *Theory and Practice of Translation*.
4. "Messianic Jews" are individuals who self-identify as both Jewish and Christian.
5. Margolis, *The Story of Bible Translations*; Orlinsky, *Essays in Biblical Culture and Bible Translation*; Orlinsky and Bratcher, *A History of Bible Translation and the North American Contribution*.
6. On this, see Greenspoon, "When Harry Met Max."
7. Greenspahn, "Why Jews Translate the Bible," among other relevant publications; Greenstein, "What Might Make a Bible Translation Jewish?" and *Essays on Biblical Method and Translation*; Hertz, "Jewish Translations of the Bible in English," and elsewhere; Katz, *God's Last Words*; Loewe and Fox, "Anglo-Jewish Versions"; Sarna and Sarna, "Jewish Bible Scholarship and Translations in the United States"; Sarna, *JPS: The Americanization of Jewish Culture 1888–1988*; and Seidman, *Faithful Renderings*.

1. The Septuagint

1. *Encyclopaedia Judaica*, produced by Keter Publishing House, Jerusalem, first appeared in sixteen-volume print format in 1972. The revised second edition, published simultaneously in print and electronic forms, came out in 2006.
2. Daniel, "Greek: The Septuagint." Daniel is probably best known for her masterful and innovative study *Recherche sur le vocabulaire du culte dans La Septante*.

3. Among contemporary scholars in Jewish studies, there is protracted debate over what, if anything, distinguishes the "Jewish" study or a "Jewish" treatment of a given topic or field. In relation to translation, two influential studies, taking different approaches and arriving at divergent results, are Orlinsky, *Essays in Biblical Culture and Bible Translation*; and Greenstein, *Essays on Biblical Method and Translation*.
4. In the first paragraph of my article I wrote: "Early on, Christians adopted the Septuagint as their Old Testament, which led to its losing favor, although not all of its status, among Jews." Greenspoon, "Greek: The Septuagint," 595.I expanded upon this idea in later paragraphs.
5. Greenspoon, "Greek: The Septuagint," 598.
6. However, the topic of the Septuagint's origins is relegated to a relatively small role in this source—vv. 9–11, 28–50, and 301–17 (out of a total of 322 verses).
7. All translations of the Letter are taken from Shutt, "Letter of Aristeas: A New Translation and Introduction."
8. For one summary and evaluation, see Troxel, *LXX-Isaiah as Translation and Interpretation*, 54–72.
9. This could well have included instruction for those who were composing or leading Greek-language prayers based on Hebrew originals. See Brock, "The Phenomenon of the Septuagint," 16.
10. The Canadian scholar Albert Pietersma has been the primary exponent of this point of view. See, among his many statements, Pietersma, "A New Paradigm for Addressing Old Questions: The Relevance of the Interlinear Model for the Study of the Septuagint." An outstanding defense of the interlinear paradigm by a younger scholar is Boyd-Taylor, *Reading between the Lines*.
11. Modrzejewski, *The Jews of Egypt*, 99–119.
12. Fernández Marcos, *The Septuagint in Context*, 63.
13. Honigman, *The Septuagint and Homeric Scholarship in Alexandria*.
14. Van der Meer, "Provenance, Profile, and Purpose of the Greek Joshua."
15. As with Josephus, for example, whose apologetic edge was not in the least dulled by his serving under Vespasian and Titus.
16. Van der Meer, "Provenance, Profile, and Purpose of the Greek Joshua," 79.
17. Thackery, *The Septuagint and Jewish Worship*.
18. Tov, "Impact of the LXX Translation of the Pentateuch," 577. Some ancient sources suggestive of the use of Greek scriptures in the synagogue are Acts 13:15; Josephus, *Antiquities*, 16:164; Josephus, *Bellum*, 2:291–92; Josephus, *Contra Apionem*, 1:91; and Philo, *Contemplative Life*, 28. From the Rabbinic side, as observed by Wasserstein and Wasserstein (*The Legend of the Septua-*

gint, chap. 3, "The Rabbis and the Greek Bible"), discussions of and references to the origin of the Greek version reflect detailed knowledge only of the Torah or Pentateuch. In my view, this may well be indicative of the widespread use of the Greek Pentateuch (and only the Pentateuch) in Jewish liturgical settings.

19. Fernández Marcos, *The Septuagint in Context*, 60.
20. Van der Meer, "Provenance, Profile, and Purpose of the Greek Joshua."
21. See Dines, *The Septuagint*, 48–50.
22. These contexts would include school, court of law, royal court, court of popular opinion, the synagogue. As Tessa Rajak (*Translation and Survival*) cogently observes, in Hellenistic Judaism (as at other times) the central activities of Judaism, including education and prayer, were tightly intertwined and difficult to separate conceptually as well as practically.
23. Orlinsky, "The Septuagint as Sacred Writ."
24. Further on in this chapter I elaborate on the view that a community's Hebrew text was the standard by which competing Greek versions were judged.
25. Rajak (*Translation and Survival*, 149–50) expresses some skepticism concerning the widely held view that Philo lacked all knowledge of the Hebrew language.
26. Philo, *De Vita Mosis* 2, 7:37–40.
27. Epiphanius, *Weights and Measures*, 3–6. I have slightly altered the translation found in Dean, *Epiphanius' Treatise on Weights and Measures* (accessed online at http://www.tertullian.org/fathers/epiphanius_weights_03_text.htm#C9).
28. This elevated status was not limited to the Pentateuch, which is the subject of the Letter of Aristeas. Rather, it, like the term "Septuagint" itself, came to include the entire Greek version of Hebrew Scriptures as well as material, also deemed sacred, that was originally composed in Greek. However, through his decision to go back to the Hebrew as the basis for an authoritative rendering into Latin, Jerome effectively undercut the Septuagint's unique status for Western Christians.
29. Honigman, *The Septuagint and Homeric Scholarship in Alexandria*, develops this theme in considerable detail.
30. This would be true whether or not we give any credence to the claim of royal patronage.
31. After more than a thousand years, MT continues to set the standard for Jewish worship and study.
32. See Margolis, "Specimen of a New Edition of the Greek Joshua."
33. See especially Orlinsky, "The Hebrew *Vorlage* of the Septuagint of the Book of Joshua."

34. Among other sources, see Ulrich, *The Dead Sea Scrolls*; Lim, *The Formation of the Jewish Canon*; and Greenspoon, "By the Letter?/Word for Word? Scripture in the Jewish Tradition."
35. See Tov, *The Greek and Hebrew Bible*, and elsewhere in his voluminous writings.
36. For more on this, see the relevant discussion in Fernández Marcos, *The Septuagint in Context*.
37. For a succinct account of the frequent (but not consistent) use of the Septuagint by writers of the New Testament, see Greenspoon, "The Septuagint," in *Jewish Annotated New Testament*.
38. The example of Justin Martyr, who lived in the second century CE, is instructive in this regard. In his writings, he strongly maintained the authority and integrity of the Septuagint over against any and all later Greek translations or revisions. Ironically, the Greek text he quoted was frequently what we attribute to the Th./*kaige* revision (from the second or first centuries BCE) or incorporated other, even later readings. Of course, from Justin's perspective, all of these readings were in Old Greek—but certainly not always the Old Greek or first rendering by the earliest translators. See, among other sources, the relevant discussions in Barnard, *St. Justin Martyr*.
39. Moatti-Fine, *Jésus (Josué)*. Where the French is translated into English, the renderings are mine.
40. See especially van der Meer, "Provenance, Profile, and Purpose of the Greek Joshua."
41. Among the foremost scholars in this field is Johann Cook, author of *The Septuagint of Proverbs*, among many other books.
42. Seeligmann, *Septuagint Version of Isaiah*. See, most recently, Troxel, *LXX-Isaiah as Translation or Interpretation*; and Wagner, *Reading the Sealed Book: Old Greek Isaiah and the Problem of Septuagint Hermeneutics*. Among Seeligmann's most effective supporters today is Arie van der Kooij.
43. When it was copied, the resultant text often lacked some or all of the signs indicating quantitative changes to be made. Origen also made numerous unmarked qualitative changes in the earlier Greek.
44. On this, see Greenspoon, "The Use and Abuse of the Term 'LXX.'"
45. See Parker, *Codex Sinaiticus*.
46. See also McDonald and Sanders, *The Canon Debate*; and Evans et al., *Exploring the Origins of the Bible*.
47. With the exception of Greek-speaking Jewish communities, where a developing form of Aquila's version was still being used well into the Byzantine period.
48. This is acknowledged and accepted in Justinian's *Novellae Constitutiones* (see, esp., 146).

49. For Theodotion's Daniel, see McLay, *The OG and Th Versions of Daniel.*
50. See Salvesen, *Symmachus in the Pentateuch.*
51. In the view of many of those who accept the reality of this second-century BCE figure, proto-Theodotion had connections (the precise nature of which is disputed) with a contemporary development in the transmission of LXX that is generally associated with *kaige*. On this and related issues, see Greenspoon, "The *Kaige* Recension."
52. Wasserstein and Wasserstein, *The Legend of the Septuagint,* provides an excellent overview and analysis of the relevant biblical material.
53. In addition to sources cited earlier, see Tov, "The Rabbinic Tradition."
54. This led to the development of Jewish Bibles, first in Aramaic and subsequently in Arabic.
55. For cogent examples, see Tov, "Midrash-Type Exegesis in the Septuagint of Joshua."
56. See Kraft, "Christian Transmission of Greek Jewish Scriptures."

2. The *Targums*

1. Many scholars identify this scroll as essentially the Torah we know to this day.
2. In addition to Rabbinic comments, we can also point to instances in the *Targums,* such as the addition (vis-à-vis MT) of "synagogues" at Ezekiel 11:16: "Because I removed them far among the Gentiles and because I scattered them among the countries, therefore I have given them synagogues, second to my sanctuary, because they are as little in the countries to which they have been exiled."
3. In this study, I consistently use *Targums* as the plural of *Targum*. Another form of the plural, *Targumim,* is also found in the secondary literature.
4. On this, see Flesher and Chilton, *The Targums,* especially chapter 1 ("Introduction") and chapter 2 ("Defining Targum").
5. Nonetheless, it is inexact and probably misleading to speak of the Aramaic version of Job found at Qumran as a *Targum*. On this, see Shepherd, *Targum and Translation.*
6. The Rabbis retrojected this practice to the far earlier time of Ezra.
7. However, directly after this (also in b. Meg. 3a), another, apparently contradictory, tradition appears that attributes the origin of a Palestinian *Targum* to Ezra. The Talmud itself resolves this seeming contradiction by attributing to Ezra the first Aramaic translation of the Pentateuch. Subsequently it was lost, but finally restored by Onkelos.
8. Flesher and Chilton, *The Targums,* 149.
9. Flesher and Chilton, *The Targums,* 130–32.
10. Grossfeld and Sperling, "Aramaic: The Targumim."

11. Flesher and Chilton, *The Targums*,10. Because large portions of this "additional . . . material" are not grounded in the Hebrew text that lay before the Targumists, it is not correct to speak of it as paraphrase.
12. See Flesher and Chilton, *The Targums*, 12–16, for their take on these developments.
13. The examples in this and the preceding paragraphs are drawn from Freedman, "The Halacha in the Targum."
14. See Flesher and Chilton, *The Targums*, 73–83, for an overview of this material.
15. Flesher and Chilton, *The Targums*, 77.
16. The name Neofiti derives from the collection of Hebrew and Aramaic manuscripts donated to the Vatican Library from Pia Domus Neophytorum in Rome.
17. In addition to the institution of this practice in the synagogue, it was also customary to make use of a *Targum* in private worship. Some Jews still do. See Grossfeld and Sperling, "Aramaic: The Targumim."
18. For careful analysis of key texts on these topics, see Flesher and Chilton, *The Targums*, 287–97.
19. We refer to these prophetic portions as *haftarot*.
20. The scholarly consensus, dating the *Targum's* composition as it does to the third century, does not support talmudic tradition (b. Meg. 3a) that it was a disciple of Hillel, Jonathan ben Uzziel, who composed this *Targum*. Jonathan's association with Hillel places him sometime in the first century. But the point of the attribution to Jonathan, and through him to Hillel, may have been more of prestige than chronological accuracy.
21. Flesher and Chilton, *The Targums*, chap. 11 ("Targum Jonathan: Former and Latter Prophets").
22. It is important to keep in mind that "late" *Targums* may well contain "early" material.
23. On this material in general, much can be learned from Flesher and Chilton, The *Targums*, chap. 12 ("Targums to the Writings").
24. A compiler may have used this approach to preserve readings from two originally distinct manuscripts, one literal, the other free (or freer).
25. Or, as in the case of the *Targum* to Job, a single compiler sought to preserve elements of two different types of translation.
26. This *Targum* was not published until the latter part of the seventeenth century. In addition, the *Targum* to Proverbs seems to have been based not on the traditional Hebrew text, but on the Syriac Peshitta.
27. Grossfeld, *The Targum Onkelos to Exodus*, 15–16.

28. As a functional equivalence translation, NJPS regularly presents the meaning of the Hebrew without adhering to its form.
29. McNamara, *Targum Neofiti I and Targum Pseudo-Jonathan: Exodus*, 29.
30. McNamara, *Targum Neofiti I and Targum Pseudo-Jonathan: Exodus*, 176.
31. This perspective is found even in the Hebrew Bible at Joshua 24:14: The Israelites are "to put away the gods that your forefathers served beyond the Euphrates and in Egypt."
32. Levey, *The Targum of Ezekiel*, 96–97.
33. Cathcart and Gordon, *The Targum of the Minor Prophets*, 139–40.
34. Cathcart and Gordon, *The Targum of the Minor Prophets*, 187–88.
35. Grossfeld, *The Two Targums of Esther*, 39–40.
36. Grossfeld, *The Two Targums of Esther*, 39–40.
37. Grossfeld, *The Two Targums of Esther*, 66.
38. Grossfeld, *The Two Targums of Esther*, 164–65.
39. In this verse Ahasuerus accuses Haman of plotting "to ravish" Esther. In fact, Haman was "pleading for his life" (so the preceding verse).
40. This is fully in line with the "primary rules" of *Targum* devised by Flesher and Chilton in *The Targums*: "Rule 1: When a Targum translates or presents the original text, it does so literally. Rule 2: When a Targum adds material into the translation, it integrates the additional material smoothly so as not to interrupt its flow" (40). These two primary rules are followed by five additional secondary rules (40–53).

3. Bible Translation into Arabic

1. A useful survey can be found in relevant sections of Ben-Sasson, *A History of the Jewish People*, among other sources. More detail can be found in Gil and Strassler, *Jews in Islamic Countries in the Middle Ages*.
2. Saadiah's place of birth is reflected in his full name and title: Saadiah ben Yosef al-Fayyumi Gaon. See Polliack, *The Karaite Tradition of Arabic Bible Translation*, 77.
3. In this chapter the terms "Rabbinic" and "Rabbanite" are used as virtual synonyms; "Rabbanite(s)" is used specifically to refer to those followers of the Rabbinic tradition who were adherents of Oral Law and stood in opposition to the Karaites, who became Saadiah's primary theological and ideological enemies.
4. By that time, this academy had been reestablished in the capital city of Baghdad, although it retained the connection with Sura.
5. In his influential work *Saadiah Gaon: His Life and Works*, 141–42, Malter states: "In all probability [Saadiah] began while he was still in Egypt, to make translations of Biblical books accompanied with commentaries and

continued this work in the following periods of his vicissitudinous life, changing, correcting, and enlarging the exegetical portions as his knowledge increased."

In the view of Polliack (*The Karaite Tradition of Arabic Bible Translation*, 77), "It is likely Saadiah began composing his Arabic Bible versions after leaving Egypt, possibly while residing in Tiberias."

6. Thus, Goodman ("Saadiah Gaon's Interpretive Technique in Translating the Book of Job," 55) speaks of "three assumptions [that] orient Saadiah's exegetical method as a translator . . . (a) the ultimate coherence of the scriptural canon, (b) the significance and intelligibility of the text, and (c) the veracity of the text. All of these are corollaries of the divine inspiration of the Torah."

   More expansively, Freidenreich ("The Use of Islamic Sources in Saadiah Gaon's *Tafsir* of the Torah," 393) enumerates "the five objectives of Saadiah in writing the *Tafsir*: To provide an Arabic rendering of the 'plain sense of Torah,' to educate and guide the assimilated masses of his day, to provide a translation of the Torah in accord with reason, to provide a translation of the Torah in accord with rabbinic tradition, to refute heretical and Karaite beliefs."

   On this, Polliack (*The Karaite Tradition of Arabic Bible Translation*, 86) writes: "Saadiah's translation methodology was bound up with his general scheme of scriptural interpretation. This scheme was meant to harmonize between the revealed text of Scripture and other sources of human knowledge. It enabled the Hebrew Bible to be presented as a text which withstands the test of logic, and so came to the defence of traditional Jewish faith whose precepts were being undermined at the time by members of other religions, agnostics and heretics. The need to draw Rabbinic tradition into this interpretive system . . . was mostly a reaction against the Karaite adherence to Scripture alone as the only binding source for Jewish religious practice."

7. See, among others, Freidenreich, "The Use of Islamic Sources," 356.
8. And thus not a text that would be read independently.
9. On this passage, see Polliack, *The Karaite Tradition of Arabic Bible Translation*, 229.
10. Polliack, *The Karaite Tradition of Arabic Bible Translation*, 86: "Saadiah's awareness of the interpretive nature of his translation of the Pentateuch may explain its designation as *tafsir*, a term which better conveys this sense than the term *tarjamah* [which usually describes a simple, straightforward translation]."
11. For those so inclined, these renderings would have been explained in some detail in the formal commentary. But they were accessible even to those who looked only at the translated text itself.

12. For Saadiah's own comments on the meaning of this passage, see Linetsky, *Rabbi Saadiah Gaon's Commentary on the Book of Creation*, 207. Freidenreich ("The Use of Islamic Sources," 378) observes that here Saadiah was "following Onkelos' lead."
13. Here NJPS reads: "One day the divine beings presented themselves before the Lord, and the Adversary came along with them."
14. For this observation, see especially Goodman, *The Book of Theodicy*, 153–55.
15. So, for example, a work of his, *'Agron* (meaning, a collection of words), dated to 913, is the first known Hebrew lexicon. See Greenslade, *The West from the Reformation to the Present Day*, 523.
16. In Linetsky's rendering (*Rabbi Saadiah Gaon's Commentary on the Book of Creation*, 164), Saadiah remarked that he translated the Hebrew expression "as 'Healing Tree,' for the word *Hayyim* in our language can mean [one of] eight things"; "healing" is one of those eight things.
17. Thus Freidenreich ("The Use of Islamic Sources," 378–79) observes: "Saadiah thus deviates from Onkelos's translation of *elohim* as great men, even though he accepts that interpretation elsewhere. Saadiah's reading of this verse has no Talmudic parallels, nor does he appear to be borrowing from the Jewish mystical tradition. . . . The association between eating from the tree and becoming like angels . . . is found instead in Qur'an 7:20. . . . [It is] a reasonable possibility [that] Saadiah's translation of Gen. 3:5 [is] an adoption of the quran'ic understanding of what happened in the Garden of Eden."
18. Freidenreich, "The Use of Islamic Sources," 382–83: "In the passage recounting Joseph's encounter with Potiphar's wife in Genesis 39, [Saadiah] repeatedly translates the word *[begged]* as *qamis*, 'shirt'. . . . [The same word is used in] Qur'an 12, the chapter about Joseph."
19. Freidenreich, "The Use of Islamic Sources," 388–93.
20. See Freidenreich, "The Use of Islamic Sources," 356–57n11, where Gen. 3:20 is cited as one of "Saadiah's examples of non-rational verses that require interpretation. . . . [Eve is not 'the mother of all the living' but merely 'the mother of all the living that are rational and mortal']."
21. So Polliack (*The Karaite Tradition of Arabic Bible Translation*, 221–22): "In Num. 22:22 the textual difficulty concerns the lack of a reason for God's anger with Balaam. Logically it could not have been aroused simply by Balaam's going with the nobles of Edom, since this is precisely what God instructed him to do earlier in the narrative (see Num. 22:20). . . . Saadiah qualif[ies] [Balaam's] going as a negative act by adding an adverbial phrase . . . which expounds the background of the verse . . . *because he went enthusiastically.*"

22. So Halkin, "Saadiah's Exegesis and Polemics," 127: "Occasionally he expands a Biblical phrase through the addition of words so as to make its intention clearer."
23. Linetsky, *Rabbi Saadiah Gaon's Commentary on the Book of Creation*, 364.
24. Linetsky, *Rabbi Saadiah Gaon's Commentary on the Book of Creation*, 228, for Saadiah's procedure here.
25. On these passages, see Freidenreich, "The Use of Islamic Sources," 357n11, and especially Goodman, "Saadiah Gaon's Interpretive Technique," 52.
26. Polliack (*The Karaite Tradition of Arabic Bible Translation*, 87–89) makes this point: "Saadiah appears to have modeled some aspects of the *Tafsir* upon [the Targum]. . . . Two characteristics of the Targum's interpretive methodology have specific relevance to Saadiah's version. They include halakhic interpretations [e.g., Exod. 23:19 and elsewhere] and the rendering of anthropomorphisms and anthropopathisms. . . . Numerous parallels have been noted between Targum Onkelos and the *Tafsir* in the translation of anthropomorphisms. In this context, it is sufficient to mention the Targum's use of 'memra' (= the word) in a construct state with the name of God, which is paralleled by the use of 'amar' (= command) in the *Tafsir*."
27. On Genesis 11:5, see Halkin, "Saadiah's Exegesis and Polemics," 126; and Linetsky, *Rabbi Saadiah Gaon's Commentary on the Book of Creation*, 235. For Genesis 18:21, see Linetsky, *Rabbi Saadiah Gaon's Commentary on the Book of Creation*, 275.
28. See Halkin, "Saadiah's Exegesis and Polemics," 126, for Genesis 6:6 and Psalm 2:4. For the psalm passage, Freidenreich ("The Use of Islamic Sources," 356) observes, as Saadiah explains in his commentary on Psalm 2:4, "verbs of action which refer to God, such as 'He descended,' 'He went up,' are rationally inadmissible and have to be transferred to agents and to be translated 'He made one descend,' 'He caused someone to go up.'"
29. Linetsky, *Rabbi Saadiah Gaon's Commentary on the Book of Creation*, 61n94: "In his *Beliefs* the Gaon explains that when the Scripture states that something was created by God's word the meaning is simply that it was done according to His wish, not by necessity."
30. Halkin, "Saadiah's Exegesis and Polemics," 125.
31. Goodman, "Saadiah Gaon's Interpretive Technique," 52.
32. Simon, *Four Approaches to the Book of Psalms*, 53n71: "Saadiah rarely makes stylistic changes from the Hebrew of Psalms." Saadiah's reluctance in this regard may be traced to his "view that the 150 psalms comprise a sort of second Pentateuch revealed to David . . . as a prophetic work of religious guidance." This view "was not based on rabbinic sources, nor was it accepted by later commentators." Simon, *Four Approaches to the Book of Psalms*, 1, 3.

33. Simon, *Four Approaches to the Book of Psalms*, 53–54n71.
34. Freidenreich, "The Use of Islamic Sources," 383.
35. Freidenreich, "The Use of Islamic Sources," 366–67.
36. Polliack (*The Karaite Tradition of Arabic Bible Translation*, 244) convincingly demonstrates that this forms a key contrast between Saadiah's translation and those produced under Karaite auspices: "Saadiah, on the other hand [contra the Karaite practice of trying to reflect 'the form as well as the function of the source text'] is primarily concerned with securing an equivalency of function between the source text and the translated text, and often rejects a translation option which preserves the form of the source text, even when it is perfectly functional in the Arabic target language." Further: "The difference may be formulated as follows: the Karaites pursue an A for A model of translation, which involves the use of as many parallel structures as possible between Hebrew and Arabic. . . . Saadiah prefers a B for A model of translation, which makes use of structures indigenous to the Arabic target language whenever possible, yet does not refrain from using existing parallel structures when these best express the function of a source language feature in a particular context" (248n6).
37. As Halkin notes ("Saadiah's Exegesis and Polemics," 124), in preparing his translation, Saadiah was not "obsessed by [a] sense of slavishness to the Hebrew. . . . On the contrary, his primary canon was that the Bible must read like an understandable, rationally tenable book."

    Or, as Malter (*Saadiah Gaon*, 143) explicates at greater length, in his translation, Saadiah's "chief thought was to make the Bible a book accessible to all; to present the Scriptures in a rational, intelligible form. Hence he does not always bind himself to the rules of the Masorah, to grammar, or to common usage; but aiming at the greatest possible clearness and consistency, often disregards all difficulties arising from rule and custom. He does not hesitate to insert words and phrases, or to divide and connect verses and sentences in his own way, when necessary to convey to the reader the intended sense. To this extent his translation is at the same time an interpretation, and Saadiah, being himself well aware of the fact, called it *tafsir*, which means both commentary and translation."
38. Goodman ("Saadiah Gaon's Interpretive Technique," 47–48): "The key to understanding Saadiah's biblical translation is the recognition that the gaon translates for referential sense. It is not his desire or intent to preserve the figures or idioms of biblical Hebrew except insofar as corresponding usages in the host language, Arabic, may shed light on the intended use."
39. Among other examples was Saadiah's translation of the Hebrew *Kohen* (priest) by the Arabic term imam, as cited earlier. Saadiah's rendering of

this term served to further his goal of producing "a target text which is oriented toward the language and culture of the reader." Freiderich, "The Use of Islamic Sources," 362.

40. As Margolis (*The Story of Bible Translations*, 53–54) observes, "Though not a paraphrase, [Saadiah's] version is by no means literal. Where necessary a word is added to bring out the sense clearly; several verses are frequently joined together in a syntactical nexus, and thus, though the original coloring is lost, the translation gains in lucidity. With a view to the same end a positive Arabic equivalent is introduced where the meaning of the Hebrew is doubtful, in order not to awaken in the laity the thought that there are obscure expressions in the Scriptures."

41. So Freidenreich ("The Use of Islamic Sources," 357): "Saadiah also rephrases biblical sentences to conform to culturally derived standards of proper literary style, without regard to the evident style of the Torah itself. This can be seen clearly in his translation of Genesis 1, in which the biblical formula which concludes each paragraph of the creation narrative, 'And there was evening and there was morning a *x* day,' is consistently recast as an introductory clause of the paragraph which follows: 'And after the evening and morning of the day *x* passed. . . .'"

42. In this instance, NJPS exhibits the paratactic style of the Hebrew. Frequently, however, NJPS, a functional equivalent translation, adopts the subordination of clauses in keeping with English usage.

43. Succinctly put, "at the core of [Saadiah's] approach lay an attempt to create an independent Arabic version which functioned, for its readers, in place of the Hebrew Pentateuch and not alongside it." Polliack, *The Karaite Tradition of Arabic Bible Translation*, 272–73.

44. In this vein, Polliack (*The Karaite Tradition of Arabic Bible Translation*) writes: "The complete absence of [lexical] alternatives in Saadiah's translation captures more than any other feature the striking difference between his approach and that of the Karaites" (264). And: The Karaites leave "the choice between several translation options open to the reader" (267). Further: "Saadiah was sharply aware of the need to consolidate standard Arabic versions of the Pentateuch and possibly of other books of the Hebrew Bible. His concept and practice of translation developed in relation to this need. . . . For this reason, Saadiah's *Tafsir* contains no translation alternatives. This cannot be otherwise, since it is meant to function as a closed self-contained version of the Pentateuch in Arabic" (272).

45. Polliack (*The Karaite Tradition of Arabic Bible Translation*, 10) speaks of this: "The Bible translations composed by Saadiah Gaon . . . were considered for a long period the earliest Arabic versions of Jewish provenance. Although

it was generally assumed he had not produced them *ex nihilo*, there was no proof for his reliance on pre-existing Jewish sources. Recently, however, some of these have come to light in the form of several Genizah fragments which contain Judaeo-Arabic translations from Proverbs, the Pentateuch and other books of the Hebrew Bible. These fragments date to the ninth century. . . . Factors suggest that the Genizah fragments represent early attempts by Jews to put down in writing their Arabic translations of the Hebrew Bible."

46. Polliack, *The Karaite Tradition of Arabic Bible Translation*, 10, 13.
47. "Saadiah's students concentrated on completing their master's work with regard to the commentary on the Pentateuch, yet did not attempt novel translations." Polliack, *The Karaite Tradition of Arabic Bible Translation*, 80n61.
48. Polliack, *The Karaite Tradition of Arabic Bible Translation*, 268n19.
49. Advocating a more cautious approach is Polliack (*The Karaite Tradition of Arabic Bible Translation*, 13n46): "There is no determining evidence that the *Tafsir* was actually recited after the reading of the Torah or alongside the Aramaic version [in the synagogue]. Though this may have occurred in Yemen."
50. Specifically on the Torah, Polliack (*The Karaite Tradition of Arabic Bible Translation*, 78–79) writes: "As to the number of Pentateuch translations Saadiah may have produced, considerable confusion is prevalent, which results from two independent factors. The first concerns Saadiah's statement in the Introduction that he was asked to compile a short *tafsir* on the Pentateuch after he had already written a long *tafsir* on the Pentateuch. The short *tafsir* appears to have consisted of his translation alone, without the commentary. . . . The long *tafsir*, which included the commentary, was eventually dropped from common usage."
51. For Polliack (*The Karaite Tradition of Arabic Bible Translation*, 79–80), these developments are best situated in the following contexts: "The question still remains, however, whether both works [i.e., the long and the short *tafsir*] contained the same translation text, or whether Saadiah changed his translation when he adapted it into a self-contained work. . . . At an early stage of its [i.e., Saadiah's translation-commentary of the Pentateuch] transmission . . . an unusual split occurred between the translation and commentary portions of this particular work. . . . This process led to the neglect of his commentary on the Pentateuch which eventually ceased to be copied. . . . The translation swiftly gained the status of an Authorized Arabic version of the Pentateuch amongst Rabbanite communities. . . . The authority of the *Tafsir* and its popular acceptance as a definitive text discouraged the writing of other translations of the Pentateuch, which explains their general absence from medieval Rabbanite sources."

52. For this translation of Maimonides' letter, see jewishhistory.org /maimonides-letter-to-a-friend/. The translator, Rabbi Berel Wein (www .RabbiWein.com), is also the sponsor of the blog *jewishhistory.org*.
53. "The external evidence is . . . in favour of Saadiah Gaon being the author of the commentary [on Ezra and Nehemiah], but is not supported by the internal evidence, which, however, certainly connects it with, if it does not be prove it to be by, the author of the commentary on Daniel formerly attributed to Saadiah Gaon." Rabbi Sa'adia, *Commentary on Ezra and Nehemiah*, ed. H. J. Mathews, vii.
54. Greenhouse, "Treasures in the Wall."

4. Bible Translation into Yiddish and German

1. Among the many comic strips in which Yiddish words and phrases appear are *Momma, B.C.*, and *Edge City*.
2. See, among many examples, the now classic Rosten, *The New Joys of Yiddish*, and Wex, *Born to Kvetch*.
3. Ashkenazi Jews initially settled in the German-speaking lands of Central Europe. Later, many moved east, where Russian and other non-German languages predominated.
4. See, among a wide range of resources, Katz, *Words on Fire*, and Kriwaczek, *Yiddish Civilisation*.
5. Also transliterated as *Tz'enah Ur'enah*, and universally pronounced by Yiddish speakers as *Tzenerene*. See Ashkenazi, *Ts'enah Ur'enah*, 2:xi.
6. See Kirsch, "Daughters of Zion": "In keeping with its intended audience, the *Tsenerene* is especially interested in using the Bible's female characters to model feminine virtues . . . that Jewish tradition honors and seeks to inculcate in women: piety and charity, humility and obedience. At the same time, however, the *Tsenerene* acknowledges that the Bible's treatment of its female characters is often sternly judgmental. We are meant to learn not just from the matriarchs' virtues but also from their faults and failures."
7. Ashkenazi, *Ts'enah Ur'enah*, 2:xii.
8. Ashkenazi, *Ts'enah Ur'enah*, 2:xiii. A slightly earlier date, in the 1590s, is also possible; see Kirsch, "Daughters of Zion."
9. See Kirsch, "Daughters of Zion."
10. For a uniquely detailed account of this phenomenon, see Kirsch, "Daughters of Zion."
11. "Yiddish."
12. Ashkenazi, *Ts'enah Ur'enah*, 2:xii.
13. Ashkenazi, *Ts'enah Ur'enah*, 2:576.
14. Ashkenazi, *Ts'enah Ur'enah*, 2:790–91.

15. Ashkenazi, *Ts'enah Ur'enah*, 2:911.
16. Gottheil, "Bible Translations," 191–92. Blitz also made extensive use of Martin Luther's German translation, which, while elevating the literary quality of his version, produced passages that were virtually incomprehensible for Eastern European Jews. Aptroot, "Notes on the Amsterdam Bible Translation," 154.
17. Even for specialists, it is not easy to sort through the privileges that the rival publishing houses sought and apparently gained. It was seemingly no easier for the major players in this seventeenth-century drama. On one occasion, Uri Phoebus and his business partner paid an enormous sum to a middleman to obtain a monopoly on sales from the Council of the Four Lands. The middleman pocketed the funds and delivered a counterfeit document. On this, see Aptroot, "Notes on the Amsterdam Yiddish Bible Translations," 137.
18. As it turns out, neither Yiddish Bible was commercially successful. Aptroot, "Notes on the Amsterdam Bible Translations," 139.
19. Gottheil, "Bible Translations," 191–92.
20. For a fuller view of the context for such activities within the Jewish community, see Goldsmith, *Modern Yiddish Culture*.
21. Orlinsky, "Yehoash's Yiddish Translation of the Bible," 174–75.
22. Orlinsky, "Yehoash's Yiddish Translation of the Bible," 175–76. See also Orlinsky, "Jewish Biblical Scholarship in America (Continued)," 345–47.
23. Orlinsky, "Yehoash's Yiddish Translation of the Bible," 176.
24. As translated from the Yiddish into English by Leonard Wolf in Manger, *The World According to Itzik*.
25. Manger, "Abishag Writes a Letter Home," *The World According to Itzik*, 26–27.
26. Manger, "The Patriarch Jacob Meets Rachel," *The World According to Itzik*, 20–21.
27. Hence the origin of the following epigram: *Si Lyra non lyrasset, Lutherus non saltasset* (If Lyra had not played the lyre, Luther would not have danced). Cited from http://www.exposition-biblique.com, which also contains a succinct analysis in French of de Lyra's pervasive influence on Luther. Commenting on this phenomenon, Margolis (*The Story of Bible Translations*, 56) writes: "Rashi's commentary was excerpted in Latin by the apostate Nicholas de Lyra (died 1340) whose 'Postillae Perpetuae,' printed in 1471–2, exercised a potent influence on Luther's German translation of the Bible."
28. The Jewish Enlightenment, or Haskalah, was a European movement of the eighteenth and nineteenth centuries. Its starting and ending dates are later than those of what is commonly called the Age of Enlightenment, although there were substantial chronological, geographical, and intellectual overlaps between these two movements and their leaders.

29. Among the many full-length studies of Mendelssohn and his multifaceted accomplishments are Altmann, *Moses Mendelssohn: A Biographical Study*; and Feiner, *Moses Mendelssohn: Sage of Modernity*. For the larger context, see now Gilman, *History of German Jewish Bible Translation*.
30. Margolis, *The Story of Bible Translations*, 86.
31. Sorkin, *Moses Mendelssohn and the Religious Enlightenment*, 53.
32. Sorkin, *Moses Mendelssohn and the Religious Enlightenment*, 175.
33. Quoted in Breuer, *The Limits of Enlightenment*, 158.
34. Sorkin, *Moses Mendelssohn and the Religious Enlightenment*, 53.
35. Quoted in Breuer, *The Limits of Enlightenment*, 159.
36. Quoted in Breuer, *The Limits of Enlightenment*, 160.
37. Quoted in Breuer, *The Limits of Enlightenment*, 161.
38. The latter were traditional and conservative, while the former sought to make Judaism "relevant" by jettisoning "outmoded" beliefs and practices and adopting others more in keeping with modern mores.
39. For an accessible introduction to this movement and its chief proponents, see Elon, *The Pity of It All*.
40. Plaut, *German-Jewish Bible Translations*, 11.
41. Belligheimer, "On Jewish Translations of the Bible in German," 6.
42. Belligheimer, "On Jewish Translations of the Bible in German," 7.
43. Belligheimer, "On Jewish Translations of the Bible in German," 8.
44. Grunfeld, "Introduction," in *Hirsch Commentary on the Torah*, xiii.
45. Grunfeld, "Introduction," in *Hirsch Commentary on the Torah*, xiii. Emphasis in original.
46. Grunfeld, "Introduction," in *Hirsch Commentary on the Torah*, xiii.
47. Grunfeld, "Introduction," in *Hirsch Commentary on the Torah*, xiii–xiv.
48. Grunfeld, "Introduction," in *Hirsch Commentary on the Torah*, xiv–xv.
49. Quoted in Grunfeld, "Introduction," in *Hirsch Commentary on the Torah*, xv.
50. Hirsch, *Hirsch Commentary on the Torah*, 3.
51. Hirsch, *Hirsch Commentary on the Torah*, 3–4.
52. Hirsch, *Hirsch Commentary on the Torah*, 4.
53. Hirsch's interpretation of *sh-ma-yim* up until this point depends on his division of the word into two parts: the first, *shem*, means "there." The second, *ayim*, is the dual ending, producing, in Hirsch's terminology, "the double 'shem.'"
54. Hirsch, *Hirsch Commentary on the Torah*, 5.
55. Plaut, *German-Jewish Bible Translations*, 13.
56. Hirsch did not offer a direct point-by-point refutation of what were, in his opinion, the deadly serious errors of the biblical critics. Were he to have taken such an approach, he would have named names, countering each fallacious assertion with the clarity of tradition. As it is, he never mentioned

a biblical critic by name; nor did he cite any of their works directly. But his familiarity with biblical criticism cannot seriously be doubted when, for example, he argued in his commentary at Genesis 2:4 against efforts by proponents of the Documentary Hypothesis to discern two separate and contrasting accounts of creation (P and J) in the first chapters of Genesis.

57. Grunfeld, "Introduction," in *Hirsch Commentary on the Torah*, xxiv.
58. Hirsch was prescient in his recognition and presentation of these concerns. They made their way into mainstream scholarship only much later and in painful hindsight. On this, see Bergen, *Twisted Cross*; Ericksen and Heschel, *Betrayal: German Churches and the Holocaust*; Heschel, *The Aryan Jesus: Christian Theologians and the Bible in Nazi Germany*.
59. Plaut, *German-Jewish Bible Translations*, 13.
60. For a perceptive analysis of Hirsch by a twenty-first-century scholar, see Levenson, "Translation versus Teaching."
61. Belligheimer, "On Jewish Translations of the Bible in German," 11–12.
62. Quoted in Plaut, *German-Jewish Bible Translations*, 13.
63. Bernfeld was especially drawn to Luzzatto's vigorously argued view that accents needed to be taken seriously into account in order to properly understand biblical Hebrew. Christian authorities Bernfeld cited included Franz Delitzsch, a prominent scholar of Assyriology.
64. Plaut, *German-Jewish Bible Translations*, 14.
65. Belligheimer, "On Jewish Translations of the Bible in German," 12–13.
66. Buber, "On Word Choice in Translating the Bible," 74.
67. Buber, "On Word Choice in Translating the Bible," 75–76.
68. Buber, "On Word Choice in Translating the Bible," 77.
69. Buber, "*Leitwort* Style in Pentateuch Narrative," 114.
70. Buber, "*Leitwort* Style in Pentateuch Narrative," 114.
71. Buber, "*Leitwort* Style in Pentateuch Narrative," 114.
72. Buber, "*Leitwort* Style in Pentateuch Narrative," 121.
73. Buber, "*Leitwort* Style in Pentateuch Narrative," 121.

5. Translations into Other Selected Languages

1. For an overview of the rich and varied history of the Jews in Spain and further insights on specific topics raised here, see Gerber, *Jews of Spain*; Mann, et al., *Convivencia*; and Sarna, "Hebrew and Bible Studies in Medieval Spain."
2. Quoted in Gottheil, "Arragel, Moses."
3. On Arragel's use of the Vulgate, see, among other sources, Metzger, "The 'Alba Bible' of Rabbi Moses Arragel"; and Lipton, "A Blurred Encounter in Moses Arragel's Epistle on the Alba Bible."
4. Gottheil, "Arragel, Moses."

5. Gottheil, "Arragel, Moses."
6. Gottheil, "Arragel, Moses."
7. Others believe there were 513 folios. For this lower figure, see Metzger, "The 'Alba Bible' of Rabbi Moses Arragel," 132.
8. Gottheil, "Arragel, Moses."
9. Metzger, "The 'Alba Bible' of Rabbi Moses Arragel," 133, indicates four full-page illustrations.
10. Among these images is the large knife in Abraham's hand in an illustration accompanying Genesis 22. This follows the usual Jewish representation; a sword figures in most Christian visual accounts of this incident. We can also point to Exodus 34:29, where rays radiate from Moses' head, in accordance with the Rabbinic understanding of this passage, but contrary to the common Christian illustration of a "horned Moses" based on the Vulgate's *cornuta facies*. A final example, taken from a number of possible ones, is the illustration accompanying Jacob's final words to Issachar in Genesis 49:14. Here Issachar is pictured as reading a book while seated on the ground. It is possible to detect that the text to which the book is opened is from Deuteronomy 33:18 (which speaks of Issachar as well as his brother Zebulun). All of this accords with a midrash that Issachar was well schooled in the Torah. Metzger, "The 'Alba Bible' of Rabbi Moses Arragel," 135–37.
11. See Metzger, "The 'Alba Bible' of Rabbi Moses Arragel," for an elegant discussion of many of the issues raised in answering this complex question.
12. To view pages from this stunning edition, visit the website www.facsimile-editions.com/en/ab.
13. On this, see Weiner, "The Ferrara Bible II," 24–25.
14. The preliminary material and the colophon add eight (in some copies, ten) pages to the larger format version. Rypins, "The Ferrara Bible at Press," 244–47.
15. Rypins, "The Ferrara Bible at Press," 248.
16. Rypins, "The Ferrara Bible at Press," 248–49.
17. Rypins, "The Ferrara Bible at Press," 249–54.
18. Rypins, "The Ferrara Bible at Press," 254–60.
19. Roth, "The Marrano Press at Ferrara, 1552–1555," 310–11, was already able to conclude: "The only thing that it seems possible to state dogmatically is that the traditional account, that *moca* figures in the 'Jewish' version and *virgen* in the 'Christian' one, cannot be maintained." Unlike Rypins, Roth did not venture a hypothesis to explain these complicated data.
20. It was revised in 1602. See Weiner, "The Ferrara Bible II," 25.
21. Broydé, "Cahen, Samuel."
22. Broydé, "Cahen, Samuel."

23. Its full title was *Archives Israélites de France: Revue Mensuelle Historique, Biographique, Bibliographique, Littéraire*. For a brief description of this publication through the early years of the twentieth century, see Weill, "Archives Israélites."
24. Delmaire ("Les traductions de la Bible au XIXe siècle et la Bible du rabbinat," 90) provides a succinct account and evaluation of this version.
25. My view is consistent with Delmaire's ("Les traductions de la Bible au XIXe siècle et la Bible du rabbinat," 91). Salomon Munk, one of the scholars working with Cahen, was responsible for learned introductions to the first volumes of Cahen's translation.
26. Among these is Cahen, *La Bible: Torah, Nevihim, Ketouvim*.
27. Among the most recent of many studies of the Dreyfus affair is Read, *The Dreyfus Affair*.
28. André, "Kahn, Zadoc." This work was later translated into German and Hebrew.
29. This article provides generally favorable accounts of Kahn and other French Jewish community leaders.
30. As quoted at http://www.dreyfus.culture.fr/en/dreyfus-and-his-family/the-support-of-family-and-friends/the-support-of-zadoc-kahn.htm.
31. Kahn likely saw his contributions as translator in the same light as his other scholarly works, his myriad philanthropic activities, and his rousing oratorical defenses of Judaism: All were essential elements in maintaining a strong Jewish community that acknowledged, practiced, and respected its heritage to the fullest and was not reluctant to assert its own worth even as it labored on others' behalf. An accessible edition of the Hebrew Bible was one of the foundations upon which any such community would be built.
32. For a history of this project and Kahn's involvement in it, see Delmaire, "Les traductions de la Bible au XIXe siècle et la Bible du rabbinat," 92–108.
33. For more details, see Gottheil, "Bible Translations."
34. This is an acronym formed from the first letters of his name in Hebrew. Similar acronyms identify other major figures in Jewish scholarship.
35. Rudavsky, "Samuel David Luzzatto and Neo-Orthodoxy," 25.
36. Greenberg, "Luzzatto, Samuel David (Shadal)."
37. Abrahams, "Samuel David Luzzatto as Exegete," 84.
38. Rudavsky, "Samuel David Luzzatto and Neo-Orthodoxy," 25.
39. For a brief summary of this correspondence, see Tobias, "Luzzatto, Samuel David," 286.
40. Rudavsky, "Samuel David Luzzatto and Neo-Orthodoxy," 38. See also Greenberg, "Luzzatto, Samuel David (Shadal)"; and Jacobs, "Samuel David Luzzatto (Shadal)."

41. In this spirit, Margolis (*The Story of Bible Translations*, 89–90) writes appreciatively that Luzzatto "unquestionably belongs [in] the first rank among modern Jewish students of the Bible. It may be said of him that he raised biblical studies among the Jews to the dignity of a specialty, requiring a man's whole time and energy and pursued as a profession."
42. Many other works by Luzzatto also first appeared or were published in revised form after his death, thanks to the efforts of his family and disciples. An accessible list of Luzzatto's publications, including his biblical translations and commentaries in Italian, appears in Seligsohn, "Samuel David (ShaDaL) Luzzatto," 225–26.
43. Abrahams, "Samuel David Luzzatto as Exegete," 98.
44. Tobias, "Luzzatto, Samuel David," 286.
45. Abrahams, "Samuel David Luzzatto as Exegete," 97–98.
46. Abrahams, "Samuel David Luzzatto as Exegete," 90–92.
47. These included Shelomoh Yehudah Rapoport, Nachman Kohen Krochmal, and Isaak Markus Jost, among others. See Seligsohn, "Samuel David (ShaDaL) Luzzatto," 225; and Abrahams, "Samuel David Luzzatto as Exegete," 97.
48. Abrahams, "Samuel David Luzzatto as Exegete," 94–95.
49. He also explained how the word *mashal* came to be associated with biblical poetry in general, while terms drawn from *shir* were restricted to poems that were sung.
50. Abrahams, "Samuel David Luzzatto as Exegete," 95.
51. Abrahams, "Samuel David Luzzatto as Exegete," 96–97.
52. Quoted in Abrahams, "Samuel David Luzzatto as Exegete," 99.
53. Silber, "Ballagi, Mór."
54. "Moritz Bloch," www.ha-gefen.org.il.
55. Silber, "Ballagi, Mór."
56. Neumann, "Bloch (Ballagi), Moritz."
57. Silber, "Ballagi, Mór."
58. Given the timing of the bestowal of this honor, officials likely took his Hungarian translation of the Bible into account—including the volumes that were in press but had not yet been published.
59. Silber, "Ballagi, Mór."
60. Silber, "Ballagi, Mór."
61. Neumann, "Bloch (Ballagi), Moritz."
62. Neumann, "Bloch (Ballagi), Moritz."
63. Silber, "Ballagi, Mór."
64. Silber, "Ballagi, Mór."
65. For an up-to-date account and analysis of such diversity, see Horowitz, *Empire Jews*.

66. Wiernik, "Mandelstamm, Leon (Aryeh Löb) B. Joseph."
67. The Jewish Enlightenment, or Haskalah, was a European movement of the eighteenth and nineteenth centuries. Its starting and ending dates are later than those of what is commonly called the Age of Enlightenment, although there were substantial chronological, geographical, and intellectual overlaps between these two movements and their leaders.
68. Slutsky, "Mandelstamm, Leon (Aryeh Loeb)."
69. Slutsky, "Mandelstamm, Leon (Aryeh Loeb)."
70. Slutsky, "Mandelstamm, Leon (Aryeh Loeb)."
71. For this translation of Mandelstamm's words, see Batalden, *Russian Bible Wars*, 167.
72. See, for example, "Collection Description—Jewish Division," www.nypl.org.
73. For a full study and assessment of Gordon and his accomplishments, see Stanislawski, *For Whom Do I Toil?*
74. Ben-Yishai, "Gordon, Judah Leib," 769.
75. Ben-Yishai, "Gordon, Judah Leib," 770–71.
76. Von Günzburg and Seligsohn, "Gordon, Leon (Judah Löb Ben Asher)."
77. Ben-Yishai, "Gordon, Judah Leib," 772.
78. Batalden, *Russian Bible Wars*, 170.
79. "Levanda stressed that the others [including Gordon] were excellent Hebraists, but that their translation could become *a bible* only after *his* stylistic labor. He claims to have had the feeling for the biblical *spirit*. . . . Presumably, after the clash with Gordon, Levanda was eliminated, and he was too proud *to claim* a part in the project started without any contractual arrangement." Perlmann, "L. O. Levanda and J. L. Gordon," 147–48. Emphasis in original.
80. Batalden, *Russian Bible Wars*, 170.
81. Batalden, *Russian Bible Wars*, 171–72.

6. English-Language Versions

1. Portions of this chapter closely follow Greenspoon, "The King James Bible and Jewish Bible Translations."
2. These psalms are listed here in the order in which they appear in the pamphlet.
3. In addition to its many other virtues, Katz's *God's Last Words* is one of very few books that mention any of the nineteenth-century Jewish Bible translators discussed in this and the following sections.
4. For the circumstances of the Jews' return to England and Menasseh ben Israel's role in this process, see Johnson, *A History of the Jews*, 275–78.

5. Loewe, "Review of A. S. Herbert, *Historical Catalogue*," 88–89. For the Moses Mendelssohn translation, see Gilman, "Between Religion and Culture," and Greenspoon, "Jewish Bible Translation in/and the Enlightenment."
6. For a concise overview of the work assignments for the various KJV companies, see "The Six Companies of Translators," in Nicolson, *God's Secretaries*, 251–59.
7. Lloyd Jones, Moore, and Reid, "Materials and Methods," 94.
8. In other words, the KJV translators had direct access to Kimchi's work in these instances.
9. For example, at Isaiah 7:14, KJV has the distinctively Christian rendering "virgin," as opposed to Kimchi's "young woman." For this and other passages, see Daiches, *The King James Version of the English Bible*, esp. 182–218.
10. Daiches, *The King James Version of the English Bible*, 146–47.
11. Lloyd Jones, Moore, and Read, "Materials and Methods," 99–100.
12. Lloyd Jones, Moore, and Reid, "Materials and Methods," 95.
13. Lloyd Jones, Moore, and Reid, "Materials and Methods," 100.
14. Daiches, *The King James Version of the English Bible*, 159.
15. Daiches, *The King James Version of the English Bible*, 153.
16. Lloyd Jones, Moore, and Reid, "Materials and Methods," 94.
17. Lloyd Jones, Moore, and Reid, "Materials and Methods," 95.
18. Lloyd Jones, Moore, and Reid, "Materials and Methods," 93–96.
19. Lloyd Jones, *The Discovery of Hebrew in Tudor England*, 115–16.
20. Lloyd Jones, *The Discovery of Hebrew in Tudor England*, 116.
21. Lloyd Jones, *The Discovery of Hebrew in Tudor England*, 117.
22. Lloyd Jones, *The Discovery of Hebrew in Tudor England*, 120.
23. Lloyd Jones, *The Discovery of Hebrew in Tudor England*, 122.
24. Lloyd Jones, *The Discovery of Hebrew in Tudor England*, 123.
25. Lloyd Jones, *The Discovery of Hebrew in Tudor England*, 124.
26. Lloyd Jones, *The Discovery of Hebrew in Tudor England*, 125–27.
27. Lloyd Jones, *The Discovery of Hebrew in Tudor England*, 129.
28. Lloyd Jones, *The Discovery of Hebrew in Tudor England*, 129–30.
29. Lloyd Jones, *The Discovery of Hebrew in Tudor England*, 130.
30. Lloyd Jones, *The Discovery of Hebrew in Tudor England*, 131.
31. Lloyd Jones, *The Discovery of Hebrew in Tudor England*, 131–32.
32. Lloyd Jones, *The Discovery of Hebrew in Tudor England*, 133–35.
33. Lloyd Jones, *The Discovery of Hebrew in Tudor England*, 135–38.
34. Lloyd Jones, *The Discovery of Hebrew in Tudor England*, 139.
35. Lloyd Jones, *The Discovery of Hebrew in Tudor England*, 140.
36. For a very accessible presentation and discussion of the translators' preface to the KJV, see Rhodes and Lupas, *The Translators to the Reader*.

37. See also Greenspoon, "The Birth of a Bible."
38. Although other individuals who were born Jewish had received such titles, prior to Goldsmid they had all converted to Christianity before the bestowal of this honor.
39. Benjamin Disraeli, a baptized Christian of Jewish parentage who was later elected prime minister (1874–80), was already a member of Parliament.
40. As, for example, the very active London Society for Promoting Christianity among the Jews, or simply the London Jews' Society.
41. See Greenspoon, "Bringing Home the Gospel."
42. On David Levi, see *The Jewish Encyclopedia* 8:25–26 and *Encyclopaedia Judaica* 11:78–79. Members of the Alexander family edited several other versions from this period. Of Levy Alexander, it is written in The *Jewish Encyclopedia* 1:348 (Jacobs, "Alexander"): "[His] translations were slovenly pieces of work, displaying ignorance alike of English and Hebrew. Levy seems to have been of a somewhat quarrelsome disposition. . . . Levy continued his abuse of the chief rabbi on the fly-leaves of the separate fascicles of his translation of the Bible." See also *Encyclopaedia Judaica* 2:571–72.
43. See Loewe, "Review of A. S. Herbert, *Historical Catalogue*," 88.
44. On this last point, see Greenspoon, "Top Dollar, Bottom Line?"
45. For more information on Newman and his career, see Lipkind, "Newman, Selig."
46. Newman, *Emendations of the Authorised Version of the Old Testament*, iv.
47. Hertz, *The Pentateuch and Haftorahs*, 217–18. See also Greenspoon, "Despoiling the Egyptians," and "The Portion: The Politics of Biblical Translation."
48. Things have not changed as much as readers might imagine. Biblical passages are still mined by those not favorably disposed to Jews and Judaism. This was equally true for avowedly atheistic Nazis as it was among the distressingly high percentage of Christian leaders who supported the racist ideologies and policies promoted by the Nazis.

    In fact, the specific Exodus imagery discussed in this chapter figured in a contemporary lawsuit, filed by an Egyptian jurist, in an effort to levy on contemporary Judaism a heavy fine supposedly equal to the cost of goods taken by the departing Hebrews. Jewish exegetes from the medieval period on, including Newman himself, would have argued that these goods are best seen as payment, and then only partial remuneration, for centuries of forced labor on the part of the Hebrews.
49. The quoted words are from Hertz, "Jewish Translations of the Bible in English."
50. Only while preparing a review of a book by Mary Wilson Carpenter, titled *Imperial Bibles, Domestic Bodies: Women, Sexuality, and Religion in the Victorian*

Market, did I learn that there existed a subgenre of Bible versions called "Family Bibles"—a Victorian phenomenon through which KJV was marketed to middle-class English men and women. Friedlander's *Jewish Family Bible* stood in this tradition. It should not have come as a surprise: Jews have not lacked acumen in marketing Bibles; on occasion they adopted techniques from the larger Christian world. Disappointingly, Carpenter does not include Friedlander's book or any other Jewish version in her otherwise comprehensive listing of British Family Bibles.

51. Hertz, "Jewish Translations of the Bible in English," 85.
52. Fisch, *Jerusalem Bible*, vii.
53. This latter passage continues to be a point of contention in some contemporary Jewish versions, where legitimate questions arise regarding fidelity to the plain meaning of the text (*peshat*) versus Rabbinic understanding.
54. As quoted in Hertz, "Jewish Translations of the Bible in English," 81.
55. Sussman, "Another Look at Isaac Leeser," 162–63.
56. Sussman, "Another Look at Isaac Leeser," 169.
57. Sussman, "Another Look at Isaac Leeser," 175.
58. Sussman, "Another Look at Isaac Leeser," 179–80.
59. These details of the history of OJPS are derived from Greenspoon, *Max Leopold Margolis*, 55–75; and Greenspoon, "Biblical Translators in Antiquity and in the Modern World." See also Sarna, *JPS: The Americanization of Jewish Culture 1888–1988*, esp. 97–116.
60. No doubt, OJPS was a stellar achievement on many levels. However, there is little evidence that one usage Margolis uniquely envisioned for it—as an impeccable guide to proper, uptown diction and vocabulary—was ever widely realized.
61. Adele Berlin, in "On Translating Proverbs 31:10," does not share my enthusiasm for the OJPS rendering here.
62. Greenspoon, "Kynge's Owne English," 54.
63. McGrath, *In the Beginning*, as quoted in Greenspoon, "A Book 'Without Blemish,'" 1–2.
64. Adler, *I Have Considered the Days*, 290.
65. On this, see Orlinsky, *Notes on the New Translation of the Torah*; and Orlinsky, *Essays in Biblical Culture and Bible Translation*, esp. 349–440.
66. In the interim Speiser died, in mid-June 1965.
67. At the same time, an important innovation, from Orlinsky's perspective, is found at the beginning of this verse (as at Gen. 11:5 and many other places) in NJPS, where the conjunction *vav*—typically translated as "and" in traditional English versions (especially KJV)—is omitted. Elsewhere in NJPS, the presence of this conjunction is signaled through the use of subordination,

where the paratactic structure of Hebrew favored coordination. By contrast, Alter consistently rendered the conjunction and structured his renderings to mirror the Hebrew's paratactic style.

68. It is instructive to compare this NJPS text with a passage from the Torah, such as the above-mentioned Deuteronomy 24:16. There NJPS retained the singular (with "person"; cf. "man" in traditional English versions), leading to the retention of the masculine singular pronoun "his." Here in the Prophets, however, NJPS succeeded in eliminating all exclusively male references.
69. Except for Speiser (see above).
70. To be precise, the JPS Writings encompassed translations from two groups. For the most part, it was the result of collaborative efforts by Greenberg, Greenfeld, Sarna, and others. But for the five books of the *megillot* it reproduced the version JPS had published (along with Jonah) in 1969. The original Torah committee (except for Speiser) produced this translation.
71. Given its importance within Judaism and the fact that its initial English-language text was published earliest, it is not surprising that the 1985 version of the JPS Torah was considerably revised from its earlier forms.
72. My language here, as elsewhere in this paragraph, closely follows the wording in the TANAKH preface itself. In this instance, such wording is, in the view of David E. S. Stein (via personal communication), "a bit of a distortion. In most cases where the 'Meaning of Heb. Uncertain' footnotes appear, the translators did arrive at one or more understandings of the word or passage in question, but they wanted readers to know that they were less sure of it (or them) than usual."
73. The volumes that make up the *JPS Torah Commentary* are as follows: *Genesis*, commentary by N. Sarna (1989); *Exodus*, commentary by N. Sarna (1991); *Leviticus*, commentary by B. A. Levine (1989); *Numbers*, commentary by J. Milgrom (1990); *Deuteronomy*, commentary by J. H. Tigay (1996). JPS commentary volumes are still being commissioned, written, and published on a regular basis.
74. Quoted in Greenspoon, *Max Leopold Margolis*, 69.
75. In addition to the inclusion of the Hebrew text, this publication also featured the second edition of the English-language translation. David E. S. Stein was the lead editor for the revision.
76. This wording is taken from the dust jacket of *The Contemporary Torah*.
77. The discussion above is based on the published text of CJPS. Subsequently, further gender-related changes have been offered, so that this verse now reads: "This is what the Eternal has commanded: 'Each household shall gather as much as it requires to eat—an *omer* to a person for as many of you as there are; each household shall fetch according to those in its tent'"

(see http://ccarpress.org/admin/manage_assetlibrary/file.asp?id=05343). In explaining the changes here, Stein stated (via personal communication): "I have come to believe that in this verse (among others), איש [*ish*] must refer to households rather than to individuals." In my view, for the desired teaching in this chapter, the net result of CJPS is the same in both the initial and the revised wording, and thus it has been retained as a relevant example.

78. This was first published in 1996, incorporating in revised form earlier editions as well as new material. Like TANAKH, *Tanach* is an acronym reflecting the traditional Jewish tripartite division of Hebrew Scripture (Torah, Nevi'im, Kethuvim).
79. The second edition of this annotated translation appeared in 1981.
80. Since Kaplan himself had translated and annotated the English-language version of the Torah, his followers used the term "Nach" to designate their renderings of the second (Nevi'im, or Prophets) and third (Kethuvim, or Writings) divisions of the Hebrew Bible: Elman, *The Living Nach: Early Prophets*; Elman and Schapiro, *The Living Nach: Later Prophets*; Schapiro, *The Living Nach: Sacred Writings*.
81. Subsequently Fox published *Give Us a King!* and *The Early Prophets*.
82. Friedman, *Commentary on the Torah*, xiii–xvi.
83. Alter, *The Five Books of Moses*, xxxii.
84. On this, see especially Greenspoon, "Between Text and Commentary."
85. Adam Kirsch, "The Alter Bible: In a Landmark New Translation, Robert Alter Revives the Literary Power of a Hebrew Masterpiece," *Tablet*, January 30, 2019. See also Hillel Halkin, "How to Judge Robert Alter's Landmark Translation of the Hebrew Bible," *Mosaic*, February 4, 2019: "A leading advocate of the view that the Bible needs to be read as great literature [Alter] has sought to bring this perspective to bear on its translation."
86. Not everyone agrees with my assessment here. So, for example, scholar and translator Edward Greenstein asserts: "Alter doesn't do any original research. He basically takes a few choice commentaries, as long as they are in relatively recent English or in Hebrew, and without himself going into any investigation just translates what seems right to him." Quoted in Elon Gilad, "How A Literature Professor Found Himself Translating the Entire Bible from Scratch," *Haaretz*, January 20, 2019. Unfortunately, Alter's response to Greenstein (as provided in the same article) is factually in error, in that Alter lumps Greenstein with some (unnamed) opponents who are participants in, or advocates for, NJPS. In fact, Greenstein's approach closely approximates the work of Everett Fox.
87. Updike, "Review of Robert Alter, *The Five Books of Moses*."

88. Regarding Updike's review and my critique of it, see Greenspoon, "Between Text and Commentary."
89. Greenspoon, "The KJV and Anglo-Jewish Translations of the Bible," explores these issues and their consequences in detail.

7. Non-Jewish Translations with Jewish Features

1. Other related examples of this phenomenon are the Alba Bible (see chapter 5) and the King James Version (discussed in the first part of chapter 6).
2. See "Note on Earlier Versions for the Jews," the source for much of the information in this section. Solomon was born in the 1790s.
3. Hershon was born in 1817 in Galicia. His conversion to Christianity took place when he was still young. In addition to preparing this version, he was involved in the London Jews' Society's activities in Palestine and wrote several studies on the Talmud.
4. This number included both complete and partial Yiddish New Testaments.
5. "Note on Earlier Versions for the Jews."
6. "Note on Earlier Versions for the Jews."
7. "The Old Testament in Yiddish."
8. Minutes of the British and Foreign Bible Society Editorial/Translation Department, vol. 5, part 5: Yiddish, as reported in early 1901. The Archives of the British and Foreign Bible Society are housed at the Cambridge University Library, where I accessed them. A catalog of the Bible Society archives is available online at janus.lib.cam.ac.uk and contains committee minutes, some Action Group materials, financial records, and important correspondence.
9. Geden, "The Yiddish Version of the New Testament," 144. A prolific writer, Geden (1857–1936) produced scholarly works on Eastern religions in addition to those on the languages of the Bible.
10. Geden, "The Yiddish Version of the New Testament," 144–45.
11. For this and other citations in this paragraph, see the Minutes of the British and Foreign Bible Society Editorial/Translation Department, vol. V, part 5: Yiddish, as reported in mid-1907.
12. BFBS Minutes, Yiddish, fall 1928.
13. "Jewish Immigrants."
14. British and Foreign Bible Society, Editorial Subcommittee Minute Cards, vol. 8: Yiddish (including Judeo-German).
15. Quoted in "The Religious Awakening among the Jews."
16. These and other similar accounts appear in "The Power of the New Testament amongst the Jews."

17. He was considered to be "still too much under the influence of Jewish expositors" (as stated in "The Power of the New Testament amongst the Jews"). Note also that even as a recent convert to Christianity, Weiss was still identified as a rabbi. For a Jewish perspective on similar activities, see Fishman, *East End 1888*.
18. As quoted in BFBS Minutes, Yiddish, September 1925.
19. As quoted in BFBS Minutes, Yiddish, May 1933.
20. This memo by the editorial superintendent, dated April 25, 1933, is quoted in BFBS Minutes, Yiddish, May 1933.
21. The edition of this Bible featured on Amazon.com was published in 2007. With its listing for each of his publications, Amazon also provides a biography of David H. Stern, which closely follows the one printed at the back of the Bible itself. Portions of this are as follows: "David H. Stern, born in Los Angeles in 1935, is the great-grandson of two of the city's first twenty Jews. . . . In 1972 he came to faith in Yeshua the Messiah. He then received a Master of Divinity degree at Fuller Theological Seminary, did graduate work at the University of Judaism, and was active in the Messianic Jewish movement. In 1979 the Stern family made aliyah (immigrated to Israel); they now live in Jerusalem."
22. The website of Congregation Shema Yisrael in suburban Detroit (https://www.shema.com) describes Messianic Judaism as "a movement of Jewish people who believe that Yeshua (Jesus's original name in Hebrew) is the Messiah of Israel and the Savior of the world."
23. I fully agree with a cautious, if not outright negative, assessment of Messianic Judaism but fully support this group's right to produce an English-language version of its Bible.
24. A brief biography of Barnstone, which references that author Jorge Luis Borges was one of his closest friends and mentors, appears at poetryfoundation.com.
25. Arguably, Stern, with "Yochanan," has done a better job than Barnstone, with "Yohanan," of reflecting the presumed original name of the author of the Fourth Gospel. His "ch" more accurately presents in transliteration the harsh guttural sound of the Hebrew letter *chet*. While there is nothing wrong with Barnstone's "h," it is less exact because it could represent the Hebrew letter *hey* as well.
26. On the significance of the consistency in this practice, see Barnstone, *The Poetics of Translation*, 74–75. In this instance, the nod goes to Barnstone, with "Ya'akov," in terms of accuracy. The Semitic original of this name has three syllables. By his insertion of what looks like an apostrophe here, Barnstone signals to careful readers that if they choose to sound out this proper name,

they'll need to pause between the two *a*'s, thus replicating the trisyllabic Hebrew nomenclature. By contrast, most English speakers would likely read the form Stern presents, "Yaakov," as bisyllabic.

27. Stern, *Jewish New Testament*, ix.
28. Stern, *Jewish New Testament*, x.
29. Stern, *Jewish New Testament*, xi.
30. Whether John's "baptism" involved immersion (with Stern) or dipping (with Barnstone) is a question of perennial disagreement among Christians. This issue is of great importance to this day, since John's practice—whether immersion or dipping—has formed something of a model for differing approaches to this central ritual for Christians.
31. Stern, *Jewish New Testament*, xx.
32. Quoted in Metzger, *The Bible in Translation*, 148n3.
33. Nonetheless, other observers appear to be more sympathetic on the matter. Among them is Bruce M. Metzger, one of the most active and best-known Bible translators of the twentieth century. In his *The Bible in Translation: Ancient and English Versions*, Metzger characterizes Stern's inclusion of Yiddish words in the New Testament as "unexpected" and concludes: "All and all [this New Testament] will certainly give the Gentile Christian readers a new perspective. It may be hoped that it will also be appreciated by its target audience, those who refer to themselves as Messianic Jews" (148).
34. The biographical information that follows in this section is drawn from Muller, *Apostle of China*, and Eber, *The Jewish Bishop*. Eber's monograph, published in 1999, draws on material not available to Muller when his book appeared in 1937; moreover, Eber's analytical framework is more sophisticated than Muller's. Nonetheless, Eber's work does not entirely replace Muller, whose narrative comes across as more immediate and compelling.
35. These quotations are found in Eber, "S. I. J. Schereschewsky's 1875 Chinese Version of Genesis," 224–25.
36. Eber, "S. I. J. Schereschewsky's 1875 Chinese Version of Genesis," 232–33.
37. Although not all of these transliterations were Schereschewsky's own construction, their consistent use was distinctive to his text and to those versions based on it.
38. Eber, "S. I. J. Schereschewsky's 1875 Chinese Version of Genesis," 231.
39. Eber, "S. I. J. Schereschewsky's 1875 Chinese Version of Genesis," 231. Like all of his notes and commentary, this one appeared in the body of the Chinese biblical text itself rather than in the margin or in a separate section at the bottom of the page.
40. This reading of Rashi is found in Scherman, *Tanach*, 10.
41. Eber, "S. I. J. Schereschewsky's 1875 Chinese Version of Genesis," 232.

42. Eber, "S. I. J. Schereschewsky's 1875 Chinese Version of Genesis," 232.
43. Fox, *The Five Books of Moses*, 23.
44. Eber, "S. I. J. Schereschewsky's 1875 Chinese Version of Genesis," 232.
45. Fox, *The Five Books of Moses*, 127.

Conclusion

1. Taylor, *Living Bible, Paraphrased.*
2. See, for example, these statements from the preface to the JPS edition of the Prophets (or Nevi'im) published in 1978 (vii–viii): "Many modern English versions [for Christians] contain translations of emended texts, sometimes without citing any departure from the traditional Hebrew text. The present translation adheres strictly to the traditional Hebrew text, but where the text remained obscure and an alteration of it provided marked clarification, a footnote is offered with a rendering of the suggested emendation."

   For our purposes, the term "variant" primarily applies to an alternative Hebrew or Greek reading actually attested in an extant manuscript or inscription. In this sense, "conjectures" refer to ancient wording that modern scholars establish as likely, even though we have no manuscript exhibiting the suggested text.
3. Nothing in the previous discussion is intended to demonstrate that the features identified are unique to Jewish versions. Rather, it is their emphasis, individually and as a group, that has served to characterize Bible versions as Jewish. See also Leonard Greenspoon, "Is the Alter Bible Jewish, in Some Definable Sense?" *Mosaic*, February 18, 2019. Compare to Hillel Halkin, "The Necessary Bad Faith in Reading the Bible as Literature," *Mosaic*, February 25, 2019.

Bibliography

Abrahams, Israel. "Samuel David Luzzatto as Exegete." *Jewish Quarterly Review* 57, no. 2 (1966): 83–100.

Adler, Cyrus. *I Have Considered the Days*. Philadelphia: The Jewish Publication Society of America, 1945.

Alter, Robert. *Ancient Israel: The Former Prophets: Joshua, Judges, Samuel, and Kings: A Translation with Commentary*. New York: Norton, 2014.

———. *The Book of Psalms: A Translation with Commentary*. New York: Norton, 2007.

———. *The David Story: A Translation with Commentary of 1 and 2 Samuel*. New York: Norton, 2000.

———. *The Five Books of Moses: A Translation with Commentary*. New York: Norton, 2004.

———. *The Hebrew Bible: A Translation with Commentary*. New York: Norton, 2018.

———. *The Wisdom Books: Job, Proverbs, and Ecclesiastes: A Translation with Commentary*. New York: Norton, 2011.

Altmann, Alexander. *Moses Mendelssohn: A Biographical Study*. London: Littman Library of Jewish Civilization, 1998.

André, Édouard. "Kahn, Zadoc." In *The Jewish Encyclopedia*, 7:414.

Aptroot, Marion. "'*In galkhes* they do not say so, but *the taytsh* is as it stands here.' Notes on the Amsterdam Yiddish Bible Translations by Blitz and Witzenhausen." *Studia Rosenthaliana* 27, no. 1/2 (1993): 136–58.

Archives of the British and Foreign Bible Society. Cambridge University Library. Catalog available online at janus.lib.cam.ac.uk.

Asher, David, trans. *The Way of Faith; or, The Abridged Bible*, by Moses Mordecai Büdinger. London: Samuel Bagster & Sons, 1848.

Ashkenazi, Yaakov ben Yitzchak. *Ts'enah Ur'enah*. Vol. 2. Translated by Miriam Stark Zakon. New York: Mesorah, 2001.

Barker, James W., Anthony Le Donne, and Joel N. Lohr, eds. *Found in Translation: Essays on Biblical Translation in Honor of Leonard J. Greenspoon*. West Lafayette IN: Purdue University Press, 2018.

Barnard, Leslie William. *St. Justin Martyr: The First and Second Apologies*. Ancient Christian Writers. Ramsey NJ: Paulist, 1997.

Barnstone, Willis. *The Poetics of Translation: History, Theory, Practice*. New Haven CT: Yale University Press, 2003.

———. *Restored New Testament: A New Translation with Commentary, Including the Gnostic Gospels Thomas, Mary, and Judas*. New York: W. W. Norton, 2009.

Batalden, Stephen K. *Russian Bible Wars: Modern Scriptural Translation and Cultural Authority*. Cambridge: Cambridge University Press, 2013.

Belligheimer, S. "On Jewish Translations of the Bible in German." *Abr-Nahrain* 7 (1967/68): 1–34.

Benisch, Abraham. *Jewish School and Family Bible*. London: Longman, Brown, Green, and Longmans, 1852.

Bennett, Solomon. *Specimen of a New Version of the Hebrew Bible*. London: printed for the author, 1834.

Ben-Sasson, Hayim, ed. *A History of the Jewish People*. Cambridge MA: Harvard University Press, 1985.

Ben-Yishai, Aharon Zeev. "Gordon, Judah Leib." In *Encyclopaedia Judaica*, 2nd ed., 7:769–72.

Bergen, Doris L. *Twisted Cross: The German Christian Movement in the Third Reich*. Chapel Hill: University of North Carolina Press, 1996.

Berlin, Adele. "On Translating Proverbs 31:10." In *Found in Translation: Essays on Biblical Translation in Honor of Leonard J. Greenspoon*, edited by James W. Barker, Anthony Le Donne, and Joel N. Lohr, 201–8. West Lafayette IN: Purdue University Press, 2018.

Berlin, Adele, and Marc Zvi Brettler, eds. *The Jewish Study Bible*. New York: Oxford, 2003.

Bobrick, Benson. *Wide as the Waters: The Story of the English Bible and the Revolution It Inspired*. New York: Simon & Schuster, 2001.

Boyd-Taylor, Cameron. *Reading between the Lines: The Interlinear Paradigm for Septuagint Studies*. Biblical Tools and Studies 8. Leuven: Peeters, 2011.

Breuer, Edward. *The Limits of Enlightenment: Jew, Germans, and the Eighteenth-Century Study of Scripture*. Cambridge MA: Harvard University Press, 1996.

Brock, Sebastian. "The Phenomenon of the Septuagint." In *Witness of Tradition: Papers Read at the Joint British-Dutch Old Testament Conference, Woudschoten, Netherlands, 1970*, edited by Martinus A. Beck, 11–36. Leiden: Brill, 1972.

Brody, Robert. *Sa'adyah Gaon*. Translated by Betsy Rosenberg. Oxford: The Littman Library of Jewish Civilization, 2013.

Broydé, Isaac. "Cahen, Samuel." In *The Jewish Encyclopedia*, 3:491–92.

Buber, Martin. "*Leitwort* Style in Pentateuch Narrative." In Martin Buber and Franz Rosenzweig, *Scripture and Translation*, translated by Lawrence Rosenwald with Everett Fox, 114–21. Bloomington: Indiana University Press, 1994.

———. "On Word Choice in Translating the Bible." In Martin Buber and Franz Rosenzweig, *Scripture and Translation*, translated by Lawrence Rosenwald with Everett Fox, 74–77. Bloomington: Indiana University Press, 1994.

Cahen, Samuel, trans. *La Bible: Torah, Nevihim, Ketouvim*. Paris: Les Belles Lettres, 1994.

Carpenter, Mary Wilson. *Imperial Bibles, Domestic Bodies: Women, Sexuality, and Religion in the Victorian Market*. Athens: Ohio University Press, 2003.

Cathcart, Kevin J., and Robert P. Gordon, trans. and annots. *The Targum of the Minor Prophets*. Vol. 14 of *The Aramaic Bible*. Wilmington DE: Michael Glazier, 1989.

Clarke, Ernest G., trans and annot. *Targum Pseudo-Jonathan: Deuteronomy*. Vol. 5B of *The Aramaic Bible*. Collegeville MN: Liturgical Press, 1998.

Cook, Johann. *The Septuagint of Proverbs: Jewish and/or Hellenistic Proverbs?: Concerning the Hellenistic Colouring of LXX Proverbs*. Supplements to *Vetus Testamentum*. Leiden: Brill, 1997.

Daiches, David. *The King James Version of the English Bible: An Account of the Development and Sources of the English Bible of 1611 with Special Reference to the Hebrew Tradition*. Chicago: University of Chicago Press, 1941.

Daniel, S. "Greek: The Septuagint." *Encyclopaedia Judaica* 1st ed. 4:851–56.

———. *Recherche sur le vocabulaire du culte dans La Septante*. Paris: C. Klincksieck, 1966.

Dean, James Elmer, ed. *Epiphanius' Treatise on Weights and Measures: The Syriac Version*. Chicago: University of Chicago Press, 1935.

Delgado, Isaac. *A New English Translation of the Pentateuch: Being a Thorough Correction of the Present Translation, Wherever it deviates from the genuine sense of the Hebrew Expressions, or where it renders obscure the Meaning of the Text; or, lastly, when it occasions a seeming Contradiction . . . together with a comment on such passages as cannot be sufficiently understood by a mere translation*. London: printed for author and sold by W. Richardson, 1789.

Delmaire, Danielle. "Les traductions de la Bible au XIXe siècle et la Bible du rabbinate." In *Zadoc Kahn: Un grand rabbin entre culture juive, affaire Dreyfus et laïcité*, edited by Jean-Philippe Chaumont and Jean-Claude Kuperminc, 89–108. Paris: Éditions de l'éclat, 2007.

De Sola, David Aaron, M. J. Raphall, Levy I. Lindenthal. *The Sacred Scriptures in Hebrew and English: A New Translation with notes*. Vol. 1: Genesis [the only volume that appeared]. London: S. Bagster & Sons, 1841.

Dines, Jennifer. *The Septuagint*. London: T & T Clark, 2004.

Eber, Irene. *The Jewish Bishop and the Chinese Bible: S. I. J. Schereschewsky (1831–1906)*. Leiden: Brill, 1999.

———. "S. I. J. Schereschewsky's 1875 Chinese Version of Genesis." *Bulletin of the School of Oriental and African Studies* 56, no. 2 (1993): 219–33.

"Editorial Echoes: Yiddish." *The Bible in the World* 10 (1914): 115–16.

Elman, Yaakov. *The Living Nach: Early Prophets*. New York: Moznaim, 1994.

Elman, Yaakov, and Moshe Schapiro. *The Living Nach: Later Prophets*. New York: Moznaim, 1995.

Elon, Amos. *The Pity of It All: A History of the Jews in Germany, 1743–1933*. New York: Metropolitan Books, 2002.

Elzas, Abraham. *The Book of Job*. London: Trübner, 1872.

———. *The Minor Prophets*. London: Trübner, 1874.

———. *Proverbs of Solomon*. London: Trübner, 1871.

Encyclopaedia Judaica. 1st ed. Edited by Cecil Roth and Geoffrey Wigoder. 17 vols. Jerusalem: Keter Publishing House Jerusalem, 1972.

Encyclopaedia Judaica. 2nd ed. Edited by Fred Skolnik. 22 vols. Jerusalem: Jerusalem Publishing House, 2006.

Ericksen, Robert P., and Susannah Heschel, eds. *Betrayal: German Churches and the Holocaust*. Minneapolis MN: Fortress Press, 1999.

Evans, Craig A., et al., eds. *Exploring the Origins of the Bible: Canon Formation in Historical, Literary, and Theological Perspective*. Acadia Studies in Bible and Theology. Grand Rapids MI: Baker, 2008.

Feiner, Shmuel. *Moses Mendelssohn: Sage of Modernity*. Translated by Anthony Berris. Jewish Lives. New Haven CT: Yale University Press, 2010.

Fernández Marcos, Natalio. *The Septuagint in Context: Introduction to the Greek Version of the Bible*. Translated by W. G. E. Watson. Leiden: Brill, 2000.

Fisch, Harold, ed. *The Jerusalem Bible*. Jerusalem: Koren, 1997.

Fishman, W. J. *East End 1888: A Year in a London Borough among the Labouring Poor*. London: Duckworth, 1988.

Flesher, Paul V. M., and Bruce Chilton. *The Targums: A Critical Introduction*. Waco TX: Baylor University Press, 2011.

Fox, Everett. *The Early Prophets: Joshua, Judges, Samuel, and Kings*. Vol. 2 of *The Schocken Bible*. New York: Schocken, 2014.

———. *The Five Books of Moses: A New Translation with Introductions, Commentary, and Notes*. Vol. 1 of *The Schocken Bible*. New York: Schocken, 1995.

———. *Give Us a King! Samuel, Saul, and David*. New York: Schocken, 1999.
Freedman, Samuel. "The Halacha in the Targum to the Torah Attributed to Yonatan ben Uzziel." PhD diss., University College London, 1999.
Freidenreich, David M. "The Use of Islamic Sources in Saadiah Gaon's *Tafsir* of the Torah." *Jewish Quarterly Review* 93 (2003): 353–95.
Friedlander, Michael. *Jewish Family Bible*. London: J. & W. Rider, 1881.
Friedman, Richard Elliott. *Commentary on the Torah with a New English Translation*. New York: HarperOne, 2001.
———. *Who Wrote the Bible?* New York: Simon & Schuster, 1987.
Geden, A. S. "The Yiddish Version of the New Testament." *The Bible in the World* 9 (1913): 143–45.
Gerber, Jane S. *Jews of Spain: A History of the Sephardic Experience*. New York: Free Press, 1994.
Gil, Moshe, and David Strassler. *Jews in Islamic Countries in the Middle Ages*. Leiden: Brill, 2004.
Gilman, Abigail E. "Between Religion and Culture: Mendelssohn, Buber, Rosenzweig and the Enterprise of Biblical Translation." In *Biblical Translation in Context*, edited by Frederick W. Knobloch, 93–114. Bethesda: University of Maryland Press, 2002.
———. *A History of German Jewish Bible Translation*. Chicago: University of Chicago Press, 2018.
Goldsmith, Emanuel S. *Modern Yiddish Culture: The Story of the Yiddish Language Movement*. New York: Fordham University Press, 1997.
Gollancz, Hermann. *The Holy Bible containing the Pentateuch, the Hagiographa, and the Former and Latter Prophets*. London: J. G. Murdoch; L. Schaap, 1880.
Goodman, L. E. "Saadiah Gaon's Interpretive Technique in Translating the Book of Job." In *Translation of Scripture*, 47–76. *Jewish Quarterly Review* supplement. Philadelphia: Annenberg Research Institute, 1990.
———, ed. and trans. *The Book of Theodicy: Translation and Commentary on the Book of Job by Saadiah ben Joseph al-Fayyumi*. New Haven CT: Yale University Press, 1988.
Gottheil, Richard. "Arragel, Moses." In *The Jewish Encyclopedia*, 2:138.
———. "Bible Translations." In *The Jewish Encyclopedia*, 3:185–97.
Greenberg, Gershon. "Luzzatto, Samuel David (Shadal)." In *Encyclopedia of Modern Jewish Culture*, edited by Glenda Abramson, 539–40. London: Routledge, 2005.
Greenhouse, Emily. "Treasures in the Wall." *The New Yorker*, March 1, 2013.
Greenslade, S. L. *The West from the Reformation to the Present Day*. Vol. 3 of *The Cambridge History of the Bible*. Cambridge: Cambridge University Press, 1963.

Greenspahn, Frederick E. "Why Jews Translate the Bible." In *Biblical Interpretation in Judaism and Christianity*, edited by Isaac Kalimi and Peter Haas, 179–95. Library of Biblical Studies. New York: T & T Clark, 2006.

Greenspoon, Leonard J. "Between Text and Commentary: A Characteristic Feature of Jewish Bible Translations." *Open Theology* 2 (2016): 476–93.

———."Biblical Translators in Antiquity and in the Modern World: A Comparative Study." *Hebrew Union College Annual* 60 (1989): 91–113.

———. "A Book 'Without Blemish': The Jewish Publication Society's Bible Translation of 1917." *Jewish Quarterly Review* 79 (1988): 1–21.

———. "Bringing Home the Gospel: Yiddish Bibles, Bible Societies, and the Jews." In *Yiddish Language and Culture: Then and Now*, edited by Leonard J. Greenspoon, 291–304. Omaha NE: Creighton University Press, 1998.

———. "By the Letter?/Word for Word? Scripture in the Jewish Tradition." In *The Hebrew Bible: New Insights and Scholarship*, edited by Frederick E. Greenspahn, 141–63. Jewish Studies in the 21st Century. New York: New York University Press, 2008.

———. "Despoiling the Egyptians: A Concerning Jewish Legacy?" TheTorah .com. https://thetorah.com/despoiling-the-egyptians-a-concerning-jewish -legacy/.

———. "Greek: Septuagint." In *Encyclopaedia Judaica*, 2nd ed.,3:595–598.

———. "Hebrew into Greek: Interpretation In, By, and Of the Septuagint." In *History of Biblical Interpretation*, vol. 1, edited by Alan Hauser and Duane F. Watson, 80–113. Grand Rapids MI: Eerdmans, 2003.

———. "Jewish Bible Translation in/and the Enlightenment." *Studia Hebraica* 2 (2003): 319–28.

———. "Jewish Translations of the Bible." In *The Jewish Study Bible*, edited by Adele Berlin and Marc Zvi Brettler, 2005–20. New York: Oxford, 2003.

———. "The *Kaige* Recension: The Life, Death, and Postmortem Existence of a Modern—and Ancient—Phenomenon." In *XII Congress of the International Organization for Septuagint and Cognate Studies, Leiden 2004*, edited by Melvin K. H. Peters, 5–16. Atlanta GA: Society of Biblical Literature, 2006.

———. "The King James Bible and Jewish Bible Translations." In *The Translation That Openeth the Window: Reflections on the History and Legacy of the King James Version*, edited by David G. Burke, 123–38. New York: American Bible Society, 2009.

———. "The KJV and Anglo-Jewish Translations of the Bible: A Unique and Uniquely Fruitful Connection." In *The King James Version at 400: Assessing Its Genius as Bible Translation and Its Literary Influence*, edited by David G. Burke, John F. Kutsko, and Philip H. Towner, 273–95. SBL Biblical Scholarship in North America 26. Atlanta GA: Society of Biblical Literature, 2013.

———. "Kynge's Owne English." *Bible Review* 19 (December 2003): 15–21, 52–54.

———. *Max Leopold Margolis: A Scholar's Scholar*. Biblical Scholarship in North America 15. Atlanta GA: Scholars Press, 1987.

———. "On the Jewishness of Modern Jewish Biblical Scholarship: The Case of Max L. Margolis." *Judaism* 39 (1990): 82–92.

———. "The Portion: The Politics of Biblical Translation." *The Forward*, January 30, 2004.

———. "'Reclaiming' the Septuagint for Jews and Judaism." In *Scripture in Transition: Essays on Septuagint, Hebrew Bible, and Dead Sea Scrolls in Honour of Raija Sollamo*, edited by Anssi Voitila and Jutta Jokiranta, 661–70. Leiden: Brill, 2008.

———. "The Septuagint." In *Jewish Annotated New Testament*, edited by Amy-Jill Levine and Marc Z. Brettler, 562–65. New York: Oxford University Press, 2011.

———. "A Short History of Bible Translation." In *The Jewish Bible*, 33–51. JPS Guides Series. Philadelphia: The Jewish Publication Society, 2008.

———. "Top Dollar, Bottom Line?: Marketing English-Language Bibles within the Jewish Community." In *Biblical Translation in Context*, edited by Frederick W. Knobloch, 115–33. Studies and Texts in Jewish History and Culture. Bethesda: University of Maryland Press, 2002.

———. "The Use and Abuse of the Term 'LXX' and Related Terminology in Recent Scholarship." *Bulletin of the International Organization for Septuagint and Cognate Studies* 20 (1987): 20–28.

———. "Versions, Jewish." In *New Interpreter's Dictionary of the Bible*, 5:760–65. Nashville TN: Abingdon: 2009.

———. "When Harry Met Max." In *New Essays in American Jewish History: Commemorating the Sixtieth Anniversary of the Founding of the American Jewish Archives*, edited by Pamela S. Nadell, Jonathan D. Sarna, and Lance J. Sussman, 289–304. Cincinnati: The Jacob Rader Marcus Center of the American Jewish Archives, 2010.

Greenstein, Edward L. "Challenges in Translating the Book of Job." In *Found in Translation: Essays on Biblical Translation in Honor of Leonard J. Greenspoon*, edited by James W. Barker, Anthony Le Donne, and Joel N. Lohr, 179–99. West Lafayette IN: Purdue University Press, 2018.

———. *Essays on Biblical Method and Translation*. Atlanta GA: Scholars Press, 1989.

———. "The Scroll of Esther: A New Translation." *Fiction* 9, no. 3 (1990): 52–81.

———. "What Might Make a Bible Translation Jewish?" In *Translation and Scripture: Proceedings of a Conference at the Annenberg Research Institute May 14–16, 1989*, 77–101. Philadelphia: Annenberg Research Institute, 1990.

Grossfeld, Bernard, trans. and annot. *The Targum Onkelos to Deuteronomy*. Vol. 9 of *The Aramaic Bible*. Wilmington DE: Michael Glazier, 1988.

———. *The Targum Onkelos to Exodus*. Vol. 7 of *The Aramaic Bible*. Wilmington DE: Michael Glazier, 1988.
———. *The Two Targums of Esther*. Vol. 18 of *The Aramaic Bible*. Collegeville MN: Liturgical Press, 1991.
Grossfeld, Bernard, and S. David Sperling. "Aramaic: The Targumim." In *Encyclopaedia Judaica*, 2nd ed., 3:588–95.
Grunfeld, I. "Introduction." In *Hirsch Commentary on the Torah* by Rabbi Samson Raphael Hirsch. New York: Judaica Press, 1966.
Halkin, A. S. "Saadiah's Exegesis and Polemics." In *Rab Saadia Gaon: Studies in His Honor*, edited by Louis Finkelstein, 117–41. New York: Arno Press, 1980.
Harrington, Daniel J., and Anthony J. Saldarini, trans. and annots. *Targum Jonathan of the Former Prophets*. Vol. 10 of *The Aramaic Bible*. Wilmington DE: Michael Glazier, 1987.
Hertz, Joseph H. "Jewish Translations of the Bible in English [being the concluding lecture in series, 'Translations of the Bible,' Toynbee Hall, 1919]." In *Addresses*, vol. 2 of *Sermons, Addresses and Studies*, 70–93. London: Soncino, 1938.
———, ed. *The Pentateuch and Haftorahs*. 2nd ed. London: Soncino, 1961.
Heschel, Susannah. *The Aryan Jesus: Christian Theologians and the Bible in Nazi Germany*. Princeton NJ: Princeton University Press, 2008.
Hirsch, Rabbi Samson Raphael. *Hirsch Commentary on the Torah*. Translated into English by Isaac Levy. New York: Judaica Press, 1966.
Honigman, Sylvie. *The Septuagint and Homeric Scholarship in Alexandria: A Study of the Narrative of the Letter of Aristeas*. London: Routledge, 2003.
Horowitz, Brian. *Empire Jews: Jewish Nationalism and Acculturation in 19th and Early 20th Century Russia*. New Approaches to Russian and East European Culture. Bloomington IN: Slavica, 2009.
———. *Jewish Philanthropy and Enlightenment in Late-Tsarist Russia*. Seattle: University of Washington Press, 2009.
Jacobs, Joseph. "Alexander." In *The Jewish Encyclopedia* 1:348.
Jacobs, Louis. "Samuel David Luzzatto (Shadal)." In *The Jewish Religion: A Companion*. Oxford: Oxford University Press, 1995.
The Jewish Encyclopedia. Edited by Isidore Singer, Cyrus Adler et al. 12 vols. New York: Funk and Wagnalls, 1901–6.
"Jewish Immigrants." *The Monthly Reporter of the* BFBS 32 (February 1903): 35.
"Jews and the Bible Society." *The Bible in the World* 13 (1917): 43.
Johnson, Paul. *A History of the Jews*. New York: Harper & Row, 1987.
Kalisch, Marcus. *A Historical and Critical Commentary on the Old Testament: Exodus*. London: Longman, Brown, Green, and Longmans, 1855
———. *A Historical and Critical Commentary on the Old Testament: Genesis*. London: Longman, Brown, Green, and Longmans, 1858

———. *A Historical and Critical Commentary on the Old Testament: Leviticus*. London: Longman, Brown, Green, and Longmans, 1872.

Kaplan, Aryeh. *The Living Torah: The Five Books of Moses*. 2nd ed. New York: Moznaim Publishing, 1981.

Katz, David S. *God's Last Words: Reading the English Bible from the Reformation to Fundamentalism*. New Haven CT: Yale University Press, 2004.

Katz, Dovid. *Words on Fire: The Unfinished Story of Yiddish*. New York: Basic Books, 2007.

Kearney, Jonathan. "The Torah of Israel in the Tongue of Ishmael: Saadia Gaon and His Arabic Translation of the Pentateuch." *Proceedings of the Irish Biblical Association* 33–34 (2011): 55–75.

Kirsch, Adam. "Daughters of Zion: The *Tsenerene* and the *Memoirs* of Glückel of Hameln." In *The People and the Books: 18 Classics of Jewish Literature*, 221–46. New York: Norton, 2017.

Komlosh, Yehuda. "Targum Sheni." In *Encyclopaedia Judaica*, 2nd ed., 19:513–15.

Kraft, Robert A. "Christian Transmission of Greek Jewish Scriptures: A Methodological Probe." In *Paganisme, Judaisme, Christianisme: Influences et affrontements dans le Monde Antique*, edited by A. Benoit et al., 207–26. Paris: De Boccard, 1978.

Kriwaczek, Paul. *Yiddish Civilisation: The Rise and Fall of a Forgotten Nation*. New York: Vintage, 2006.

Leeser, Isaac. *The Law of God: Edited, and with Former Translations Diligently Compared and Revised*. Philadelphia: C. Sherman for Isaac Leeser, 1845 (initially published in five volumes, one for each of the books of the Torah).

———. *The Twenty-Four Books of the Holy Scriptures: Carefully Translated According to the Massoretic Text, on the Basis of the English Version, After the Best Jewish Authorities and Supplied with Short Explanatory Notes*. Philadelphia: Sherman for A. De Sola, 1853.

Levenson, Alan T. "Translation versus Teaching: Competing Agendas in Samson Raphael Hirsch's Bible Project." In *Found in Translation: Essays on Biblical Translation in Honor of Leonard J. Greenspoon*, edited by James W. Barker, Anthony Le Donne, and Joel N. Lohr, 227–41. West Lafayette IN: Purdue University Press, 2018.

Levey, Samson H., trans. and annot. *The Targum of Ezekiel*. Vol. 13 of *The Aramaic Bible*. Wilmington DE: Michael Glazier, 1987.

Levi, David. *The First Book of Moses, called Genesis, in the Hebrew, with English Translation on the Opposite Page. With Notes, Explanatory, Exegetical, Practical, Critical, and Grammatical*. London: Lion Soesmans, 1787.

Levine, Baruch A. *Leviticus. JPS Torah Commentary*. Philadelphia: The Jewish Publication Society, 1989.

Lewis, Jack P. *The English Bible from KJV to NIV: A History and Evaluation*. Grand Rapids MI: Baker, 1981.
Lieber, David L., Jules Harlow, et al. *ETZ HAYIM: Torah and Commentary*. Philadelphia: The Jewish Publication Society, 2001.
Lim, Timothy H. *The Formation of the Jewish Canon*. Anchor Yale Bible Reference Library. New Haven CT: Yale University Press, 2013.
Linetsky, Michael, ed. and trans. *Rabbi Saadiah Gaon's Commentary on the Book of Creation*. Northvale NJ: Jason Aronson, 2002.
Lipkind, Goodman. "Newman, Selig." In *The Jewish Encyclopedia*, 9:294.
Lipton, Walter S. "A Blurred Encounter in Moses Arragel's Epistle on the Alba Bible." *Modern Language Notes* 84, no. 2 (1969): 298–304.
Loewe, Raphael. "Review of A. S. Herbert, *Historical Catalogue of Printed Editions of the English Bible 1525–1961*." *Journal of Jewish Studies* 21 (1970): 88–89.
Loewe, Raphael, and Everett Fox. "Anglo-Jewish Versions." In *Encyclopaedia Judaica*, 2nd ed., 3:614.
Lloyd Jones, Gareth. *The Discovery of Hebrew in Tudor England: A Third Language*. Manchester: Manchester University Press, 1983.
Lloyd Jones, Gareth, Helen Moore, and Julian Reid. "Materials and Methods." In *Manifold Greatness: The Making of the King James Bible*, edited by Helen Moore and Julian Reid, 94–100. Oxford: Bodleian Library, 2011.
Malter, Henry. *Saadiah Gaon: His Life and Works*. New York: Hermon Press, 1969. Originally published 1926.
Manger, Isaac. *The World According to Itzik: Selected Poetry and Prose*. Translated and edited by Leonard Wolf. New Yiddish Library. New Haven CT: Yale University Press, 2002.
Mann, Vivian, et al., eds. *Convivencia: Jews, Muslims, and Christians in Medieval Spain*. New York: George Braziller, 2007.
Margolis, Max L. "Specimen of a New Edition of the Greek Joshua." In *Jewish Studies in Memory of Israel Abrahams*, edited by Alexander Kahut Memorial Foundation, 307–23. New York: Jewish Institute of Religion, 1927.
———. *The Story of Bible Translations*. Philadelphia: The Jewish Publication Society, 1917.
McDonald, Lee Martin, and James A. Sanders, eds. *The Canon Debate*. Peabody, MA: Hendrickson, 2002.
McGrath, Alister. *In the Beginning: The Story of the King James Bible and How It Changed a Nation, a Language, and a Culture*. New York: Doubleday, 2001.
McLay, R. Timothy. *The OG and Th Versions of Daniel*. Septuagint and Cognate Studies 43. Atlanta GA: Scholars Press, 1996.
McNamara, Martin, trans. and annot. *Targum Neofiti I: Deuteronomy*. Vol. 5A of *The Aramaic Bible*. Collegeville MN: Liturgical Press, 1997.

McNamara, Martin, trans., Michael Maher and Robert Haywood, annots. *Targums Neofiti I and Pseudo-Jonathan: Exodus*. Vol. 2 of *The Aramaic Bible*. Collegeville MN: Liturgical Press, 1994.
Metzger, Bruce M. *The Bible in Translation: Ancient and English Versions*. Grand Rapids MI: Baker, 2001.
Metzger, Thérèse. "The 'Alba Bible' of Rabbi Moses Arragel." *Bulletin of the Institute of Jewish Studies* 3 (1975): 131–55.
Milgrom, Jacob. *Numbers. JPS Torah Commentary*. Philadelphia: The Jewish Publication Society, 1990.
Moatti-Fine, Jacqueline. *Jésus (Josué)*. La Bible d'Alexandrie 6. Paris: Cerf, 1996.
Modrzejewski, Joseph Mélèze. *The Jews of Egypt: From Rameses II to Emperor Hadrian*. Translated by Robert Cornman. Philadelphia: The Jewish Publication Society, 1995.
Moore, Helen, and Julian Reid, eds. *Manifold Greatness: The Making of the King James Bible*. Oxford: Bodleian Library, 2011.
Muller, James Arthur. *Apostle of China, Samuel Isaac Joseph Schwereschewsky*. New York: Morehouse, 1937.
Neumann, Eduard. "Bloch (Ballagi), Moritz." In *The Jewish Encyclopedia*, 3:256.
Newman, Selig. *Emendations of the Authorised Version of the Old Testament*. London: B. Wertheim, 1839.
Nicolson, Adam. *God's Secretaries: The Making of the King James Bible*. New York: HarperCollins, 2003.
Nida, Eugene A., and C. R. Taber. *The Theory and Practice of Translation*. Leiden: Brill, 1969.
"Note on Earlier Versions for the Jews." *The Bible in the World* 9 (1913): 146.
"The Old Testament in Yiddish." *The Bible in the World* 24 (1920): 121.
Orlinsky, Harry M. *Essays in Biblical Culture and Bible Translation*. New York: KTAV, 1974.
———. "The Hebrew *Vorlage* of the Septuagint of the Book of Joshua." In *Congress Volume (Rome 1968)*, 187–95. Leiden: Brill, 1969.
———. "Jewish Biblical Scholarship in America." *Jewish Quarterly Review* 45 (1955): 374–412.
———. "Jewish Biblical Scholarship in America (Continued)." *Jewish Quarterly Review* 47 (1957): 345–353.
———. "The Septuagint as Sacred Writ and the Philosophy of the Translators." *Hebrew Union College Annual* 46 (1975): 89–114.
———. "Yehoash's Yiddish Translation of the Bible." *Journal of Biblical Literature* 60 (1941): 173–77.
———, ed. *Notes on the New Translation of the Torah*. Philadelphia: The Jewish Publication Society of America, 1969.

Orlinsky, Harry M., and Roger G. Bratcher. *A History of Bible Translation and the North American Contribution*. Atlanta GA: Scholars Press, 1991.

Parker, D. C. *Codex Sinaiticus: The Story of the World's Oldest Bible*. Peabody MA: Hendrickson, 2010.

Perlmann, Moshe. "L. O. Levanda and J. L. Gordon: Levanda's Letters to Gordon, 1873–75." *Proceedings of the American Academy for Jewish Research* 30 (1967): 139–85.

Pietersma, Albert. "A New Paradigm for Addressing Old Questions: The Relevance of the Interlinear Model for the Study of the Septuagint." In *Bible and Computer: The Stellenbosch AIBI-6 Conference*, edited by Johann Cook, 337–64. Leiden: Brill, 2002.

Plaut, W. Gunter. *German-Jewish Bible Translations: Linguistic Theology as a Political Phenomenon*. The Leo Baeck Memorial Lecture 36. New York: Leo Baeck Institute, 1992.

———, ed. *The Torah: A Modern Commentary*. New York: Union of American Hebrew Congregations, 1981.

Polliack, Meira. *The Karaite Tradition of Arabic Bible Translation: A Linguistic and Exegetical Study of Karaite Translations of the Pentateuch from the Tenth and Eleventh Centuries C.E.* Études Sur le Judäisme Médiéval, vol. 17. Leiden: Brill, 1997.

"The Power of the New Testament amongst the Jews." *Monthly Reporter of the BFBS* 15 (December 1886): 207–09.

Rajak, Tessa. *Translation and Survival: The Greek Bible of the Ancient Jewish Diaspora*. Oxford: Oxford University Press, 2009.

Read, Piers Paul. *The Dreyfus Affair: The Scandal That Tore France in Two*. London: Bloomsbury, 2012.

"The Religious Awakening among the Jews." *Monthly Reporter of the BFBS* 14 (March 1885): 33–34.

Rhodes, Erroll F., and Liana Lupas, eds. *The Translators to the Reader: The Original Preface of the King James Version of 1611 Revisited*. New York: American Bible Society, 1997.

Rosten, Leo, with Lawrence Bush. *The New Joys of Yiddish: Completely Updated*. New York: Three Rivers Press, 2003.

Roth, Cecil. "The Marrano Press at Ferrara, 1552–1555." *The Modern Language Review* 38, no. 4 (October 1943): 310–11.

Rudavsky, David. "Samuel David Luzzatto and Neo-orthodoxy." *Tradition* 73 (1965): 21–44.

Rypins, Stanley. "The Ferrara Bible at Press." *The Library: Transactions of the Bibliographical Society* (1955): 244–60.

Sa'adia, Rabbi. *Commentary on Ezra and Nehemiah by Rabbi Saadiah*. Edited by H. J. Mathews. Oxford: Clarendon Press, 1882.

Salvesen, Alison. *Symmachus in the Pentateuch*. JSS Monograph 15. Manchester: University of Manchester Press, 1991.

Sarna, Jonathan D. *JPS: The Americanization of Jewish Culture 1888–1988*. Philadelphia: The Jewish Publication Society of America, 1989.

Sarna, Jonathan D., and Nahum Sarna. "Jewish Bible Scholarship and Translations in the United States." In *The Bible and Bibles in America*, edited by Ernest S. Frerichs, 83–116. Atlanta GA: Scholars Press, 1988.

Sarna, Nahum. *Exodus*. *JPS Torah Commentary*. Philadelphia: The Jewish Publication Society, 1991.

———. *Genesis*. *JPS Torah Commentary*. Philadelphia: The Jewish Publication Society, 1989.

———. "Hebrew and Bible Studies in Medieval Spain." In *Sephardi Heritage*, vol. 1, edited by R. D. Barnett, 323–66. New York: KTAV, 1971.

Schapiro, Moshe. *The Living Nach: Sacred Writings*. New York: Moznaim, 1998.

Scherman, Nosson, ed. *Tanach*. Brooklyn: Mesorah, 1996.

Seeligmann, Isaac Leo. *The Septuagint Version of Isaiah: A Discussion of Its Problems*. Leiden: Brill, 1948.

Seidman, Naomi. *Faithful Renderings: Jewish-Christian Difference and the Politics of Translation*. Chicago: University of Chicago Press, 2006.

———. "'A New Garb for the Jewish Soul': The JPS Bible in the Light of the King James Bible." In *The King James Version at 400: Assessing Its Genius as Bible Translation and Its Literary Influence*, edited by David G. Burke, John F. Kutsko, and Philip H. Towner, 475–98. SBL Biblical Scholarship in North America 26. Atlanta GA: Society of Biblical Literature, 2013.

Seligsohn, Max. "Samuel David (ShaDaL) Luzzatto." In *The Jewish Encyclopedia*, 8:224–26.

Shepherd, David. *Targum and Translation: A Reconsideration of the Qumran Aramaic Version of Job*. Studia Semitica Neerlandica. Assen, Netherlands: Van Gorcum, 2004.

Shutt, R. J. H. "Letter of Aristeas: A New Translation and Introduction." In *The Old Testament Pseudepigrapha*, vol. 2, edited by James H. Charlesworth, 7–34. Garden City NY: Doubleday, 1985.

Silber, Michael K. "Ballagi, Mór." In *The YIVO Encyclopedia of Jews in Eastern Europe*, edited by Gershon David Hundert, 841–43. New Haven CT: Yale University Press, 2008.

Simon, Uriel. *Four Approaches to the Book of Psalms: From Saadiah Gaon to Abraham Ibn Ezra*. Translated by Lenn J. Schramm. Albany: State University of New York Press, 1991.

Slutsky, Yehuda. “Mandelstamm, Leon (Aryeh Loeb).” In *Encyclopaedia Judaica,* 2nd ed.,13:465.
Sorkin, David. *Moses Mendelssohn and the Religious Enlightenment.* Berkeley: University of California Press, 1996.
Stanislawski, Michael. *For Whom Do I Toil?: Judah Leib Gordon and the Crisis of Russian Jewry.* Studies in Jewish History. New York: Oxford University Press, 1988.
Stein, David E. S., ed. *The Contemporary Torah: A Gender-Sensitive Adaptation of the JPS Translation.* Philadelphia: The Jewish Publication Society, 2006.
Steinsaltz, Adin Even-Israel, commentary. *The Steinsaltz Humash: Humash Translation and Commentary.* 2nd ed. Jerusalem: Koren, 2018.
Stern, David H. *Complete Jewish Bible.* Jerusalem: Messianic Jewish Publisher, 2007.
———. *Jewish New Testament: A Translation of the New Testament That Expresses Its Jewishness.* Jerusalem: Jewish New Testament Publications, 1989.
Tanach. The ArtScroll Series. Stone Edition. Brooklyn NY: Mesorah Publications, 1996.
Taylor, Kenneth N. *The Living Bible, Paraphrased.* Wheaton IL: Tyndale House, 1971.
Sussman, Lance. “Another Look at Isaac Leeser and the First Jewish Translation of the Bible in the United States.” *Modern Judaism* 5, no. 2 (1985): 159–90.
Thackery, H. St. John. *The Septuagint and Jewish Worship: A Study in Origins.* London: Oxford University Press, 1923.
Tigay, Jeffrey H. *Deuteronomy. JPS Torah Commentary.* Philadelphia: The Jewish Publication Society, 1996.
Tobias, Alexander. “Luzzatto, Samuel David.” In *Encyclopaedia Judaica,* 2nd ed., 13:286–87.
Tov, Emanuel. *The Greek and Hebrew Bible: Collected Essays on the Septuagint.* Supplements to Vetus Testament 72. Leiden: Brill, 1999.
———. “The Impact of the LXX Translation of the Pentateuch on the Translation of the Other Books.” In *Mélanges Dominique Barthélemy,* edited by P. Casetti, O. Keel, and A. Schenker, 577–92. OBO 38. Fribourg: Éditions universitaires, 1981.
———. “Midrash-Type Exegesis in the Book of Joshua.” *Revue Biblique* 85 (1978): 50–61.
———. “The Rabbinic Tradition Concerning the ‘Alterations’ Inserted into the Greek Pentateuch and Their Relation to the Original Text of the LXX.” *Journal for the Study of Judaism* 15 (1984): 65–89.
———. *The Text-Critical Use of the Septuagint in Biblical Research.* 3rd ed. Grand Rapids MI: Eisenbrauns, 2015.
Troxel, Ronald L. *LXX-Isaiah as Translation and Interpretation: The Strategies of the Translator of the Septuagint of Isaiah.* Leiden: Brill, 2007.

Ulrich, Eugene C. *The Dead Sea Scrolls and the Origins of the Bible*. Studies in the Dead Sea Scrolls and Related Literature. Grand Rapids MI: Eerdmans, 1999.

Updike, John. "Review of Robert Alter, *The Five Books of Moses*." *The New Yorker*, November 1, 2004.

Van der Meer, Michael. "Provenance, Profile, and Purpose of the Greek Joshua." In *XII Congress of the International Organization for Septuagint and Cognate Studies*, edited by Melvin K. H. Peters, 55–80. Atlanta GA: Scholars Press, 2006.

Von Günzburg, Baron David, and Max Seligsohn. "Gordon, Leon (Judah Löb Ben Asher)." In *The Jewish Encyclopedia*, 6:47–48.

Wasserstein, Abraham, and David J. Wasserstein. *The Legend of the Septuagint: From Classical Antiquity to Today*. Cambridge: Cambridge University Press, 2006.

Weill, Julien. "Archives Israélites." In *The Jewish Encyclopedia*, 2:87.

Weiner, L. "The Ferrara Bible II." *Modern Language Notes* 11, no. 1 (January 1896): 24–42.

Wex, Max. *Born to Kvetch: Yiddish Language and Culture in All of Its Moods*. New York: Harper Perennial, 2006.

Wiernik, Peter. "Mandelstamm, Leon (Aryeh Löb) B. Joseph." In *The Jewish Encyclopedia*, 8:289.

"Yiddish." In *Encyclopaedia Judaica*, 2nd ed., 3:610–11.

Subject Index

Index of Bible Passages and Other Ancient and Religious Texts

Bible

New Testament

Babylonian Talmud

Classical Period Authors

Qur'an